THE QUEEN'S STAMPS

H.M. the Queen examining stamps produced by
the Crown Agents Stamp Bureau to mark her
Golden Jubilee in 2002.

THE
QUEEN'S STAMPS

The Authorised History of the Royal Philatelic Collection

❖·❖·❖

NICHOLAS COURTNEY

Methuen

Published in 2004 by Methuen

1 3 5 7 9 10 8 6 4 2

Text copyright © 2004 Nicholas Courtney

First published in Great Britain in 2004 by Methuen Publishing Ltd
215 Vauxhall Bridge Road
London SW1V 1EJ

Methuen Publishing Limited Reg. No. 3543167

A CIP catalogue record for this book is available from the British Library.

ISBN 0 413 77228 4

Designed by Bryony Newhouse

Printed and bound in Great Britain by
Butler & Tanner Limited, Frome and London

CONTENTS

Since Tudor times, there has always been a tradition of collecting within the Royal Family. It was Charles I who was the first true collector; with taste, refinement and knowledge, he laid the foundation of the Royal Collection, one that was added to greatly by Charles II, George III and George IV. Royal collecting gained an added dimension with the accession of Queen Victoria, who was greatly influenced and encouraged by Prince Albert, the Prince Consort.

My great-grandfather, George V, was a true collector from the same mould, carrying on the family tradition, maybe not in old masters and antiquities, but more specifically in postage stamps. Throughout his life he built up one of the foremost collections of Great Britain and Empire, through dedication and great scholarship. His knowledge rivalled any of the top philatelists of his day. As in the past, his collection has been assiduously added to, with the postage stamps of George VI, and throughout her reign by The Queen, to make it one of, if not the, finest in the world.

Great works within the Royal Collection are exhibited and enjoyed, both in the United Kingdom and abroad, so too is the Royal Philatelic Collection becoming more accessible to a wider public – hobby stamp collector and specialist alike.

This work, *The Queen's Stamps: The Authorised History of the Royal Philatelic Collection*, will bring the great collection of a former Duke of York within reach of an even wider audience.

ACKNOWLEDGEMENTS

Grateful acknowledgement is made to Her Majesty Queen Elizabeth II for her permission to study and quote from the Royal Archives, and for access to the Royal Philatelic Collection. I am further indebted to Her Majesty for her gracious permission to reproduce the photograph of a pair of cuff-links belonging to George V (p. 34) and the Prince of Wales with his brother, Prince Alfred (p. 25).

In addition, I would like to thank John Murray Publishers for permission to quote from *John Betjeman's Collected Poems*; and Hutchinson, an imprint of Random House UK Limited, for permission to quote from Tony Benn's *Out of the Wilderness: Diaries 1963–67*.

In the writing of this official history of this incomparable collection, there were many who contributed in making what could well have been a daunting project into a fascinating and enjoyable study. Nothing seemed to be too much trouble for Miss Allison Derrett, Assistant Registrar of the Royal Archives, Windsor, who plied me with countless Royal diaries and files, and above all, minutely read the text. The book certainly could not have been written without the help and guidance of the fellows, members and staff of the Royal Philatelic Society London. Access to their library was invaluable, pleasurable too with the aid of the librarian Philip Lindley and his assistant Caroline Bossowska, along with Joanna Williamson and Paul Moorcroft.

John Inestone added much to the passage on the Siege of Mafeking stamps. Nigel Fordham, Head of the Crown Agents Stamp Bureau (along with his assistant Jo Gray), provided much interesting material for both current and historical material. Both the Rt Hon. Tony Benn and the Earl of Snowdon gave invaluable help with the stamps of the current reign, as did Douglas Muir, Curator of Philately at the Postal Heritage Trust.

Sir David Wilson Bt kindly provided the drawing of his father, Sir John Wilson Bt (p. 259). Likewise Lady Marriott supplied the photograph of her late husband, Sir John Marriott (p. 300). The photographs on pages 311 and 313 were taken by Caroline Forbes.

To David Beech, Curator and Head of the Philatelic Collections at the British Library and President of the Royal Philatelic Society London, my deep thanks for his unstinting advice so freely given, and humour.

But it is to the Keepers of the Royal Philatelic Collection that I owe so much, both Charles Goodwyn, the former Keeper, who at the very outset gave advice and encouragement, and the present Keeper, Michael Sefi, who notwithstanding his heavy workload with putting together the Smithsonian Exhibition and multifarious other duties still made the time to steer me through a difficult path and to scrutinise the text, as did Patrick Pearson, Chairman of the Expert Committee of the Royal Philatelic Society London. Any errors that remain are naturally my own. The Deputy Keeper, Surésh Dhargalkar, with his encyclopaedic knowledge of the workings of the Royal Household and the Royal Palaces added much to the research of the book: it was he who collated the illustrations. Sir Edward Ford was most illuminating on the inner workings of the Private Secretary's office.

The contribution of Hazel Orme went far beyond her role as editor. Finally, I would like to thank my wife, Vanessa, still a non-philatelist who did not overly complain at the enthusiasm of the convert and to whom this book is dedicated.

AUTHOR'S NOTE

As there appears to be no hard and fast style as to how to describe the face value of a stamp, I have repeated exactly what is printed on the stamp. Thus, a penny-halfpenny stamp appears variously as 1½d., 1½d, 1½^d or THREE HALFPENCE. Likewise, a five cents stamp is described as either 5 CENTS or 5 cents, sometimes just 5 c. Although apparently inconsistent, it cannot, however, be wrong.

PHILATELIC MAP

CANADA

ONTARIO

QUEBEC

NEWFOUND-LAND

Prince Edward I.
NOVA SCOTIA
NEW BRUNSWICK

CARIBBEAN

PERU

GUYANA

FALKLANDS

1859
HELIGOLAND
(Brit.)

GREAT
BRITAIN
1840

• Ber

• W

ION
(Br

MALTA •

GAMBIA 1869
(Brit.)
SIERRA
LEONE (Brit.)
Freetown

GOLD COAST (Brit.)
TOGOLAND 1892
BENIN 1888

NIGERIA

U

LIBERIA 1860

Lagos
(Brit.Col.1861)
1874

CAMEROUN
(Brit.1915 Fr.1915)

ASCENSION IS.

ST HELENA

TRISTAN DA CUNHA

S
A

CARIBBEAN INSET

TURKS Is.
(Brit.1678)
1867

VIRGIN Is .
Brit.1866

•ANTIGUA

ST KITTS
1870
NEVIS
1861

BARBADOS
(Brit.1852)
1851

ST LUCIA (Brit.1814)
1860
ST VINCENT (Brit.1783)
1861
GRENADA (Brit.1783)
1861

TOBAGO
(Brit.1814)
1879

TRINIDAD
(Brit.1802)
1851

BRITISH GUIANA
1850

SOUTH AFRICA INSET

Pietersburg 1901 •
Pretoria S.AFRICAN
Mafeking 1900 •
REP.
TRANSVAAL
ORANGE RIVER
COLONY

Lydenburg
• 1901

SWAZI-
LAND

BRITISH
BECHUANALAND
GRIQUALAND
WEST

Blood
River

ZULU-
LAND

BASUTOLAND

NATAL

CAPE OF GOOD HOPE
1853
UNION OF S.AFRICA
1910

Cape Town

BRITISH ANTARCTIC
TERRITORY
1963

OF THE WORLD

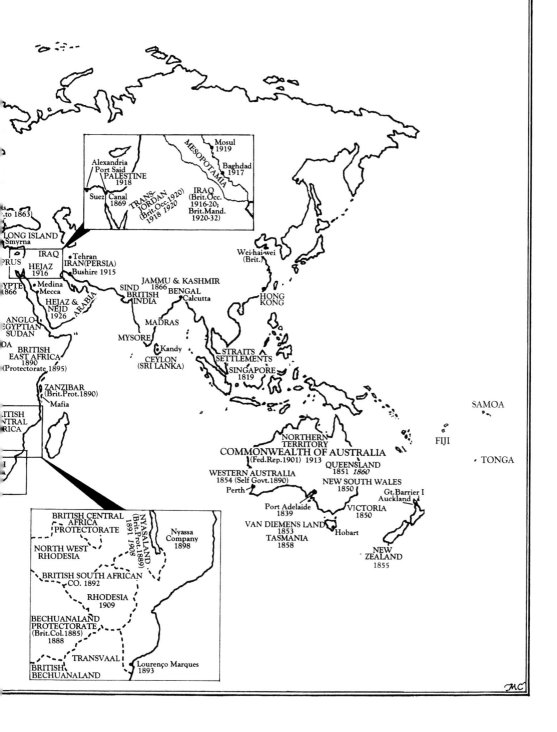

Mosul
1919

MESOPOTAMIA

Alexandria
Port Said
PALESTINE
1918

Baghdad
1917

Suez Canal
1869

TRANS-
JORDAN
(Brit.Occ.1920)
1918 1920

IRAQ
(Brit.Occ.
1916-20;
Brit.Mand.
1920-32)

..to 1863)

LONG ISLAND
Smyrna

IRAQ

PRUS

HEJAZ
1916

•Tehran
IRAN(PERSIA)
•Bushire 1915

Wei-hai-wei
(Brit.)

YPTE
866

•Medina
•Mecca

JAMMU & KASHMIR
1866

SIND   BENGAL
BRITISH •Calcutta
INDIA

HONG
KONG

HEJAZ &
NEJD
1926

ARABIA

ANGLO-
EGYPTIAN
SUDAN

MADRAS

DA

MYSORE

BRITISH
EAST AFRICA
1890
(Protectorate 1895)

•Kandy
CEYLON
(SRI LANKA)

STRAITS
SETTLEMENTS
SINGAPORE
1819

ZANZIBAR
(Brit.Prot.1890)
•Mafia

SAMOA

ITISH
NTRAL
RICA

FIJI

NORTHERN
TERRITORY

• TONGA

COMMONWEALTH OF AUSTRALIA
(Fed.Rep.1901) 1913   QUEENSLAND
                       1851 1860
WESTERN AUSTRALIA
1854 (Self Govt.1890)   NEW SOUTH WALES
Perth   1850

BRITISH CENTRAL
AFRICA
PROTECTORATE

NYASALAND
(Brit.Prot.1889)
1891 1908

Nyassa
Company
1898

Gt.Barrier I
Auckland

NORTH WEST
RHODESIA

Port Adelaide
1839

VICTORIA
1850

BRITISH SOUTH AFRICAN
CO. 1892

VAN DIEMENS LAND
1853
TASMANIA
1858

Hobart

RHODESIA
1909

NEW
ZEALAND
1855

BECHUANALAND
PROTECTORATE
(Brit.Col.1885)
1888

TRANSVAAL

Lourenço Marques
1893

BRITISH
BECHUANALAND

MC

PREFACE

'Eyes to the cross, please, ma'am.'

Her Majesty Queen Elizabeth II sat motionless, gazing at tiny strips of black camera tape stuck to the wall of the Red Corridor, the first-floor landing that leads to her private rooms in Buckingham Palace where her cousin, the 5th Earl of Lichfield, had been commissioned to take one of the official photographs for her Golden Jubilee. The set-up had been meticulously researched, tried and tested for he had just five minutes to capture the images of both the Queen and the Duke of Edinburgh. He worked quickly, but by using digital photography he managed it with twenty seconds to spare.

Patrick Lichfield took the Queen and the Duke of Edinburgh in profile and, before their eyes, he merged the two separate photographs on the screen. The Queen was delighted with this portrayal, which Lichfield likened to 'a Wedgwood relief', although he admitted later that he had 'not consciously seen the single profile of The Queen as a stamp'.[1]

But the photograph, which now hangs in the National Portrait Gallery, was seen very much as a stamp by Nigel Fordham, Head of the Crown Agents Stamp Bureau. It was he who chose the single image of the Queen for the stamp to mark the fiftieth anniversary of the Coronation for ten of the fifteen Overseas Territories the Crown Agents look after philatelically. The use of this profile of the Queen was twofold: for the image itself to be created into a stamp and for the silhouette to be used in the corner of every subsequent stamp issued by them (except when the Royal Cipher is employed).

The designer began by playing around with the digital image on a computer, experimenting with different colours and lettering. Then a shadow was created around the head to accentuate the profile. He also tried various depths of detail, from blank to full relief, but decided to return to the days when stamps had a single image of the sovereign, with a different colour to indicate denomination. It was decided to return to the original script too, Goudy Old Style Extra Bold, to complete the

classic look of the new stamps. The option of embossing was abandoned, as was thermography, where heavier ink is layed on parts of the stamp to give an engraved look, as both forms of embellishment were thought unnecessary with such a fine stamp.

The Royal Mail, the Great Britain Offshore Islands and the Overseas Territories all submit the artworks to the Queen for her approval before printing their stamps, and over the years she has frequently made suggestions on how they might be improved. With this new issue, the timing was so tight that Fordham sought the informal opinion of the Queen for the proposed stamp design and was told that if final designs were formally submitted the Queen would view them favourably.

The design, values, quantities and different background colours were discussed and agreed with the various Overseas Territories Post Offices and final artwork or essays were prepared. Ascension Island went for a £3 stamp, the British Antarctic Territory £2, Bermuda $25, British Indian Ocean Territory $2.50, British Virgin Islands US$5, Cayman Islands CI$4, Falkland Islands £2, South Georgia & the South Sandwich Islands £2 and St Helena £2.50, while Tristan da Cunha decided on £2.80 – each one being used as a definitive, rather than a commemorative, stamp.

The finished designs or essays were passed to the Protocol Division, Foreign and Commonwealth Office for formal submission to the Queen for her approval. Once the approval was received by the Crown Agents, ten

United Kingdom Overseas Territories: 2003. The Crown Agents chose the fiftieth anniversary of the Coronation to launch the new Queen's Head stamps for ten Overseas Territories. For the first time, the silhouette of the Queen's head was used for the 'traffic lights' in the margin (opposite). The photograph was taken by the Earl of Lichfield, the direct descendant of the 1st Earl, Postmaster General at the time of the introduction of the uniform Penny Post.

individual contracts to print all the countries' stamps went to the Dublin firm of BDT International Security Printers. They used a lithography four colour printing process on Crown Agents' own watermarked paper – a crown with a CA below, laid deep into the paper. Once the proofs were agreed by the Crown Agents' production staff, permission was granted to print the stamps. These stamps were sent to the Territories for sale from their Post Offices and also to the Crown Agents for sale to stamp dealers and collectors world wide.

It was a race to produce them in time for the launch day, 2 June 2003, the fiftieth anniversary of the Coronation. While the new stamps could be air-freighted to most Overseas Territories – those for the British Antarctic Territory went first to the Falkland Islands, then on by Otter seaplane to the Antarctic bases, while St Helena, with no airport, had to rely on the sailing of RMS *St Helena* from Portland in Dorset to collect the mail from Jamestown, the Ascension Island to which it had been flown by the British Forces Post Office. The Tristan da Cunha stamps were flown to South Africa then picked up by fishing boat and delivered sometime later. At least those islands have a port. When Pitcairn Islands receive their stamps, they are sealed in a large drum and tipped overboard by a passing freighter for the islanders to collect by long boat.

The Crown Agents today are following a long tradition in the production of British Colonial issues. But however fine these stamps are, with their skilful computer design and sophisticated production, they cannot begin to match the artistry or variety of the nineteenth-century issues, with their infinite combinations of papers, watermarks, colours, inks and printing.

The early Colonial stamps usually began with a delicate watercolour sketch, then translated to a die for line-engraved printing. The artist worked closely with the portrait engraver, then passed his work to the framing, or background, specialist, who gave it to the lettering engraver to complete. With line-engraved printing – also known as *taille douce*, intaglio or, simply, the copperplate process – the ink is transferred to the paper from the cut recesses on the plate; very fine detail is possible with this method of printing. With surface printing, the process is reversed. Here, the image is raised on the plate, and when inked, the design is transferred to the paper. Sometimes with surface-printed stamps, the sharp edges of the pattern presses into the paper so that the back seems almost embossed with the design. Lithography is an alternative method of surface printing, but here the design is laid down, or transferred, to a lithographic stone with a special ink. The stone is then treated so as to repel the ink except where it is required for printing. Some early stamps were embossed with two dies – one in reverse on top, the other in relief below.

The paper used in early issues was as diverse as the printing. The straight-forward wove was the most common form with no distinguishing feature, unlike laid paper, which has a series of parallel lines (and the occasional right-angled line) running through it, made during manufacture by the wires at the bottom of the mould. It is tough and often used in line engraved stamps. Ribbed paper is a form of wove that has been treated with a serrated roller to give parallel lines on one side of the paper only, while Dickinson, the proprietary brand of John Dickinson and Co., has an arrangement of silk threads running through each sheet. On chalk-surfaced paper a layer of chalky material guarded against the removal of cancellations from a stamp as it broke up when moistened.

The vagaries of materials used in stamps and their production methods have fascinated millions of collectors since the beginning of philately. Great collections have been formed through scholarship (and, to a lesser extent, money), but nowhere in the world is there a more complete collection of Great Britain and the Commonwealth, her former Dominions, Colonies and Protectorates, than the Queen's Stamps, the Royal Philatelic Collection.

Normally, a block of four (very occasionally six) of each value of each new issue produced by the Crown Agents is sent to the Keeper of the Royal Philatelic Collection in the Stamp Room, tucked into a courtyard of St James's Palace, London. However, these Overseas Territories' new Queen's Head stamps, being very exceptional, were mounted in a fine album and pre-sented to the Queen in 2004. In this setting, the colour code in the margin, known as the 'traffic-lights', appeared for the first time in the same silhouettes of the Queen's head rather than as circles or other commercial devices. The sheets of these issues were also numbered in the margin, and the sheet numbered 001 from each country was mounted in a special album to be presented to the Queen. The usual corner block of four with margins were sent to Michael Sefi, the keeper of the Royal Philatelic Collection, where they will remain, in special conservation envelopes, until mounted in the appropriate album, bound in green leather, the colour for Queen Elizabeth II. Her albums, known as the 'Green Collection', join those that hold the stamps collected in George VI's reign, which are bound in dark blue (the 'Blue Collection'), and the red volumes, which contain the bulk of the collection, all 328 of them, amassed by George V. They are uniform in size and each a masterly example of binding in three-quarter morocco leather of the appropriate colour. The Queen's albums bear in gold leaf the EIIR cipher, the word 'STAMPS' and the volume number on the spine, with the Queen's Arms on the front and back of both the album and the slip cover. The albums of George VI are exactly the same except the Arms are his. Likewise, the albums of George V (the 'Red Collection') are just the same excepting the cipher on the spine.

The Royal Philatelic Collection is shelved in a vast strong room, under carefully controlled environmental conditions, to be seen, to be studied, to be exhibited, to be compared. This fine Overseas Territories issue, the first to bear the new profile of the Queen, became part of an ever-expanding collection. The choice of the image of the Queen by Lichfield for this special stamp issue was particularly appropriate as the 1st Earl of Lichfield, his forebear, was Postmaster General during the time of the postal reforms and responsible for the introduction of Sir Rowland Hill's Penny Post, where it all began.

INTRODUCTION

'The Postmaster General and Mr Rowland Hill await your Majesty's pleasure,' declares the Groom of the Chamber.

Queen Victoria is in the Council Chamber at Windsor Castle, seated at a large table strewn with pamphlets – *Reports on Postage*, copies of the *Post Circular*, and the annual reports of the French and American post offices. Lord Melbourne, her Prime Minister hovers at her shoulder as she reads Rowland Hill's most famous work, *Post Office Reform, Its Importance and Practicality*, a pamphlet that championed the 'Uniform Penny Postage Plan'.

The Queen directs that the Earl of Lichfield, her Postmaster General, and Rowland Hill be seated, then continues: 'I have been reading carefully and with great interest, the late discussions and evidence on the postage question, and I now wish to hear what is my Post Master's opinion on the plan, which I therefore beg you, Mr Hill, to describe in a few words.'

Rowland Hill launches into his speech. 'With Your Majesty's leave, I will say nothing about the dearness and hardship of the present Post Office rates, or of Post Office management itself, but confine myself, according to Your Majesty's commands, to the plan you have honoured me by noticing. My plan is that all letters not weighing more than half an ounce should be charged one penny; and heavier letters one penny for each additional half ounce, whatever may be the distance they are carried. The postage to be paid when the letter is sent, and not when received, as at the present.'[1]

'With regard to the scheme set forth by Mr Hill, of all the wild and visionary schemes which I had ever heard or read of, it was the most extravagant,'[2] Lichfield replied.

This encounter appears in a short play written by Henry Cole in April 1839. Although the scene was imaginary, the issues and much of the dialogue were real enough: Lichfield's were the exact words he had spoken just two years before to damn Hill's proposals at a House of Commons Select Committee. On a sensitive subject, the play was hugely popular and published in many forms; one was bound into Part XIII of *Nicholas Nickleby* – at that time Charles Dickens issued his novels in instalments.

By then, the postal system was in a sorry state through the mismanagement of the Post Office and a complicated, unwieldy tariff system. Revenue was down, despite an increasing population, and high charges put the post out of reach of most at a time when there was wide scale migration from country to town and the economy was expanding. The need for postal reform had long been recognised, but it was only after the tireless efforts of Robert Wallace, the first elected Member of Parliament for the new constituency of Greenock, that the Duncannon Commission 'to enquire into the management of the Post Office' was finally set up in 1835. Over the next two years, evidence was considered by the three members of the committee, and a series of reports was produced. When Rowland Hill's *Post Office Reform* appeared in January 1837, the cause was considerably advanced.

Rowland Hill was born in Kidderminster in 1795, the son of a prosperous owner of a private school in Birmingham. He too became a headmaster, but left teaching to become, at the age of forty, secretary to the South Australian Commission, which chartered ships to transport emigrants to the Colony. It was at that time that he met Robert Wallace, who supplied much of the ammunition for his pamphlet. In it, Hill presented his case for the reduction of postal charges and a uniform penny post – as paraphrased in Cole's play – with well-reasoned argument. He even came up with such innovations as the letterbox 'into which the Letter Carrier would drop the letters, and, having knocked, he would pass on as fast as he could walk'.[3]

Despite opposition led by the Duke of Wellington, Lichfield and Colonel Maberly, the Secretary of the Post Office, Hill's campaign gathered momentum. National support for his plan was largely orchestrated by the City of London Mercantile Committee on Postage, a consortium of City merchants set up in 1828 whose secretary was none other than Henry Cole. A

Parliamentary Select Committee, under the chairmanship of Robert Wallace, met in 1838 at which evidence was heard on both sides. Its findings and the voice of the public, echoed by the reformers, finally led a reluctant government – it feared loss of revenue – to pass the Penny Postage Bill in August 1839. The mandarins of the Post Office had been defeated – in Cole's play the Queen has the lines, 'It appears to me, my lord, that the loss of Colonel Maberly to the Post Office would be another great gain to the public,' and 'It is clear to me that Lord Lichfield had better retire from the Post Office.' Rowland Hill was rewarded by Francis Baring, the Chancellor of the Exchequer, with a post at the Treasury (rather than at the Post Office where he was deeply unpopular) to supervise the introduction of the penny post, and chose Henry Cole as his assistant.

Hill's first problem was how effectively to collect the prepaid postage. In his pamphlet he had advanced the idea of Charles Knight: the 'stamped covers or sheets of papers be supplied to the public from the Stamp Office or Post Office, as may be most convenient and sold at such a price as to include the postage... Covers, at various prices, would be required for packets of various weights; and each should have the weight it is entitled to carry legibly printed with the stamp.'[4] It was decided that the public should be invited to submit ideas too, and in September 1839 the Treasury placed a notice in *The Times*:

THE TREASURY COMPETITION

Before My Lords can decide on the adoption of any course either by stamps or otherwise, they feel it would be useful that artists, men of science, and the public in general, may have the opportunity of offering any suggestions or proposals as to the manner in which the stamp may best be brought into use. With this view, My Lords will be prepared to receive and consider any proposal which may be sent to them on or before the 15 October 1839.[5]

A premium, or prize, of £200 was offered for the 'most deserving' proposal, with £100 for the runner-up. The contestants were to consider convenience, security against forgery, easy recognition at the Post Office, and expense. The Treasury recorded over 2,600 replies (in his journal Hill put it nearer three thousand) with only a small percentage connected with designs for actual stamps. There are over 100 'Treasury Essays' or entries in the Royal Philatelic Collection from seventy-eight different contestants. While some of the suggestions were bizarre, many others displayed 'much ingenuity', although 'their lordships did not think that it would be advisable to adopt any of the specific plans proposed'.[6] However, the prize money was increased to £400 and divided equally between Benjamin Chevington, Henry Cole, Charles Whiting, and a

Great Britain: 1839 Treasury Essay number 22,897 submitted by Charles Whiting.

joint entry from Francis Coffin and James Bogardus. Examples of the Treasury Essay from each winner are in the Royal Philatelic Collection.

Throughout his campaign, Hill had mooted the idea of 'a bit of paper just large enough to bear the stamp, and covered at the back with a glutinous wash which the user might, by applying a little moisture, attach to the back of the letter'.[7] Although no design was thought entirely suitable in the Treasury Essay competition for a new stamp, one entry, number 20,639 submitted by Sir George Mackenzie of Coul, the noted mineralogist, was of a watercolour showing the young Queen Victoria in silhouette on a black background.

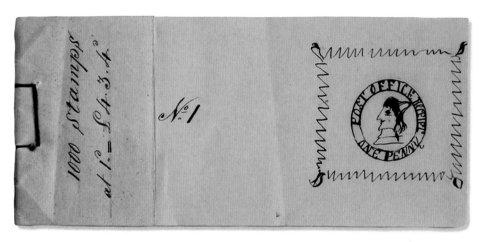

Above: Great Britain: 1839 Treasury Essay number 23,043 for a stamp booklet submitted by John Little.

Treasury Essay number 20,639 submitted by Sir George Mackenzie of Coul. This watercolour, showing the young Queen Victoria in profile, could well have influenced Hill in the final design for the Penny Black.

Great Britain: 1840 sketch of 1d and 2d stamps made for Rowland Hill to submit to Francis Baring, Chancellor of the Exchequer.

Hill must have had Mackenzie's design in mind when he had something similar drawn up to illustrate his notion of the ONE PENNY black and the TWO PENCE blue. The watercolours of the stamps appear, side by side, on a scrap of paper, and again show the Queen's head in silhouetted profile. Across the head of the first design (coloured black) is written 1d. in pencil in his handwriting, while the other, coloured blue, is similarly marked in pencil, 2d. Hill presented it to the Chancellor of the Exchequer for approval. The sketch survived, and was given to George V, then Duke of York, by Baring's son, the Earl of Northbrook. Like the Mackenzie essay, it is now in the Royal Philatelic Collection. However, four sketches went to the Chancellor for his approval. An identical pair (only marginally smaller) painted by the same hand came to light and were bought by R. M. Phillips for his collection (now part of the Postal Heritage Trust). This scrap of paper has clearly been torn off the top of the one in the Royal Philatelic Collection, the length and rough edges top and bottom fitting exactly. Thus, this one piece of paper showed what the proposed stamps would look like in two sizes. The Chancellor went for the larger option.

Once the concept of the Penny Black and the Twopenny Blue had been agreed, Rowland Hill commissioned the artist Henry Corbould to prepare drawings for the engravers. The young Queen Victoria's head was taken from a medal by William Wyon, struck by the Corporation of London to commemorate her visit to the Guildhall shortly after her accession. Wyon had, in fact, used Corbould's portrait of the Queen for his medal, but it was thought that by using the portrait head in relief as it appeared on the medal, rather than the original, it was less likely to be forged. There is a drawing in the Royal Philatelic Collection marked 'Original sketch for the Postage Stamp

Great Britain: 1840 ONE PENNY black Plate 1, imprimatur before the plate was hardened.

Opposite: Great Britain: 1840 TWO PENCE blue, Plate 1, an unused block of 38. The largest known multiple from that plate, the block was purchased by George V in 1924.

In Wetting the Back be careful not to remove the Cement.

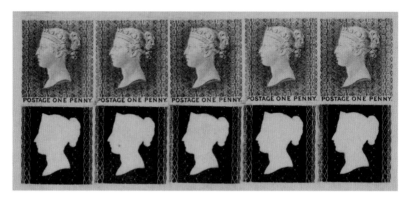

Great Britain: 1840 (January) proof in deep blue of Die I set above the new Die
for comparison of the backgrounds.

(by Wyon)' but this is now thought to have been Corbould's work. What is
certain, however, is that Corbould's essay, for which he was paid £12, was sent
to the engravers, Charles and Frederick Heath. It is most likely that it was
worked by Frederick Heath alone, for by that time his father's eyesight was
failing. The engine-turned background, similar to that used on banknotes,
was added by the printers, Perkins, Bacon and Petch.

The original die, from which proofs were printed on a handmade paper,
were deemed unsatisfactory. It was sent to Colonel Maberly with the inscription 'The face is of course unfinished. The stamps will be printed in sheets
each containing 240. On the margin [of] the sheet will be an instruction to
place the stamp over the address. The back will be gummed.'[8] On the new
die, the final version, stars were added to the top corners, and, at the suggestion of Francis Baring, the word POSTAGE above the head, ONE PENNY or TWO
PENCE below. As Great Britain was the first country to issue stamps, it was,
of course, unnecessary to specify its name on the stamp – a unique practice
that still holds today.

The proofs from the finished plates were finally approved by Baring on
2 April 1840. The issue, the product of the initial two plates (out of a total
of eleven plates), went on sale on 1 May and £2,500 worth of stamps were
sold, but they were not valid until the first day of postage, 6 May 1840. As a
precaution against forgery, each stamp had a watermark crown. Each sheet

contained twenty rows of twelve stamps, so the first row had the letters AA, AB, AC up to AL, the next BA, BB, BC, and so on through the sheet of 240. The check letters were designed to deter the forger, although with the volume of incoming post to the receiving offices, and the poor light, detection of forgery was virtually impossible.

What went unforeseen was the ease with which the red Maltese cross, used to cancel the stamp, could be removed, and a cottage industry grew up in recycling used stamps. 'All sorts of tricks,' Hill wrote in his diary, 'are being played by the public who are exercising their ingenuity in devising contrivances for removal of the obliterating of the stamp by chemical agents and other means.'[9] The Royal Philatelic Collection holds a Penny Black that had been cleaned and put through the system three times.

Rowland Hill consulted the renowned chemist, Professor Richard Phillips for a solution to the problem. Perkins, Bacon and Petch made two plates and filled the top right-hand corner of each *intaglio* stamp with wax, then printed off a trial block of three, and another of twelve stamps with an assortment of inks. Hill and Phillips then experimented with different cancellation inks and their removal from the stamps. Among many examples of these trial printings, the Royal Philatelic Collection includes a block of six stamps when a solution of tartaric acid, prussic acid and potash or turpentine was used, ineffectually, to 'clean' the stamp; however Phillips successfully managed to restore another pair to their pristine unused state (not in the Collection). The other use of these doctored plates was for colour trials – later known as 'the Rainbow Trials'. The printers produced a complete series of stamps in shades of red through to brown, and in an assortment of blues. They mounted a sample of each specimen colour on a sheet and sent it to Hill and Phillips. Hill then recommended that the Penny Black be replaced with the Penny Red: trials showed that it was more difficult to remove the cancellation mark from the red ink than the black. The Penny Red, with minor alterations, remained in service until 1880. The actual trial sheet studied by Hill and Phillips, with the chosen colour – number 16G – is another historic item in the Collection.

The other method of prepayment, originally preferred by Rowland Hill, was the pre-stamped envelope and letter sheet. His assistant Henry Cole, initiated the scheme. Cole informed J. Thompson, the renowned wood

Great Britain: 1840 Mulready, May 1840.

engraver, that 'there is a wish to have all the beauty possible to be got into the stamped envelope'[10] and to this end, he asked the President of the Royal Academy to suggest some artists to submit a suitable design. The Chancellor, Baring, put forward William Wyon, but Hill and Cole decided on William Mulready, an Irish-born Academician, with Thompson as the engraver.

Mulready produced his initial design, and after a little input from Hill, Cole and Thompson, an interim rather faint pencil sketch was prepared, which is now in the Collection. It is beautifully drawn, and 'although some parts of it are somewhat incongruous, it is eminently suitable as an emblematic design, showing the benefits of cheap postage and plainly destined to spread to all parts of the world'.[11] The allegorical design of the 'Mulready', as the envelope became known, was well meant, but the effect is ludicrous. The figure of a somewhat bewildered-looking Britannia is seated on a rock in the middle of the ocean, with a lion and shield at her feet. She is dispatching winged messengers to the four corners of the earth, improbably represented by such scenes as William Penn entreating a group of Indians, a Laplander in a sleigh drawn by reindeer, laden camels and elephants, coolies and a planter in a large hat under a palm tree. On one side, a mother reads good news to her children, and on the other, a parent receives what is evidently bad news.

From its first issue, also 6 May 1840, the Mulready was 'abused and ridiculed on all sides'[12] – particularly in the press. Derisive caricatures of it by famous artists appeared by the dozen, alongside a mass of other unrelated illustrated envelopes. Just six days after its issue, Rowland Hill admitted its failure. In his journal he wrote: 'The conduct of the public, however, shows that although our attempt to diffuse a taste for fine art may have been imprudent, such diffusion is very much wasted.'[13] The Mulready one penny envelope was withdrawn from sale at the end of January 1841, to be replaced by an envelope with an embossed one penny stamp. Major Edward Evans put together the most important collection of Mulready envelopes, caricatures and proofs and it was sold in its entirety to George V in June 1917.

With the introduction of the uniform Penny Post, Members of Parliament lost one of their most closely guarded privileges: free postage. Through Rowland Hill, it was arranged that printed Parliamentary Envelopes would be available for Members to use if they signed their names in the bottom left-hand corner and posted them within the Palace of Westminster. The Royal Philatelic Collection has a good holding of these including eight examples from the Commons, and four, including one from the Duke of Wellington, from the House of Lords. The system was open to abuse, although largely by accident with missed signatures, or letters posted outside the House.

The Royal Household also enjoyed free post, but Queen Victoria insisted on paying for her private correspondence. One fine example of her high moral stand, a letter to her aunt Queen Adelaide, which is stamped and signed on the envelope is now in the Collection. There was, however, a move for a special issue of the Penny Black exclusively for Government departmental use. A design was produced, with the letters v and r – Victoria Regina – placed in the top corners. The stamps were never issued, although there are examples of them in the Collection, including one that was mysteriously used on a letter posted in Ireland on 28 February 1841.

With the demise of the Mulready, the embossed envelope and a die 'for stamping the letter paper furnished by the public'[14] was brought in to replace it. Rowland Hill commissioned William Wyon in December 1839 to produce them, and he teamed up with Charles Whiting of the Beaufort House Press, who had shared the Treasury competition prize. Wyon produced a fine head, like the Penny Black facing left, while Whiting created a variety of engine-turned surrounds and the lettering. Whiting was hoping for the contract to print the envelopes (he was too expensive) and produced another die, this time with the head of the Queen facing right. After 'much blundering by Whiting'[15] and delays, a sheet of six sample embossed stamps was presented to Hill so that he could make the final choice for the envelope – this 'Postage Experiment' is also in the Collection. The embossed envelope came into use in 1841, and its successor has only comparatively recently been phased out. The embossed letter sheet was thought open to forgery so it was never produced.

Opposite: Great Britain: 1840 Parliamentary Envelope One Penny, used on 16 January, initialled in left-hand corner by the sender.

Above: Great Britain: 1841–51 ONE PENNY red-brown pair on cover. The letter, posted in Cowes and cancelled on 25 May 1849, was from Queen Victoria to her aunt, Queen Adelaide at Marlborough House London. It is signed 'The Queen' in the bottom left hand corner. She was insistent on paying for all her postage.

There are several examples of Wyon and Whiting's work in the Collection.

The penny post was an instant success and the mania for letter-writing spread throughout the country, although, as Colonel Maberly had prophesied, it was not until the mid-1870s that the revenue matched pre-1840 levels. Letters were often kept intact with their stamps. In 1841 when 'A young lady being desirous of covering her dressing room with cancelled postage-stamps,'[16] advertised for them in *The Times*, the used stamp took on an importance of its own. *Punch* took a jaundiced view of this fad, stating that the 'mysterious illusions [*sic*] to collections that are in progress of old stamps, under the pretext of papering rooms, are really with the intention of defrauding the Post-office and ruining the revenue'[17] by cleaning and reusing them. Other decorative schemes, where stamps were used, like *tesserae*, in a mosaic, followed. A popular form of 'collecting' at that time was 'the snake' where the stamp was threaded on a string and trimmed. Another piece appeared in *Punch* in 1842 informing its readers that 'the ladies of England betrayed more anxiety to treasure up the Queen's heads than Henry VIII did to get rid of them'.[18] It was a play on words: throughout Queen Victoria's reign, stamps were known as 'Queen's Heads'.

Stamps were first collected for themselves in Britain during the 1850s. 'Foreign stamp collecting' began with schoolboys, for whom overseas examples had a fascination that the commonplace stamps of Great Britain lacked. At around the same time in France, a geography master at a school in Paris encouraged his pupils to collect foreign stamps and to paste them on to the relevant pages of their atlases and exercise books; this might well have been the first systematic classification of stamps in a collection. Soon, this 'hobbyhorsical' interest in collecting stamps was no longer the preserve of the schoolboy. One of the earliest British collectors was a Dr C. W. Viner who began in 1855, and went on to edit both the *Stamp Collector's Magazine* and the *Philatelist*. Collections were built up largely through swaps and, from 1860 onwards, a regular exchange of stamps took place in Birchin Lane, in the City of London. In an evening, up to one hundred collectors would congregate there, of all 'ages and ranks' and of both sexes, even including, as reported in the *Stamp Collector's Magazine*, 'one of Her Majesty's Ministry'. Eventually the over-zealous police intervened, and the exchanges were made surreptitiously in back lanes, or conducted through a female stamp dealer in Birchin Lane.

The interest in collecting and the serious study of stamps was not confined to London. In the 1860s, societies had formed in Brussels and Paris, where the members were known as either *timbreophiles*, as members of the Société Française de Timbrologie, or the Philatèle, from the Greek φιλος (philos: lover of), ατελεια (ateleia: exemption from tax) – in other words, interest in 'the little labels that tax or postage has been paid'. *Philatèle* was anglicised to 'philately'.

In London, a coterie of the more intellectual collectors began to frequent the rectory of the City church Allhallows Staining – Dickens described it as 'a stuffy little place' – at the invitation of the perpetual curate in charge. The Reverend Francis J. Stainforth was a 'zealous collector' who had built up a fine collection (for its day) through his 'well-known readiness to bid high for any real or supposed rarity'. The group of those 'seeking information on the subject of stamps, and for those who had information to impart'[19] met on Saturday afternoons. They included such men as Dr Viner, Mount Brown (who produced the *Catalogue of British Colonial and Foreign Stamps*, based on Stainforth's collection), Sir Daniel Cooper, the first Speaker of the New South Wales Legislature, and Judge Frederick Philbrick. In 1869 and after much discussion, out of this group of learned collectors The Philatelic Society, London emerged. In November 1906, Edward VII 'graciously allowed the Society the style and dignity of the prefix *Royal*' and it became known as the Royal Philatelic Society, London.

A little before the Society's formation, there was another important philatelic date. On 3 June 1865, Prince George of Wales was born at Marlborough House, London. He was the second son of the then Prince and Princess of Wales. Prince George – later Duke of York, Prince of Wales, then King George V – was to become one of the foremost collectors of his generation. Now his unrivalled collection, which forms part of the royal heritage, is the basis of the Royal Philatelic Collection, The Queen's Stamps.

CHAPTER ONE

❖❖❖

For Edward, Prince of Wales, keeping up his diary was obviously a chore. The entries are little more than a brief record of the day's main activity such as 'In the morning we walked out with Papa and Mama, in the afternoon it rained hard',[1] 'Paid Aunt Gloucester a visit' or an account of 'an educational visit' when he went 'to Town to hear Faraday's lecture; Col. Phipps went with us; when we came home Capt. Sayer came in our Railway Carriage'.[2] The entry for 8 April 1856, when the Prince was fifteen was little different: he and his brother, Prince Alfred, 'Dearest Affie', were taken by their long-suffering tutor Frederick Gibbs, for another educational visit: 'London: A rainy day. In the afternoon we went to De la Rue's Manufactory which was very interesting'.[3]

The royal party was shown round by Joseph Coggins, described as 'an Officer of the Inland Revenue'. At that time, the Inland Revenue, not the Post Office, commissioned all new issues of postage stamps, and for their surface-printed or letter-press stamps, they had gone to De La Rue. The princes followed each stage of the printing process, starting with a huge roll of standard emblems watermarked paper, then lingered at the press as it printed off sheets of the lilac '6d. Postage Labels'. Coggins took up a freshly printed sheet of 240 stamps, and with a pair of scissors cut off a block of forty in two equal panes of twenty, four wide and five deep. With a flourish, Coggins endorsed the two blocks of stamps in the margin with his signature and an account of the visit, and handed it to the Princes as a souvenir. Later during the tour, he pulled off another sheet, 240 ONE PENNY revenue stamps, signed them as before: every stamp had to be accounted for, otherwise the printer was liable for the shortfall. In all probability, they were taken by Prince Alfred who, on later evidence, was more interested in stamps than his elder brother. Unfortunately, his account of the visit has not survived. But the two panes of SIX PENCE lilac have, and are the first recorded stamps to enter the Royal Philatelic Collection. Also of interest in the Collection connected with the visit is a specimen of the comb perforation made by Henry Archer's third machine on plain paper. On the margin at the top in manuscript is 'Presented by the inventor. This specimen being one of the first on which the plan of perforation was tried.'[4] The 'presentation' was in fact to a niece whose son sold it to the Collection.

Another stamp with early royal connections is the reprint of the Penny Black by Perkins, Bacon, printers of the original stamp which was phased out in 1841. Legend has it (although discounted by Edward Bacon) that these specimen stamps were ordered in 1864 from the Board of Inland Revenue 'for some younger members of the Royal Family' who had started to form collections, there being no spare copies left of the original. The 'Royal Reprints', as they are known by some, were 'reprinted in black, on paper watermarked Large Crown, from one of the plates of the Retouched Die of the One Penny with crosses in the upper corners'.[5]

Great Britain: 1865 ONE PENNY black. This horizontal pair, known as the 'Royal Reprints', were taken from Plate 66.

The particular plate (Plate 66, Die II) had recently been withdrawn from printing the Penny Red, and had been sent to Somerset House, home of the Inland Revenue, where just four sheets of the stamps were printed on paper with a Large Crown inverted watermark.

It is not known who these 'younger members' of the Royal Family were, although it has always been assumed that one was Prince Alfred. At the time of their printing (now thought to be 1865) he was twenty-one, a student at the University of Bonn and a year away from becoming a captain in the Royal Navy and being created Duke of Edinburgh, thus hardly fitting the description of a 'younger member'. Of Queen Victoria's extended family, the twelve-year-old Prince Leopold and his sister Princess Beatrice might well have been the recipients of the 'Royal Reprint', but Prince Arthur, then aged

Albert Edward, Prince of Wales (left) with his brother Prince Alfred
at Osborne, Isle of Wight, August 1855.

Prince Alfred, Duke of Edinburgh, KG, 1844–1900.
[Photo: RPSL]

fifteen, is the most likely candidate: he had started a collection. He was buying on his own account as seen by a letter from his governor (tutor) Major Howard Elphinstone to Stafford Smith, a firm of stamp dealers in Brighton: '…H.R.H. Prince Arthur has retained a n^r of the stamps in your album amounting to about £3 15. A detailed list of these will be sent to you by tomorrow's post together with a post office order for the amount.'[6] Of the single, two pairs and block of six 'Royal Reprints' in the Collection, none can be positively identified as coming from any of these sources, the fine corner pair was certainly bought at a later date. However, a single example might well have come from Prince Alfred: like most collectors of his day, he acquired on a 'one of everything' basis.

Notwithstanding the recipient of these early 'royal' stamps, Prince Alfred, Duke of Edinburgh, is acknowledged as the founder of the Royal Philatelic Collection. The second son of Queen Victoria and Prince Albert, he set his heart from an early age on the Royal Navy with 'a passion which we, as his parents, believe not to have the right to subdue'.[7] At fourteen, he was a midshipman aboard HMS *Euryalus* in the Mediterranean. His letters home bore the stamps of each country he visited, just as his letters from home were sent with the latest issue. In this early exchange of letters, the content was more important than the stamp. Lucrative too, for the Prince 'was either kept very short of money or was very extravagant, and consequently very hard up, so he soon discovered that he could make capital out of his royal mother's letters and put them up for sale. One day, he came among the mids [midshipmen] with a new letter, crying out, "I'm sure you ought to give me £5 for this one – there is such a lot of good advice in it!"'[8]

Promotion came rapidly for the newly created Duke of Edinburgh who was given his own command, HMS *Galatea* at the age of twenty-two. He had already served throughout the Mediterranean, and over the next few years he went to the West Indies, South Africa, Australia (where he was shot), New Zealand and South America. But his naval career could have been over early, not by the assassin's bullet but by the offer to become King of Greece. Alfred was an attractive proposition to the Greeks, as he would have brought with him the Ionian Islands, then a British protectorate. Although Queen Victoria was in favour of the idea, Palmerston, her Prime Minister, would have none of it. Throughout his sea-time, the Duke was collecting almost exclusively foreign issues. In 1890, he opened the Jubilee Philatelic Exhibition at the Portman Rooms, where he was also one of the exhibitors. That year, he had also been elected the first Honorary President of The Philatelic Society, London, which could account for the reaction of the judges, who were much impressed by the 'excellence' of the exhibits, and the Duke establishing 'himself publicly as an assiduous and ardent collector'.[9]

His collection was described as being 'one on general lines, [with] a large range of countries and colonies'.[10] In many ways, the countries in which he specialised reflected his past career. He was particularly strong, for instance, on Malta, where he had spent much time, latterly as commander-in-chief of the Mediterranean fleet, also Greece and the Ionian Islands, along with Cyprus and Gibraltar. Other groups of countries centred round the Baltic, with Norway, Denmark, Sweden, and Heligoland, even Iceland, and the Balkans with Serbia, Bulgaria and Montenegro. He had also served in the West Indies, hence Cuba and Puerto Rico. Fernando Po, which he also collected, was a port of call on the way to Cape Town, like the island of Tristan da Cunha which had fêted him and renamed the settlement Edinburgh in his honour. In 1967, the island issued a set of four pictorial stamps celebrating the centenary of his visit.

Over the next decade, the quality and content of the Duke's collection seems to have become more specialised. Judging by his entries in the London Philatelic Exhibition at the Institute of Painters in Watercolours in 1897, it would appear that he had abandoned his chosen countries for such rarities as the United States 1851–57 5 CENT red-brown and the 1857–61 90 CENT blue, along with the 1853 3 CUARTOS 'bear' stamps of Madrid. There was also an example of the rare 'Neuchâtel stamp of Switzerland, unused'. He displayed various British and Colonial stamps, including a pair of the Penny Black VR stamps, some rare Nevis, including the 1876–78 SIX PENCE lithographed and the surface printed 1882–90 SIX PENCE green. Unused were the St Vincent 1880 FIVE SHILLINGS, watermarked star and the New South Wales 1850 ONE PENNY, Sydney view, Plate I. Two more stamps of note were the 1863–71 Hong Kong 96 CENTS olive-bistre (a form of yellow-brown) and the TWELVE PENCE black of Canada.

These two stamps can
be positively identified
in the Red Collection as
coming from Alfred, Duke
of Edinburgh's collection.

Hong Kong: 1863–71
96 CENTS olive-bistre, unused.

New Zealand: 1855
ONE SHILLING imperforate.

The Duke's display shows him to have been an astute collector, and even in 1897 these rarities were comparatively expensive. Throughout his life he was always short of money – he even charged social climbers to lunch with his brother, the Prince of Wales. By 1900, after years of extravagant living, his finances became so strained that he was forced to sell his beloved stamp collection to his brother for an undisclosed sum. The Prince of Wales promptly passed it on, in its entirety, to his son, Prince George, and parts of it were eventually amalgamated into his own collection. Today only the Hong Kong 96 CENTS olive-bistre, the New Zealand 1855 ONE SHILLING imperforate and the unused Sierra Leone 1860 grey-lilac SIX PENCE imperforate in the Collection can be positively identified as from the Duke's collection, although there must be other unrecorded examples. Shortly after he had disposed of his collection, the Duke died.

Today, he is little remembered for his active career in the Royal Navy although, through his own ability and hard work, he ended up as Admiral of the Fleet. He is, however, well remembered in philatelic circles, not only as an enthusiastic collector and active honorary President of The Philatelic Society, London but also for his encouragement of others. When his ship, HMS *Galatea*, was paid off, he remet and fell in love with the Grand Duchess Marie Alexandrovina, daughter of Tsar Alexander II. They married in St Petersburg in 1874, and although they lived in England (in Coburg after 1893), the Tsar allowed the Duke and Duchess the use of Farm Palace, a large, romantic, neo-Gothic style cottage near St Petersburg. It was a blissful retreat, set in rolling countryside beside the Gulf of Finland. The Gothic

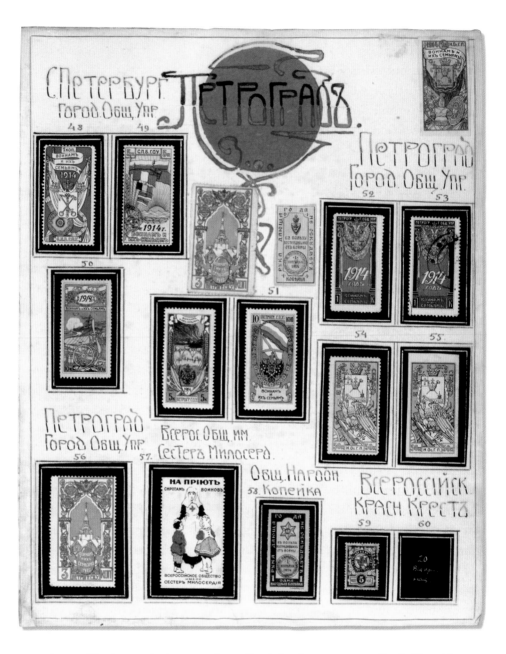

A page of Russian war charity stamps. Legend has it that they were prepared by the Tsarevich, the Grand Duke Alexei.

Cottage Palace stood close by, and beyond it the Palace of Peterhov, and it was here that various members of the Romanov family congregated each summer. There, in the 'land of the midnight sun', Prince Alfred would enthuse about his stamp collection to those who were interested and, more often, those who were not – even then he was acquiring the reputation of being a terrible bore.

Those who did listen, though – like Marie's first cousin, Grand Duke Alexis Michaelovich – went on to form collections of their own. Proposed by the Duke of York and seconded by the honorary assistant secretary, John Tilleard, the Grand Duke was delighted to become an ordinary member of The Philatelic Society, London rather than 'an honorary one'. [11]

The Duke of Edinburgh's mother-in-law, the Tsarina, was another convert; not so Tsar Alexander, although it was often rumoured that he was a keen collector. However, sitting somewhat uneasily in the Collection there is an album of Russian war charity 'stamps', sold in aid of military hospitals and for the care of the wounded. According to a handwritten annotation on the margin of the first sheet, the 'Russian War Stamp Album, [was] personally prepared and hand painted by the last Tsesarevich [the Grand Duke Alexei] at Tobolsk and Ekaterinburg (1917 – July 1918)'. The album pages are well illustrated, though far beyond the capabilities of that fourteen-year-old boy so would have been executed by another hand. According to the annotation, the album was looted by a Red Army gunner from the light artillery, who kept it rolled up in a large tomato tin. It is said to have been purchased by an English trader living in Odessa, who brought it to England in 1923. It remained in his family until it was presented to the Queen in 1981.

When the Duke of York received the Duke of Edinburgh's precious albums, he was already a dedicated collector with the solid basis of a good collection. He also had a good grasp of the *science* of philately. That he had progressed so far was in part due to his uncle's encouragement: Prince George had served in HMS *Alexandra*, the Duke of Edinburgh's flagship under him. But the Duke's interest in stamps had been sparked in early adolescence.

After his time in HMS *Britannia*, the comfortless naval training ship 'that had survived from Nelson's day, …anchored in the river Dart, in Devon',[12] Prince George and his brother, Prince Albert Victor, known as Eddy, were sent as cadets to HMS *Bacchante*, a fully rigged corvette of 4,000 tons with auxiliary engines. They were accompanied by their tutor, the Reverend John Neale Dalton, who as a curate at Whippingham, the nearest church to Osborne, Isle of Wight, had come to the notice of Queen Victoria, a local parishioner. The brothers spent a total of three years in the *Bacchante*, with three separate cruises, the last round the world.

It was during that final voyage that Prince George, a midshipman of sixteen made the first reference to stamp-collecting in his diary on 3 November 1881: 'Put some stamps in my book'.[13] The *Bacchante* had anchored in Osaka Bay, and the Prince was occupying his time while he waited to hear if shore leave was to be granted. This first reference to his book presupposes that this was a new pastime. But as he had visited exotic places all over the world during the previous thirty months, he had had plenty of opportunity to pick up any number of foreign issues, and thus might have started his collection earlier. Furthermore, it would appear that Dalton was also a collector – later he offered his pupil some stamps, for which Prince George wrote, 'Thank you so much for sending me those New South Wales "Centenary" stamps which I wanted for my book very much,' adding 'only I don't like to take them away from you.'[14] There can have been little time for recreation throughout the cruise of the *Bacchante* and entries in Prince George's diaries such as 'Stuck a few stamps in my book'[15] are few and often confined to when he was in the sick bay.

However, just as their father had visited De La Rue, Princes Albert Victor and George had been to the Government Printing Office, Bent Street, Sydney, on 19 July 1881. There, they saw 'the printing presses at work, for a great deal of the work which is done for Government by contract in England under private firms is here done by the Colonial Government for themselves... We saw the postage and receipt stamps being printed, and the railway tickets for the Government lines...'.[16] As a memento, Prince Albert Victor was given the design for the latest issue of Fiji's ONE SHILLING stamp, which had been engraved by T. Richards. The die had just been completed, and it would appear that the Prince took the first impression himself, using a white wove paper and red-brown ink. At some stage, he gave it to his brother as it is now in the Royal Philatelic Collection.

Fiji: 1881–91 ONE SHILLING. Prince Albert Victor took the first impression of this stamp during a visit to the Government Printers in Sydney.

While he was serving as a lieutenant in the Mediterranean under his uncle, Admiral H.R.H. the Duke of Edinburgh, Prince George appears to have had more time for his collection. From January 1887 onwards, there are frequent references in his diary to 'arranging stamps with Uncle Alfred'.[17] Stamps obviously occupied a significant part of his life then, and show him at his most contented: 'another lovely day. Arranging stamps'[18] or 'Uncle Alfred put a few stamps in my book & I finished *She* [Rider Haggard].'[19] Also he stayed at his uncle's official residence, San Antonia Palace, Malta, where he enjoyed a close friendship with his uncle and the rest of the family. The Duke relished his nephew's company too, possibly as his own son was far younger and did not share his philatelic interest. When Prince George went on leave to Cannes to meet up with his parents, he visited a dealer, Kanie, and bought a few stamps. Back in Malta, it was more of the same: 'arranged stamps with uncle Alfred. I brought him some from Cannes.'[20]

At that time, the Prince used a printed album for his collection of adhesives, envelopes and postcards. Although both collections were composed largely of foreign issues, it would appear that Prince George was also interested in current issues of Great Britain. He wrote to Dalton from HMS *Dreadnought*, Malta, asking for 'two complete sets of the new English stamps which have just come out, as I have not got them yet, and I want to give one set to uncle Alfred who collects too. You better buy them new, they look nicer, and I will pay you when I come home, get a 5 shilling one too if there is one.'[21] He was asking Dalton to buy a complete set of the Jubilee stamps that had been issued a month before, on 1 January 1887, and were the last designs to be printed in Queen Victoria's reign. Bicoloured, they are a most attractive set, and while there was no five-shilling stamp as the Prince had hoped, there was a one-pound value. The set, which ranges from ONE HALFPENNY up to ONE SHILLING, along with the fine oblong ONE POUND, is well represented in the Royal Philatelic Collection.

The bicoloured issue was prepared by De La Rue and sent to Windsor Castle for Queen Victoria's approval. A slightly embarrassed J. S. Purcell, the Controller of Stamps at the Inland Revenue, replied that he was commanded by the Queen to thank De La Rue for the stamps and for 'giving her notice of the proposed change of design. The Queen looked at the new stamps but did not give any opinion upon them. Perhaps she may do so later.' He went on to explain that the Queen 'is more set upon the Churchill incident than about stamps'.[22] She approved them once Lord Randolph Churchill, the Chancellor of the Exchequer, had resigned from the Government, the Queen indignant that he had used Windsor writing paper 'that vy night, in my House'.[23]

Among George V's personal effects is a pair of beautiful nine-carat gold cuff-links: on each of the four plates there is a facsimile of a stamp bearing the

Pair of cuff-links made up of Great Britain stamps from the latter part of Queen Victoria's reign belonging to George V.

head of Queen Victoria in enamel, taken from the set that Dalton had bought for him. One shows a representation of the dull purple and blue 9^d stamp and a 2^d green and carmine, while the other has the green and purple brown 4^d and a lilac ONE PENNY from the 1881 issue. The origin of the cuff-links is unknown, but they could well have been a specially commissioned present from his philatelist uncle, the Duke of Edinburgh, or even Dalton, who remained on close terms with his former pupil throughout their lives.

Prince George's interest in stamps was little known, and at that time he would have been grateful for any gift, like that from a Mrs Williams, to whom he wrote, 'Thank you so much for sending me those stamps, I have taken some and am sending you back the rest'.[24] However, news of his interest in stamp collecting reached a far wider and specialised audience when the Duke of Edinburgh, Honorary President of The Philatelic Society, London, opened the London Philatelic Exhibition on 19 May 1890. In his speech he announced proudly: 'Today, Prince George of Wales starts – nay probably has started – from Chatham in the *Thrush* to the command of which he has been appointed. I am sure you will join me in wishing him a prosperous and pleasant cruise. He is also a stamp collector and I hope he will return with a goodly number of additions from North America and the West Indies.'[25] Lieutenant H.R.H. Prince George of Wales had indeed taken command of HMS *Thrush*, a first-class gunboat, and already embarked on what turned out to be a hazardous voyage to Gibraltar with a torpedo boat in tow. After repairs, he crossed the Atlantic to join the West Indian station. There, he cruised the islands, from Trinidad to Bermuda, spending some time in Barbados and St Vincent, and the Leeward Islands. As his uncle suspected, he scoured each island for stamps, often co-opting the Governor or the island's postmaster in his search.

When he reached Trinidad on 19 February 1891, for example, the General Post Office went one stage further and issued a whole set of the current stamps and postal stationery surcharged with a large 9^d. Another set, also overprinted thus, was cancelled TRINIDAD, Fe 23 1891 solely in his honour. In his enthusiasm over the commemorative surcharges, the postmaster forgot to pass on the current 1883–94 issue, so when the *Thrush* reached Bermuda, the Prince wrote to H. E. W. Grant, Governor of Trinidad: 'I am sorry to trouble you again about those blessed stamps; but I find that the Post Master didn't give me any post cards, envelopes & wrappers of the present issue, but only those surcharged with 9d., so I am going to ask you if you would mind getting a set & sending them up to Bermuda when you send the Tobago stamps.'[26] Grant duly obliged the Prince, and that complete set is mounted in the Collection.

Trinidad: 1883–94 value surcharged 9[d].
The whole range of postage, postage due, envelopes, wrappers, postcards and reply postcards
were similarly surcharged to mark the visit of Prince George of Wales,
Captain of HMS *Thrush*.

Not all of Prince George's stamps were gifts. From Barbados, he wrote to John Dalton 'I have been very busy since I have been in the West Indies collecting stamps & I have been lucky enough to pick up some rather good ones, but had to pay a long price for them.'[26] Long periods in port, mostly Bermuda, meant that he could spend time with his collection. 'Wrote some letters and did some stamps'[27] or 'Put some stamps in my book with Dyer [his second in command]'[28] were typical diary entries. On 24 July 1891 on the way from Halifax to Plymouth, he recorded 'no wind quite calm, read prayers. General Qts. put stamps in my book with Dyer all day & counted them. I have got just 5000. The album completely arranged by the next day.'[29]

The *Thrush* returned to England and was paid off in August 1891. Lieutenant H.R.H. the Prince George of Wales's life was about to change dramatically, and with it his approach to his passion for collecting stamps.

CHAPTER TWO

⚜⚜⚜

For its age, the Stanley Gibbons catalogue of stamps of 1891 is in remarkably good condition. The gilt letter G, surmounted by a crown of a prince of England, is stamped deep into the black morocco leather covering. It was bound as a gift to Prince George, and accompanied him on the later stages of the *Thrush* cruise. On each page is marked off each stamp in his Collection with a right-handed tick in red ink. Not surprisingly, the West Indies is best represented. Nearly every Barbados stamp, for instance, is marked as being in the Collection, although some ticks were undoubtedly added at a later date. These neat red ticks show not only the numbers but, more importantly, the sophisticated level his collection had reached at that time: 'A collection which contained the Double Geneva and the 4 centimes of Vaud, as it was then known, was not that of a beginner.'[1]

The early 1890s were a philatelic watershed, where the science and style of collecting was changing. Slowly, the vogue for 'one of everything', regardless of condition, and the emphasis on rarity (like the renowned Thomas Tapling Collection), gave way to the 'study collection'. Here, the advanced student went for 'specialised' collecting better to understand the historical aspects of the design of each issue, the minutiae of its production, and the technique of the printer. A good collection was a balanced one, put together with specialised knowledge and full understanding of everything in it, where as much

The Stanley Gibbons catalogue for 1891 was specially bound in black morocco leather for Prince George of Wales.

39

care went into the selection and study of the 'humblest stamp as the acknow-ledged rarity of a country'.[2] With this new fashion and the rash of new collectors, prices inevitably spiralled. Rarities had always commanded high prices, but with the demand for completeness, scarcity made rarities out of even the most moderate examples.

The move to a more sophisticated form of collecting required time, scholarship, money and opportunity, and for Prince George his change of for-tune came at exactly the right time. In mid-January 1892, Prince Albert Victor died of pneumonia and his brother was desolate. At the same time, at the age of twenty-six, he found himself transformed from a comparatively impecu-nious naval officer to second in line to the throne. In her birthday honours in May, Queen Victoria created him Duke of York, Earl of Inverness and Baron Killarney. He moved into a suite of rooms within St James's Palace, which became known as York House, and had the use of the Bachelors' Cottage at Sandringham. With a comptroller who doubled as a treasurer and an equerry in waiting, the Duke began a not too onerous programme of royal duties. He was allowed one brief farewell cruise, manoeuvres off the coast of Ireland, then retired from the Navy after nearly sixteen years service. With his own and the Duke of Clarence's portion of a Parliamentary grant of £36,000 a year, sober needs, and time on his hands, the Duke had both the opportunity and the money to indulge himself as he pleased. Throughout the rest of his life, his stamp collection became an escalating part of that indulgence.

Although he had been an established collector for a decade, the Duke of York was on the 'ground floor' of the new style of collecting. In addition, as heir to the heir to the throne, the idea of collecting the stamps of Great Britain, her Dominions and the Crown Colonies took on a whole new meaning for him. When he studied a particular stamp of the Empire, he had the added familial interest in the design and craftsmanship used to portray the Sovereign's head to honour, but not always to flatter, his grandmother, later his father and himself.

He began by asking The Philatelic Society, London for their latest work on the stamps of the West Indies. A copy was specially bound and 'offered for his acceptance'. It was a good start, and the gift reminded the Society's officers that he was a serious collector. Yet, however much he collected and studied on his own, or read books and journals on philately, the Duke recognised that his collection could not advance as he wished unless he had help. On 28 February 1893, at York House, he duly recorded in his diary the most important event yet in his career as a collector: 'Mr Tilleard came to see me about my stamps'.[3] John Alexander Tilleard was assistant honorary secretary of The Philatelic Society, London, and it was he who had encouraged the Duke of Edinburgh to become a member and subsequently Honorary President. The Duke, in turn, put forward Tilleard as philatelic adviser to his nephew.

Tilleard, then aged forty-three, and the Duke of York took to each other immediately, and a firm friendship grew between them that lasted for over twenty years. Tilleard was a successful solicitor, with his own busy practice in the City of London. Whatever time he had to himself, he devoted to philately. His knowledge was encyclopedic, and he 'had the unerring instinct of the true collector in assimilating what is really fine and scarce'.[4] Before his involvement with the Duke of York, he had formed a noted collection of his own but gave it up to concentrate on the Duke's. After his collection – which 'contained some splendid stamps' – was dispersed, he kept in close touch with the philatelic world for twenty years as honorary secretary of The Philatelic Society, London. His numerous learned contributions to philatelic literature (India and Prince Edward Island, Canada, were his areas of particular expertise) and his annual reports for the Society on the activities of the members and philatelic subjects were an inspiration to all his successors.

Tilleard served the Duke of York for the rest of his life. A man of 'considerable taste in his choice of specimens',[5] he was an ideal tutor, who set his own exacting standards on his pupil, condition being the most important criterion. Tilleard's charm and easy manner endeared him to all, particularly his fellow collectors and the principal stamp dealers, and it was through these contacts that he was able to acquire 'very many superb and desirable stamps at prices that excited the envy of us all'.[6] Although Tilleard gave as much time to his royal position as he could afford, he spent most of it acquiring stamps, rather than mounting and writing them up. In the main, when a whole collection was bought, it was left in its original album, and subsequent stamps were added to it.

He also enjoyed an easy friendship with the Duke's Household. He was a frequent guest of the comptroller and treasurer, Major General Sir Francis de Winton, a veteran of the Crimean War, who had a house, Congham Lodge, just two miles from Sandringham. The Duke recorded: 'de Winton brought Tilleard over to lunch. In [the] afternoon took him & Williams the usual Sunday rounds & showed them all the animals. After tea, Tilleard showed me some stamps he has just got for me.'[7]

Tilleard's first act was to suggest that the Duke of York became a member of The Philatelic Society, London, and his election came through on 10 March 1893. At the same time, he was immediately elected honorary vice president. Although, strictly speaking, he was an honorary member, he always paid his subscription as an ordinary member – then one guinea a year, which had risen to three guineas by his death in 1936. Tilleard was frequently summoned to York House by the Duke, so often that Harold Nicolson, George V's official biographer, observed that 'it must be admitted that the visits of Mr Tanner [the Duke's tutor on the law and practices of the Constitution] to York House are recorded with less frequency than those of Mr Tilleard, the philatelist'.[8]

For the Duke of York, the benefits of membership of The Philatelic Society, London were immediate. On 3 May 1893, he became engaged to his late brother's fiancée, Princess May of Teck, and a hundred members of the Society, including some from Europe, the United States and Canada, clubbed together for a one-sided wedding present of a 'handsome volume' containing 1,500 stamps. The names of the contributors, headed by the President, the Earl of Kingston, and J. N. Keynes, father of Lord (Maynard) Keynes and such philatelic luminaries as Philippe La Renotière von Ferrari, were entered at the front, with a list of the stamps at the end. The gift was supposed to reflect the Duke's areas of collecting, 'great care having been taken to ensure that they would be acceptable as additions to the collection of His Royal Highness'. [9] The majority of the stamps were unused and in pristine condition. The idea was that they would be removed from the finely tooled morocco-bound volume and arranged in the Duke's albums, which eventually they were, except for a few Russian rural posts which had no place in his collection so remained in the volume and are there today. As the Duke transferred his wedding present to his collection, each stamp was marked off in his Stanley Gibbons catalogue.

In the 'wedding present' album the stamps were mounted by country in alphabetical order, beginning with Afghanistan and Austria. Under British East Africa, he received the dull purple HALF PENNY and ONE PENNY 1881 Great Britain Queen Victoria stamps, surcharged 'British East Africa Company HALF ANNA' and 'British East Africa Company 1 ANNA'. Thirty-one years later, in 1924, he must have enjoyed seeing another HALF ANNA surcharge in his album, that one a unique version with the error HALΓ for HALF, a present from his sister, Princess Victoria.

Under Canada, the Duke received two handsome imperforate SIX PENCE stamps, one 1851 slate violet/brown purple on laid paper, the other, the 1852–57 slate violet/grey brownish on handmade wove paper. Ceylon was well represented too with such delights as the HALF PENNY reddish-lilac private roulette on blued glazed paper of 1857–64 and an inverted 1855 5 cents

British East Africa
Company 1890
HALF ANNA on ONE
PENNY, error HALΓ
for HALF, a present
from Princess Victoria
to her brother,
George V.

Ceylon: 1857–64 (1855)
SIXTEEN CENTS pale violet,
FIVE CENTS surcharge, inverted.
Crown CA watermark.

Ceylon: 1857–64 ONE HALF
PENNY reddish-lilac rouletted
on blued glazed paper of 1857.

Ceylon: 1885 pale violet FIVE CENTS
surchage on SIXTEEN CENTS.

British East Africa Company:
1890 1 ANNA on 2d.

Four examples of the rare stamps from the Duke of York's wedding
present donated by members of The Philatelic Society, London.

Great Britain: 1841 pair
of ONE PENNY red-brown
on Dickinson silk-thread paper,
Plate 11 trial printing.

Great Britain: Hertford College Oxford on cover 1879 (½ᵈ). Some Oxford and Cambridge Colleges
had their own stamps, but the Post Office stopped the practice in 1886.

surcharge on SIXTEEN CENTS pale violet. There were also rarities like those of the 1870–71 *Fiji Times* Express – the I PENNY black on very deep rose, and the THREE PENCE black on the pale rose on laid bâttonné paper that had been typeset and printed at their offices at Levuka, Ovalau Island.

In the Collection, a selection of the 1850–54 ONE PENNY and TWO PENCE on Dickinson silk-thread paper was also included in the wedding present album, along with numerous other rare and desirable examples, such as the 'proof on card in black and red of the 1d. and the 2d. with letters in the corners, a strip of 6 of the (1867–80) 3d. (spray of rose watermark), several copies of the (1865–7) 6d., 9d., and 1s. (large letters)'.[10] There were two 1840 Mulready sheets and eleven stamps of the Oxford and Cambridge colleges, issued for inter-college messenger services in the 1870s and 1880s; they were never accepted as legitimate postage stamps, and were dropped after the intervention of the Post Office.

The Duke of York would have been delighted to see so many West Indian stamps in his gift for like most of the St Vincent, they were 'very numerous and fine being nearly all unused, and amongst the latter were the [1875–78], FOUR PENCE blue (star watermark) FOUR PENCE yellow, ONE SHILLING brown, [1869], FIVE SHILLINGS (1880) and the unbelievably rare ½d in red on each half of the SIX PENCE (1881).'[11]

Recalling his own time in the Caribbean, the Duke can only have been delighted when he received 'A very fine copy of the rare (November 1880) 1d surcharged in ink on the six pence orange of Tobago, used on part of the original envelope, together with the scarce [1882–84] six pence ochre (now stone) of the same colony'.[12] The Duke's collection of Trinidad stamps was considerably increased with a fine, unused set of the ONE PENNY first issue of 1851–6, on blued paper, but to his already good collection of Turks Islands, was added an entire sheet of 1881 surcharge '½d on a ONE PENNY, and a half sheet showing all the varieties of another setting of the ½d on the ONE SHILLING plum'. He must have been proud of his Turks Islands collection as it was frequently exhibited, especially those two items.

Australia too was well represented in the gift, with some acceptable 1850 'Sydney Views' from New South Wales, and some later issues from

St Vincent: 1875–78 FOUR PENCE blue, 1869 FOUR PENCE yellow, the ONE SHILLING brown, and the 1880 FIVE SHILLINGS rose red. These were all welcome wedding presents, more so, the rare St Vincent: 1881 ½ᵈ on half SIX PENCE bright green, a horizontal pair.

Turks Island: 1881 ½ on ONE PENNY dull red, block of 30. Having spent some time in the West Indies whilst in the Royal Navy, the islands were always prized in the Duke of York's Collection. This block came as a wedding present and greatly enhanced his already good collection.

Western Australia: 1857–59 SIX PENCE black-bronze, rouletted. Part of his extensive wedding present, such stamps not only enhanced the Duke of York's collection, but opened up new areas of study.

Victoria. The rare rouletted SIX PENCE black/bronze of 1857–59 of Western Australia stood out among them.

In October 1893, the Duke of York and Tilleard together selected his exhibits for The Philatelic Society's London Exhibition of West Indian stamps. It was held in the Society's rooms in Arundel Street, London. As well as the fine displays, the exhibition was marked by 'the electric light, which was provided temporarily; a decided improvement, and one that will no doubt be capable of still further amelioration if supplied by a permanent installation'.[13] Another innovation was the glass display cases. A constant stream of visitors filed past the exhibits, and accounts appeared in the national press, the exhibition 'an especially gratifying evidence of the increasing spread of the appreciation of Philately'.[14] Perhaps the Duke's participation fuelled the public's keen interest.

If the public was impressed, the Duke's fellow philatelists were delighted with his exhibits. Diplomatically, he showed part of his wedding present, the Turks surcharges, which, as Tilleard observed, 'there being only one or two copies known and altogether this exhibit will be found a very instructive one'.[15] Another exciting entry was the Pacific Steam Navigation Company Stamps. Under letters patent the Company had been incorporated in 1840 to carry British mails along the west coast of South America. It began with two wooden paddle-steamers, but by 1852 the fleet had acquired four more for the bi-monthly service between Valparaíso and Panama. The operation was expanded in 1867, with monthly sailings from Liverpool through the Straits of Magellan for a new mail service. Such was the success of the operation that the Company continued to expand – by 1891 there were thirty-six mail-carrying vessels. Finally, in 1910 the Royal Mail Steam Packet Company absorbed it into its larger operation.

In 1847 William Wheelright, one of the founders of the Pacific Steam Navigation Company, had written to his cousin Joshua Butters Bacon, of the printers Perkins, Bacon and Petch, to ask him to come up with some designs for a stamp. Bacon replied with 'one or two sketches for a stamp such as you describe in your letter': a representation of Commerce with the value set in the surrounding engine-turning. Wheelright and his company secretary William Taggart were not satisfied and sent a 'rough outline' of what they wanted: a 'print of the Company's steamers'.[16] Bacon said that this was impractical and open to forgery, but in the end the Company had its way using the two pioneer paddlers, the *Chile* and the *Peru*, for the ONE REAL and TWO REALES respectively. In the Royal Mail Steam Packet Company section of the Royal Philatelic Collection, there is a fine block of thirty, 1875 deep rose TEN CENTS stamps.

Naturally, at the West Indian Exhibition the Duke was keen to show his complete set of Trinidad surcharged 9[d], cancelled 23 February 1891, which commemorated his visit on HMS *Thrush*. He also exhibited a fine copy of the 1847 5 cents 'Lady McLeod' on a folded letter dated 2 June 1847. It is likely that he bought it in Trinidad (it was ticked in his 1891 catalogue as being in his collection), which was farsighted of him: the stamp had only recently been

Trinidad: 1847 (5 cents) blue, on entire, uncancelled.
This comparatively rare example (on a folded letter dated 2 June 1847), is known as a 'Lady McLeod'
after the name of the ship that carried the mails from Port of Spain to San Fernando.

recognised as a comparative rarity when, soon after his return, one sold for thirteen guineas.

The 'Lady McLeod', as this classic private local postage stamp is known, was a native-printed lithograph in deep blue on yellowish paper. It portrays the paddle steamer, the *Lady McLeod,* with most of her sails set, in a choppy sea above the interlaced, upper-case initials *LMcL*. The background has vertical and horizontal lines within a framework of interlaced semicircles. The ship was named after the wife of the then Governor, Sir Henry McLeod, but he retired shortly before the ship came into service in November 1845. At sixty tons displacement with engines producing forty horsepower, the *Lady McLeod* plied the twenty-five miles between Port of Spain and San Fernando as the road was virtually impassable. Soon after her inaugural run, a notice appeared in the *Port of Spain Gazette*:

Steamer *Lady McLeod*

LETTERS, MONEY, AND SMALL PARCELS

Will be carried from this date for subscribers only at one dollar per month from each Subscriber or Estate, payable quarterly in advance; letters of non-subscribers will be charged ten cents each. Letter Box at Michael Maxwell's, San Fernando, and Turnbull, Stewart & Co., Port of Spain.

Turnbull, Stewart & Co., the owners, found that subscribers were few, as most preferred to turn up on the day and pay the ten cents in cash for each letter, as did the next owner, David Bryce, the *Lady McLeod*'s master, who placed another notice in the *Port of Spain Gazette* on 16 April 1847:

The Subscriber experiencing inconvenience in Collecting the Money for Letters of Non-Subscribers, has procured Labels, which may be had of him or the Agents for the Steamer, at 5 cents each, or Four Dollars per Hundred.

No other letters but those of subscribers who have paid *in advance*, or such as have these labels attached, will be carried, from and after the 24th instant.

Freight for parcels and small packages as heretofore.

DAVID BRYCE

Proprietor

For almost thirty months, Bryce ran the *Lady McLeod* regularly between Port of Spain and San Fernando and beyond carrying mails. Throughout that time, the labels were cancelled by hand with a pen, usually in the form of a cross. Alternatively, the corner of the stamp was torn off to cancel it, 'reminding one of the method employed to signify use of the early stamps of Afghanistan'.[17] There are some rare examples of these stamps like the one in the Royal Philatelic Collection on a folded letter dated 2 June 1847 that escaped the postmaster's cancellation pen. Bryce sold the *Lady McLeod* to a consortium from San Fernando, and when her monopoly to carry letters ended so that she had to compete with the Americans and the Dutch, she was sold on, and finally foundered on a bank near San Fernando in 1854. She was not, however, entirely forgotten: the ship's bell was recovered and is sometimes shown at meetings of the Trinidad Philatelic Society. The 125th anniversary of the first sailing of the *Lady McLeod* was marked by a three-set commemorative issue in 1972, examples of which are also in the Collection.

When the Duke of York visited De La Rue, the Government printers, he was rather more expansive than his father in the subsequent diary entry:

> At 11.45 went with de Winton and Cust to the City to see De la Rue's Manufactory. Mr Purcell & Mr Tilleard were there. Mr De la Rue showed us the whole process of Postage Stamp making & it was most interesting, he makes 20 millions (sterling) worth of stamps a year & employs 2000 people. We lunched with him. Home at 6.0.[18]

Unlike his father thirty-eight years before him who wrote 'very' interesting, the Duke meant it: he stayed 'not only to lunch, but tea as well'.[19] The chairman, Warren William De la Rue, showed the Duke around, accompanied by de Winton and Cust, J. S. Purcell, Controller of Stamps, and his own stamp adviser. While his staff did not generally share his enthusiasm for stamps, the Duke was enthralled, and left with a better understanding of the technical aspects of stamp production and printing.

Succinct as ever, the Duke of York recorded on 10 May 1894 that he: 'went with uncle Alfred to Effingham House to see an exhibition of very rare Postage stamps, sent by members of the Philatelic Society. I sent some too.'[20] The exhibition of rarities was staged to celebrate the twenty-fifth anniversary of the founding of The Philatelic Society, London, where, in the overblown language that marked philatelic writing of the day, 'the leading Philatelists have disclosed in friendly self-abnegation some of the hidden valuables, that by their knowledge and experience can now be marked out for search and future acquisition by their less fortunate *confrères*'.[21] The exhibition was arranged in alphabetical order of the exhibitors, starting with the Grand Duke Alexis Michaelovich, the Duke of Saxe Coburg and Gotha's protégé, who displayed some fine Russian essays, followed by W. B. Avery, a leading collector.

The Duke of York had already admired Avery's collection of Nevis at the West Indies exhibition the previous year, but it is likely that this was the first time he had ever set eyes on the famous Mauritius 'Post Offices' of 1847, whose laconic catalogue entry; 'One each, Issue I. (Post Office), 1 d. and 2 d.; unused' belied the importance of these romantic stamps. Although he did not yet own anything of such magnitude, it must have given the Duke considerable pleasure to see just how well his contributions compared with those of the great collectors of his day. His exhibits also showed how far he had advanced in his collecting, though some, like the pair of one penny red-brown on Dickinson silk-thread paper had been included in his wedding present. However, Tilleard's influence can already be seen: some of the Duke's exhibits were not marked off in the '1891 catalogue' and therefore were not part of it.

Once again Tilleard, with the connivance of the Duke, made an extensive selection of imperforate Great Britain, including a pair of the unissued vr Penny Black official stamps of 1840 and the surface printed stamps of all values and issues to that date, including the THREE PENCE with the shaded spandrels, and two examples of the FOUR PENCE small garter watermarks 1855–57 in lake, matchless shades. This important exhibition was the only occasion when the Duke exhibited foreign (that is non-colonial) stamps such as the fine United States block of six 'City Despatch' post of New York.

Great Britain: 1840 VR ONE PENNY black official stamps, registered but never used.

★ ★ ★

Despite the 'transient flicker of a recovery', the Earl of Kingston died in Cairo in the middle of January 1896 after an operation. He had been President of The Philatelic Society, London, for nearly four years, adding 'lustre to it by his Philatelic abilities [a collection of Great Britain and Colonies] and noble birth'.[22] Tilleard, by then honorary secretary of the Society, intimated to its Council that the Duke of York, if offered, would accept the Presidency. He was duly elected on 29 May.

From the beginning, the Duke, whose 'knowledge of matters philatelic was in no sense a perfunctory one',[23] was far more to the Society than a mere royal figurehead. At that time, for example, there was heated debate about the variations of colour and the difference in shape of the figure '2' of the 1851–4 2 RIGSBANK SKILLING blue of Denmark. During a seemingly interminable summer visit to his mother's Danish relations, the Duke addressed the problem. On his return home, he wrote a paper on his findings, which was read by Tilleard at the Society's November meeting. The Duke had taken the question to the General Post Office in Copenhagen, where he discovered that plaster casts from the original single die, engraved on steel of the 2 RIGSBANK SKILLING, had been taken to form the matrix in the production of the plates. He then worked out that the discrepancies in colour and the numeral differ-ence were due to defects in the casting, where clearly some portions of the die had not been filled in properly with the plaster. Further research revealed that ten blocks of these defective plaster matrices, each two stamps wide and five long, had been joined together to form a single block, and cast by the stereo-type process in type metal – a composition of tin, lead and antimony. Ten of the stereotypes were soldered together and mounted in a mahogany frame to form the printing plate, so compounding the error, which explained the variety in printing that recurred so regularly on the plate. As all agreed at the Society's next meeting, their President had successfully resolved the question on his own – or, as the editor of the London Philatelist had it in the purple philatelic prose of the day, 'The entire question had been one both of interest and utility, and the successful entrance of the President into the arena of discussion will be hailed by all Philatelists as the happiest of dénouements.'[24]

At home, in one of his first public acts as President, the Duke of York opened the London Philatelic Exhibition at the Royal Institute of Painters in Watercolour of the Diamond Jubilee year. His own exhibit 'a complete collection of the De La Rue series [of India], represented by imperforate copies of each plate registered on being put to press, and including the new 6 a.[nnas] stamp prepared many years ago, but not yet issued',[25] was not entered for competition; neither was the selection of essays and proofs from his Collection. He was in his element: he returned twice more, once with his father, the Prince of Wales, and once with his wife. As they moved from country to country, the stamps entered by exhibitors from all over the world, he pointed out to her 'the lion of the Exhibition', W. B. Avery's Mauritius POST OFFICE ONE PENNY and TWO PENCE, while the Duchess remarked on the pair of unused SIX PENCE Canadian, slate-violet on thin wove paper bearing the image of the Prince Consort, one of the attractions of Henry Duveen's exhibit. She asked the Duke if he possessed such a stamp: he replied, 'with a superior Philatelic smile', that it was the TWELVE PENCE 'of the same issue that he lacked'.

Even in 1897, philatelists viewed the 'TWELVE PENCE black' with a certain awe. It was the highest denomination of Canada's first postage stamps which first came into use on 23 April 1851 although the TWELVE PENCE was not issued until 14 June. The THREE PENCE in red showed a beaver, the SIX PENCE in purple, as the Duchess of York rightly pointed out, portrayed Prince Albert, while the TWELVE PENCE black bore the head of Queen Victoria.

The TWELVE PENCE covered just a few destinations. Thus, many fewer of these than the lower values were printed and only warranted a single printing on laid and wove paper. The latter are extremely rare, and consequently expensive; they were only issued when those on the laid paper were running out. For some reason, the new postal system of Canada was not an instant success and of the 51,400 TWELVE PENCE black, only 1,510 were sold and the remainder destroyed in 1857.

The TWELVE PENCE black was one of the first stamps to be classed as a rarity. It appeared in Alfred Potiquet's catalogue in 1862, later changing hands for as much as £1 – a considerable sum in 1865. It is also a stamp surrounded by anecdote. An old man living in a log cabin on the banks of the St Lawrence bought what must have been one of the first TWELVE PENCE blacks to be sold

Canada: 1851 TWELVE PENCE black, one of the earliest stamps to be classed as a rarity.

because he wanted to send an important document to a banking house in New York. He placed the letter in a strongbox, intending to deliver it to the nearest post office several miles downstream. Before he could leave his home, his nephew, 'a good for nothing scoundrel', jumped the old man, who hurled the box into the river outside. In the resulting struggle, the oil lamp fell over and smashed, setting the log cabin alight. The nephew fled and the old man perished, but not before he had named the culprit to his neighbours. In 1892, that part of the St Lawrence was dredged, and the strongbox was found. The contents, still miraculously in reasonable condition, were identified and returned to his heir, who sold the cover for £70.

The Duke finally managed to secure the coveted Canadian TWELVE PENCE black, which was among the selection of Canadian stamps shown to the Royal Philatelic Society, London in 1912. One of only six known copies on cover, it was on a folded letter to Wall Street dated 13 January 1853. There is an unused copy in the Collection with a left sheet margin. He might have been able to buy an example earlier, had a cache not been lost by dealers.

One very hot, airless day, a London dealer was examining five TWELVE PENCE blacks spread out on a table beside an open window. He had recently bought them in a mixed lot, and was particularly pleased with his haul as he had paid little for them, and looked forward to selling them at auction the next week. He was so engrossed that he did not hear the door open. A rush of air blew the stamps out of the window. They fluttered down three storeys and onto the Strand, never to be seen again. Another dealer had bought the Lachlan Gibbs collection of Canada, which included no less than a dozen TWELVE PENCE blacks, five on covers, the rest used. They were stuffed into a drawer of his desk, which was already overflowing with papers. When a client wanted to see them, the drawer was turned out, the office safe searched but to no avail. The envelope with the stamps and the covers had fallen out of the drawer, into the wastepaper basket and been thrown away. The two losses increased the value of the remainder – not that value is an issue with the Royal Philatelic Collection: these rarities would never be sold.

To mark the centenary of the first Canadian issue, an appropriate selection of stamps was sent from the Royal Philatelic Collection to the Capex International Philatelic Exhibition held in Toronto in 1951. The exhibit included a handsome album with the complete imprimatur set of stamps printed by Canada to celebrate the Diamond Jubilee of Queen Victoria in 1897. The event was marked enthusiastically throughout the Empire. Up to that time, stamps had been, for the most part, purely functional, a means of showing that postage had been prepaid, as Rowland Hill had envisaged at the beginning of the Queen's long reign. But in the United States, the government, for the first time ever, issued sixteen different stamps to commemorate the four-hundredth anniversary of the landing of Christopher Columbus in the New World; this issue doubtless inspired Canada (and six other countries) to follow its example to mark the Diamond Jubilee.

Canada produced a set of stamps, of uniform design with sixteen values from HALF CENT to FIVE DOLLARS in a fine assortment of colours using the famous 1837 portrait by Alfred E. Chalon alongside Heinrich von Angeli's 1886 portrait. A complete set of these stamps was presented to the Duke

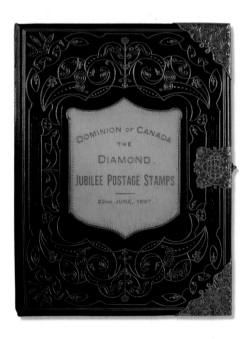

Canada: 1897 volume to commemorate Queen Victoria's Diamond Jubilee, 'bound and illuminated in the taste of the time', presented to the Duke of York.

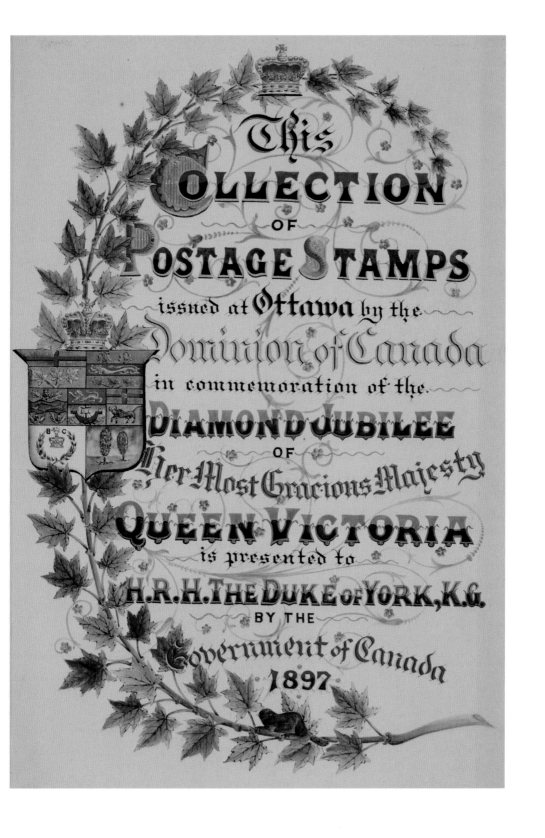

This
COLLECTION
OF
POSTAGE STAMPS
issued at Ottawa by the
Dominion of Canada
in commemoration of the
DIAMOND JUBILEE
OF
Her Most Gracious Majesty
QUEEN VICTORIA
is presented to
H.R.H. THE DUKE OF YORK, K.G.
BY THE
Government of Canada
1897

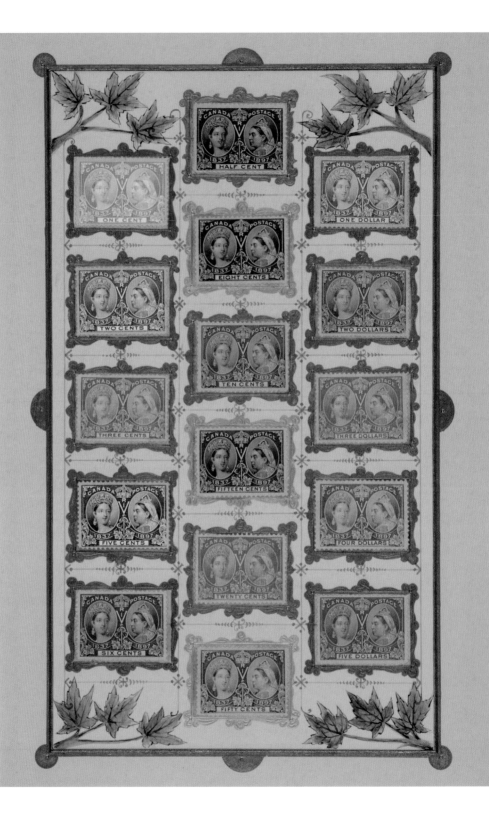

of York, 'bound and illuminated in the taste of the time'[26] The album is covered in blue morocco leather, heavily embossed with gold leaf, with solid Canadian gold corners and a clasp in the form of oak leaves with the Duke's entwined monogram, GFEA – George Frederick Ernest Albert. It is dated 22ND June 1897, in a raised white shield. Inside, there is a beautiful calligraphic inscription, with the arms of Ottawa, decorated with sprays of the Canadian maple leaf, as is the page set with the Jubilee stamps. The last page was left blank for the certificate of destruction of the plates in the presence of the Postmaster General of Canada, the Hon. William Mulock. Although the certificate was never issued, there is a letter in the Royal Philatelic Collection confirming the destruction of the plates.

The Queen survived her Diamond Jubilee by three and a half years. She died peacefully at Osborne House, on the Isle of Wight on 22 January 1901. The Duke of York, present at her bedside, wrote that night 'Our beloved Queen & Grandmama, one of the greatest women that ever lived, passed peacefully away.'[27] Her death at the dawn of the new century heralded a new era: her eldest son, the Prince of Wales, acceded to the throne as Edward VII.

CHAPTER THREE

⚜ ⚜ ⚜

The *Alberta*, Queen Victoria's favourite yacht, glided through the flat, oily water towards Portsmouth to the strains of funereal music and the deafening salutes of a vast array of Royal Navy ships that lined the Roads from Cowes to Portsmouth. Her coffin lay on the quarterdeck, covered in white and gold, with the Imperial crown at its head, guarded by four of her A.D.C.s. A convoy of mourners, led by the Royal Yacht *Victoria and Albert* followed in her wake, HMY *Osborne* and the Kaiser's yacht, SMY *Hohenzollern*, at either side. The King and Queen were aboard the *Victoria and Albert,* and shortly after they left Cowes, Edward VII sent for the captain to demand why the Royal Standard was flying at half-mast. The Captain explained: 'The Queen is dead, sir.' 'The King of England lives,' came his swift reply, and the Royal Standard was immediately hoisted to the truck.

The Royal Standard that flew at the masthead served for both Queen Victoria and the new king. Where it had been easy enough to transform the Prince of Wales's standard to that of sovereign (by simply removing the appliquéd white label with three pendants) the first issue of Edward VII stamps was not so simple, and was to take a whole year to produce. Nor did the new king have the help of his philatelist son to advise him as the Duke and Duchess of York were abroad. It had long been arranged that he would represent Queen Victoria at the opening of the Australian Parliament in Melbourne, and although his father was unwilling to let him go so soon after his accession, the tour went ahead as planned and the couple sailed in HMS *Ophir*, a liner chartered from the Orient Line by the Admiralty, in March 1901. On the accession of his father, the Duke became Duke of Cornwall, and with the title came the revenues provided by the Duchy properties to add to his already adequate income from Parliament.

The voyage out was comfortable and although the Duke and Duchess hated leaving home, the trip offered some compensations – at least for him. In Malta, he invested Ugo Testeferrata, Baron of Gomerino, with the Companion of the Order of St Michael and St George, and in return received 'a most valuable collection of stamps which the Baron had collected for some forty years'.[1] Throughout his life, the Duke with his methodical mind and accurate memory could remember where most of the important stamps in his collection had come from, even though his albums were written up by others. He did not see the need to keep a philatelic diary, and only the occasional stamp-related entry crept into his personal diary or correspondence. Even then, it was invariably less than specific. In a typical extract from one of his letters to Tilleard he wrote: 'I am sending you two stamps which I received yesterday from F. R. Ginn (whom no doubt you know) asking if I wish to buy them. They appear to me to be two very good unused specimens…'.[2] There is no way of telling what these stamps were, or if they were incorporated into the Collection, or indeed if the Testeferrata gift was. However, if the Baron was collecting Malta, some of the early Crown Colony stamps, like the HALF PENNY buff on blued paper, might well have come from this source. A halfpenny was the standard rate for the internal post within the island and was printed by De La Rue in London. The overseas post was the responsibility of the British Post Office, hence Great Britain stamps were utilised and cancelled with the A25 postmark. These are all well represented in the Collection, along with every shade of the HALF PENNY, in blocks of four, pairs, and on covers along with other values. As elsewhere on the cruise of the *Ophir*, the Duke bought (or, more usually, was presented with) all the current stamps of the country when ashore.

The *Ophir* reached Ceylon where the Duke undertook more official duties and accepted a collection of unspecified stamps, and left on 16 April for Singapore. For the whole ship's company, it was a 'very hot day, with occasional showers which do not cool the air much. We have all had enough of the tropics, but we must possess our souls in patience, for we have still a long run, almost parallel with the Equator.'[3] But for the Duke it was less of a trial as he had his beloved stamps to distract him: shortly before Singapore and the next day, he was closeted in his day cabin with one of his friends and equerry, Commander Sir Bryan Godfrey-Faussett, where they arranged his stamps 'in ... between blotting paper to prevent them sticking together'.[4] There must have been a sizeable number if it took two of them two afternoons to lay them out. And there were many more to come.

At last the *Ophir* reached Melbourne, the capital of Victoria, and the then seat of the Australian Government. On 9 May, the Duke inaugurated the first Commonwealth parliament, the prime purpose of his tour. Despite the heavy call on his time of official duties, though, he managed to fit in a little philatelic research. The settlement around Port Phillip Bay, the present Melbourne, in the south of New South Wales had grown so fast during the first four decades of the nineteenth century that its representatives had petitioned the British government for permission to form their own separate Colony, to be called Victoria in honour of the Queen. Even before the Colony was formally declared in 1851, the legislative council of New South Wales had introduced its own postal reforms, which included stamps inscribed VICTORIA for the Port Phillip Bay settlement. They were printed locally, under licence, by Thomas Ham of Melbourne from January 1850 until the end of 1859. Ham's first printings, which became known as the 'Half Lengths', of the ONE PENNY, TWO PENCE and THREE PENCE values, were produced all together on a steel die – there is an original proof of the ONE PENNY in black on thin glazed card from this die in the Collection. By the time of the Duke's visit in 1901, most of the plates of the original issues of the Victoria

Victoria: 1850–53 (Half Length), ONE PENNY black, die proof of the Ham first setting.

Victoria: 1850–53 (Half Length) THREE PENCE bright blue, pair unused. Coming from the first Ham setting, this issue is known as a 'Half Length' as opposed to the later full length portrait, the 'Queen on Throne'.

stamps had been destroyed, but the first steel die was found and reprints made 'in black with impressions with the 2d, 3d and 1d … from the original steel plate'.⁵ The pull, marked 'No 1 Impression', was presented to the Duke, along with the No 4 impression of the ONE SHILLING.

Similarly, the original steel plate of the TWO PENCE 'Queen on Throne' of 1852 also came to light, and the reprint from that plate (in black on white glazed paper) is in the Collection with the original Ham plate proofs, in red-brown on soft card. The stamp is well represented with many examples of the TWO PENCE reddish-brown and TWO PENCE purple-brown, along with the 1891 reprint, both the pale-brown and the grey-brown. Increased postal rates required larger denominations, and in 1854 the contract to print a ONE SHILLING value went to another local firm, Campbell and Fergusson (who

Victoria: 1901 'Queen on Throne' TWO PENCE black, reprint, detail from a sheet of 50, with margins and inscriptions. This reprint was made during the Duke of York's visit to Melbourne and, along with the ONE PENNY and THREE PENCE values, it is marked 'No 1 Impression from the original steel plate'.

Opposite: Victoria: 1850–53 (Half Length), ONE PENNY vermilion and THREE PENCE blue on cover. It is dated 11 January 1850 and, at just ten days after the first die proof, is the earliest recorded date.

also took over the original Ham plates). In the Collection, the reprint in black (No 4 Impression from the original steel plate) was set beside the proof from the plate of 1854 with '5 designs horiz[ontal]. First design with bold lettering rejected; second design accepted lettering; the other three designs without lettering.'[6] The collection of Victoria that the Duke and his advisers put together is almost complete, with many splendid examples of all the early issues and printings. However, the pair of the unused Half Length, THREE PENCE blue (shades) of Ham's fourth setting Veil shaded stamps of January 1853 that must have given him the greatest pleasure was a present from his wife, Queen Mary in 1924.

The royal party left Melbourne for Brisbane by train, then returned to Sydney, the final leg, in the *Ophir*, which had come round to meet them. There, it was more of the same – receptions, reviews, shaking hands, all in the line of duty. Just once in the line of pleasure the Duke shook hands with the committee of the Sydney Philatelic Club. The President, S. H. Lampton, offered the Society's 'most cordial and affectionate welcome', thanked the Duke for becoming their Patron and asked him to accept 'the accompanying selection of the stamps of this the Mother State [New South Wales] of Australia, and trust that they might find a position amongst your philatelic treasures'.[7] It was a truly handsome gift. The sunk-mounted leaves were bound in an album of maroon morocco leather, 'simply but chastely ornamented'. The names of the thirty-six members who contributed were entered alphabetically along with the loyal address. The Duke was delighted – as well he might be to receive such a fine collection of Sydney Views, Laureates and later issues. (See Appendix 1, page 317)

The Sydney Philatelic Club received the 'gratifying acknowledgement of the souvenir' from Sir Brian Godfrey-Faussett; the honorary secretary, A. F. Basset-Hull, regarded the gift as 'eminently satisfactory to those members of the club who contributed some of their cherished possessions'. However, those who did not contribute were censured, as 'a little more effort would have amounted in rendering the collection almost complete in the type of varieties of New South Wales issues'.[8]

Two days later, on 31 May, the Duke and Duchess had a particularly busy day: they laid a foundation stone for a hospital, the Duke received an honorary degree from the university, they visited the National Gallery and attended a concert in the evening, but philatelically the Duke merely recorded: 'Bought some stamps from a dealer.'[9] As ever, he did not record what they were.

The first day back at sea, 7 June on the way to New Zealand, the Duke of York was 'Busy all [the] morning with Godfrey [-Faussett] choosing and putting away stamps.'[10] As usual he was presented with a set of current stamps when they reached Auckland, but the gift that doubtless intrigued him the most was the 1898–99 Pigeon Post stamps of the Great Barrier Island.

Although they were just sixty-five miles north-east of Auckland, the inhabitants of Great Barrier Island (the descendants of miners and loggers who had come for copper and the kauri tree), were dependent on the weekly sailing of the supply ship for any contact with the outside world. Thus an answer to a letter took, at best, sixteen days to arrive. Their isolation from the mainland was further highlighted when the SS *Wairarapa* foundered off Great Barrier Island on her way from Sydney to Auckland and many lives were lost. It was more than three days before news of the wreck reached her home port. A year after the disaster, an excursion to the site was organised for the relatives of the dead and in order to publish the account in the *New Zealand Herald* the next day, a 'sturdy little pigeon, named "Ariel" carried the record weight message of that period (five sheets of letter-sized paper – three tissue and two ordinary sheets)'.[11] Ariel was owned by Walter Fricker, who had soon established a regular pigeon post.

Fricker's pigeons flew between his loft in Auckland to a Miss R. E. Spring-hall, daughter of the official postmistress at Okupu, on Great Barrier Island. In February 1897, his Great Barrier Pigeon Agency opened for business, taking mail between Auckland and the newly established gold and silver mines of Okupu and Oreville. The cost was two shillings per message. There were six to eight 'flights' per week and each bird could carry up to eight messages, tied with cotton to its legs.

Soon after a rival service was being operated by Mr J. E. Parkin, whose pigeons were delivered by mistake to Miss Springhall; after much wrangling, she switched her allegiance from Fricker to Parkin. In the end two services ran to different ends of the island, and a fine of £5 was imposed on anyone

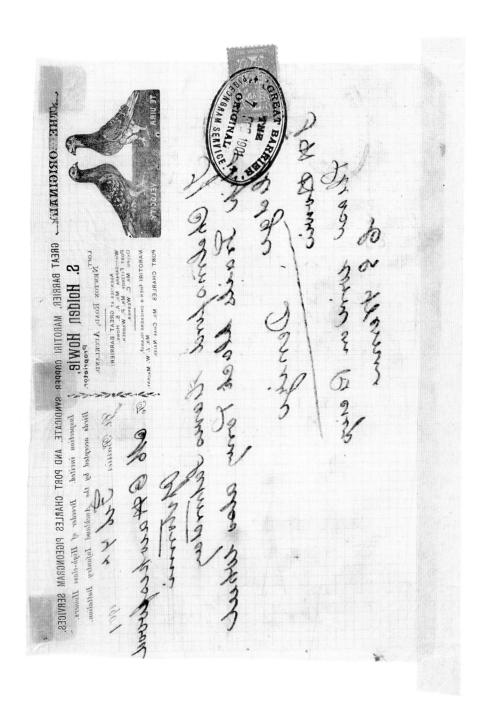

who shot a carrier pigeon. The first stamps were issued the next year, on 19 November 1898, by Mr H. Howie who had taken over Parkin's service, followed by a second issue in January 1899. However, the New Zealand government who held the monopoly on postal services, naturally objected to the use of the word 'post' appearing on the stamps, so the third issue, May 1899, had the words 'PIGEON GRAM' overprinted in black. A new printing followed with 'Pigeongram' substituting 'Special Post' in the design in August 1899. By 1908 technology had caught up: a telegraph cable was laid from the island to the mainland and the pigeon post became obsolete. The Duke of York also received examples of all the ONE SHILLING and SIX PENCE triangular stamps from the rival Great Barrier Pigeongram Agency, and another including a September 1899 ONE SHILLING pale blue, overprinted MAROTIRI PIGEONGRAM from the Marotiri Island copper mine.

When the *Ophir* reached Tasmania, the Duke could indulge himself again. There he was visited by a Mr Park and saw his 'splendid collection of Australian stamps'[12]. It could well have been Mr Park who was instrumental in arranging for the Duke to receive the four plate proofs of the 1863–80 George and Dragon postal fiscal stamps of Tasmania, in black, of the THREE PENCE and TWO SHILLINGS & SIXPENCE values in part sheets, and the FIVE SHILLINGS and TEN SHILLINGS values in complete sheets all taken off in 1888.

Tasmania Postal Fiscals: 1863–80 THREE PENCE green, TWO SHILLINGS & SIXPENCE carmine or lake, TEN SHILLINGS orange or salmon, postal fiscal stamps, plate proofs. The Duke of York received these 'George and Dragon' postal fiscals during his visit to Tasmania on the cruise of the *Ophir*, 1901.

Opposite: New Zealand: Great Barrier Island Pigeon Post 1899 (January) ONE SHILLING bluish green on flimsy paper. Letters went to Auckland and back attached to the legs of pigeons. There was a £5 fine for shooting a carrier pigeon.

But the real gem came from Western Australia. The lithographic stone of the famous black swan SIX PENCE imperforate of 1857–59 had recently been discovered in use as a doorstop, and was returned to the government printer, A. Hillman. As the first impression was taken, the stone cracked, so only two more were taken, and the exercise was abandoned.

He bought some more stamps in Adelaide, but no more were recorded until his homeward journey, although the *Ophir* called at Mauritius, South Africa and most of the provinces of Canada.

It was only when the ship left St John's, Newfoundland, that an uncharacteristic hint of excitement crept into the Duke's diary. Of the first day at sea, he wrote: 'Busy with Godfrey[-Faussett] making of statistics of our journey & put away all my stamps, beautifully arranged for Tilleard.'[13] The Colonial tour, the Duke computed, lasted 231 days and covered 50,718 miles. He had laid twenty-one foundation stones, received 544 addresses, reviewed 62,174 troops, and shaken hands with around thirty-thousand people. With his interest in philately so well known, the stamps with which he returned from such an epic tour must have been considerable in number and importance.

The royal party arrived home on 2 November. The Duke could hardly contain himself. The very next day, he recorded, 'Spent all the afternoon & evening showing & handing over all the stamps I collected to Tilleard, who was very pleased with them.'[14] A further reward was waiting for him: a week later, on his father's birthday he was created Prince of Wales.

The new Prince of Wales obviously relished being back at home among his friends and able to enjoy his favourite pursuits of shooting and stamps. There were the cosy meetings with Tilleard, who often came to dine and twice 'looked [at] a beautiful collection of Lord Kintore's'.[15] The 9th Earl was a friend and courtier having been a lord-in-waiting to Queen Victoria and Edward VII. This collection, part of which the Prince of Wales bought later, would have been of particular interest as Kintore had been Governor of South Australia.

However just as Tilleard had advanced the Prince of Wales's collection and become a friend, so the Earl of Crawford was to change his style of collecting and focus on philately. Ludovic Lindsay, 26th Earl of Crawford, was a truly remarkable man. Tall and thin as a rail, with 'a full beard and striking red hair',[16] he was a polymath. From his father, he had inherited charm, a fortune, a rich varied library, to which he added throughout his life, and an enquiring and scientific mind. At fifteen, his tutor wrote to his mother that her son was 'remarkably intelligent and had a very unusual degree of aptitude for anything that takes his fancy'.[17] On inheriting in 1880, Crawford built his own observatory, financed and led astronomical expeditions to Spain and Mauritius, and was elected a Fellow of the Royal Society at the age of thirty. His friendship with the Prince of Wales was initially founded on their mutual love of yachting – both were members of the Royal Yacht Squadron.

Crawford's boyhood enthusiasm for stamp-collecting had evaporated, until by chance when buying some Arabic and Greek manuscripts at Sotheby's in 1899, 'a fat album, containing a number of stamps came up for disposal ... and his curiosity was aroused at the sight of the album, which he instantly determined to purchase'.[18] A year later, Crawford was an active member of The Philatelic Society, London, Vice President in 1902, and President in 1910.

The 'fat album' in question had come from the estate of Colonel John Chard VC, (played by Stanley Baker in the film *Zulu*) a hero of Rorke's Drift in the Zulu War, which Crawford purchased for £73. It was enough to spawn one of the finest collections of its day. Crawford was surprised by how far stamp-collecting had advanced since his schooldays, and the number of books, periodicals and related matter available to the serious collector. Despite his slight frame and ruddy appearance, it was his 'lot to live in close communication with two inseparable hangers-on, the one rheumatism, the other asthma'.[19] He found relief in spending winters at sea in his yacht, the last being MV *Valhalla* of 1700 tons displacement with a crew of sixty-five. He invariably took with him 'some stamps for study and arrangement', which provided him with 'interesting and unfailing occupation'.[20] On his travels he found that the 'The Stamp Album was of itself an admirable letter of introduction or passport to the kindest welcome, always extended by the members of this great family, the one to the other.' The Prince of Wales was indeed fortunate to be included within that 'family', for he had been fired by the Earl's genius style of collecting.

What set Crawford apart as an exceptional collector was his approach to the subject. He applied his phenomenal scientific and analytical mind to it and, with his deep understanding of history, turned stamp-collecting into a technical exercise. Added to that, he was dedicated and wealthy – in the first two years of collecting he spent £10,000 with Stanley Gibbons alone. With these attributes, he took the 'study collection' to new heights. He put together everything 'connected with the production of the design and its subsequent development, with the incorporation of all essays, proof colour trials, and original drawings and prints connected with the several issues',[21] concentrating on unissued stamps. In the long passages at sea, the Earl mounted his collection himself, and annotated each page. Thus, it became the 'historical epitome of the stamps from their conception to their super-session, and comprised – with the magnificent luxury of issued varieties – specialised collections that for scientific study and completeness have been the admiration of the whole philatelic world'.

Stamp-collecting had always had its detractors – particularly when huge prices were paid for 'little scraps of paper', or the collective worth of an exhibition was published. But when a distinguished bibliophile and Fellow of the Royal Society, the Earl of Crawford, and the Prince of Wales took such a keen interest, philately could hardly be counted as a childish hobby.

The Prince of Wales, supported by Tilleard, began to follow the pattern his friend had set. Again, the move came at exactly the right time in his collecting career. Apart from a little philatelic study in Australia, the Colonial tour had merely resulted in an accumulation of a great number of stamps from every country visited. While the Prince was proud of his acquisitions, he could well appreciate the added appeal of this more sophisticated approach that became known as the French style of collecting; in the English School the 'collection of postage stamps should be nothing more nor less than the accumulation of the printed designs'.[22] With his additional income from the Duchy of Cornwall, he could afford to buy anything that came on the market, regard-less of price – although he was astute enough to realise the investment potential of stamps – and that delay would mean paying a higher price in the future. His adoption of the Crawford style of collecting exactly coincided with the inception of the stamps of the new reign.

The Prince of Wales enlisted the help of his father. Edward VII was never interested in stamp collecting (apart from his own issues) but was always keen to promote his son's involvement, and consequently wrote to the Inland Revenue. He arranged that corner pairs of all new printings, including the essays and proofs, from both the Post Office and the Crown Agents for the Colonies be sent to his son. Later, when the Prince moved to collecting blocks of four, these were also supplied, usually a corner block. He also received examples of all stamps registered at the headquarters of the Universal Postal Union at Berne, although at that time all Great Britain stamps of more than one shilling in value were generally overprinted 'Specimen', as were the Crown Agents' stamps, but not those of the Dominions. The Prince was delighted, and passed on the good news to Tilleard: 'I am glad to hear that the Deputy Chairman of the Commissioners of the Inland Revenue has promised to send me the new stamps, proofs, and essays from Somerset House.'[23]

It is strange, though, with the Prince's new approach to collecting that he did not ask for the die proof and progress proofs of the stamps for the Empire as well: like any other less privileged collector he bought most of those that are in the Collection. But the Prince of Wales was in the unique position of being able to study the stamps of his father's reign and, typically, he was only too willing to share his research, knowledge and good fortune with his fellow philatelists.

'Marlborough House: at 8.30 went to the Examination Hall on the Thames Embankment' the Prince of Wales recorded in his diary on 4 March 1904, 'where I presided at a meeting of the Philatelic Society of London, & read them a paper "Notes on the Postal Issues of the United Kingdom during the present reign", and also showed them the essays, proofs & stamps belonging to me to illustrate their history.'[24] As a description of the first Edward VII stamps, the paper written and read by the Prince of Wales to over sixty members of the Society can hardly be bettered. It was accurate and instructive in content and supporting exhibits, and showed him the equal of his mentor, the Earl of Crawford.

Shortly before the Prince had left on his Colonial tour, the Secretary to the Treasury, a Mr [John] Henniker Heaton, assured the House of Commons that the design for the new stamps of Edward VII's reign was well in hand.

However, a month later a notice appeared in the *London Gazette* announcing that it was intended that certain of the Queen Victoria stamps were to remain in use, namely 'the 1d. of December, 1881; the 5s., 10s. and £1 of April, 1884; the £5 of March 1882; the 10d. of 1890, and the other values comprised in the "Jubilee" issue of 1887' The rest of the issues left over from her reign were demonetised, but somehow the orange EIGHT PENCE of 1876 – the Collection holds the proofs and examples of this value, and copies of the unissued purple-brown EIGHT PENCE – and the TWO SHILLINGS brown 1867–80, seemed to have been forgotten and remained valid for use. The Prince, in his

Great Britain:
1881 Die II ONE PENNY deep purple, a rare version on blued paper.
1883–84 FIVE SHILLINGS rose another rare version on blued paper.
1883–84 TEN SHILLINGS.
1884 ONE POUND brown-lilac.
1867–83 FIVE POUNDS orange.
These issues remained in use during the reign of Edward VII.

Great Britain:
1876 EIGHT PENCE
purple-brown, prepared
for use but unissued.

Great Britain: 1867–80
TWO SHILLINGS brown.
A very rare complete pane.

paper to the Society, thought that 'philatelists would probably hesitate to pass through the post their unused copies of the brown 2s.!' The 1867–80 TWO SHILLING blue also remained valid.

Meanwhile, De La Rue produced four designs for the Postmaster General of the new ONE PENNY stamp, with a three-quarter face and a quarter-face portrait of the King looking to the right, and the same with the portrait reversed, along with a set of 'unified' stamps, from ONE HALF PENNY to ONE SHILLING with similar portraits looking right. The images had been taken from a photograph, and turned into an essay lithographically. None of these designs was adopted. The essays of the rejects, along with many others, were shown to members of the Society by the Prince to illustrate his paper, and are still in the Collection.

The Prince continued. De La Rue came up with their own idea, to use the existing frames of the still current Queen Victoria Jubilee issue stamps, but substitute the head and crown of Edward VII for that of the late Queen. This idea seemed sound and the attractive bicoloured stamps were adopted for the $1\frac{1}{2}^d$, 2^d, 4^d, 5^d, 9^d, 10^d, and 1^s values. This meant that brand new stamps were required for the remaining values – $\frac{1}{2}^d$, 1^d, $2\frac{1}{2}^d$, and 6^d, while 7^d came in 1910 possibly to cater for the reduction of the parcel rate. Naturally, for both sets of stamps, a new image of Edward VII was required.

The choice of the artist for the Sovereign's new image aroused high indignation, with questions even being asked in the House of Commons as to why the President of the Royal Academy had not been consulted. But the King himself had decided on Emil Füchs, an Austrian sculptor living in London, whose portrait of him made the year before, he considered 'specially well adapted for the purpose'. The King granted Füchs another sitting, and the Prince of Wales borrowed the resulting sketch from the Board of the Inland Revenue to show to his audience.

Füchs also designed a new frame and border, with a choice of style for the ONE PENNY value, and supervised their production by De La Rue. Proofs were prepared with the King's profile inserted in them, and subsequently photographed, side by side. These, marked 'A' and 'B', were submitted for his approval. The King initialled his assent for Proof 'A', the comments 'head leaning too far forward' and 'pose of head correct' are written in another

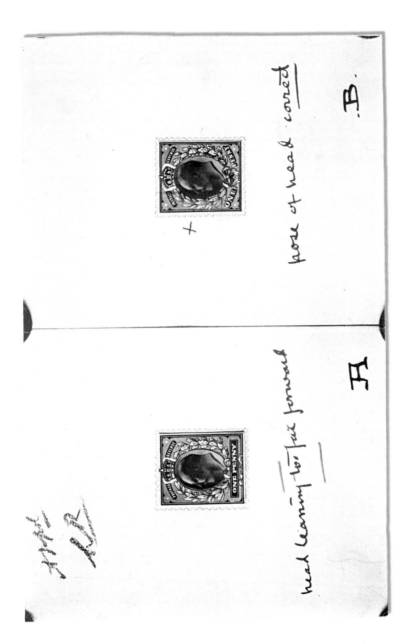

Great Britain: 1902 photograph of two variations of Füch's ONE PENNY with Edward VII's initialled approval – 'head leaning too far forward' and 'pose of head correct' – is in another hand. The original is in the Postal Heritage Trust.

hand. There are three further bromides in the Collection together with two die proofs, one in red on white and the other purple on red, none with the fnally completed head.

The Prince informed his rapt audience that night that the eventual narrowing of the wreath was Queen Alexandra's idea, but that the King and Queen felt that much of the character and expression of the original portrait was lost between the temporary plate and the working dies. Nonetheless, the head was adopted for the HALF PENNY, ONE PENNY, 2½ᵈ and SIX PENCE stamps. Again, the proofs of all four values were shown to the Society that night.

On 26 September 1901, the HALF PENNY was registered at Somerset House with the ONE PENNY following on 14 October. Colour trials of these had been prepared in a variety of colours with impressions in 'mauve on white paper, two tints of mauve on red paper, and seven distinct shades of pink, lake, or red, on white paper'.[25] All these colour trials were produced for the members to see, save the carmine, which was the colour actually adopted. The 2½ᵈ and SIX PENCE values were registered on 3 December 1901 (missing the King's birthday on 9 November). However, the 2½ᵈ was in mauve on blue paper, and a few thousand sheets were printed before it was decided to switch to a blue stamp on white paper. Nine colour trials in varying shades of blue were produced and the chosen one registered on 17 December. The sheets of the unissued mauve were destroyed, but the Collection holds an imprimatur corner block and a perforated corner pair together with copies of all the colour trials on white paper.

All was set for the launch of the new stamps on 1 January 1902, followed by the remaining values soon after. The higher values, the TWO SHILLINGS AND SIXPENCE to ONE POUND were released later in the year. A die was produced for the highest value of all, a POSTAGE FIVE POUNDS stamp in early 1902, but before it advanced to a printing plate it was abandoned. However, a proof was taken from the die and found its way into the Collection.

To Edward VII, his Great Britain stamp was always a compromise. The public were also disappointed, 'the production, they urged, was crude and lacked dignity' – and 'Much adverse comment resulted when it was learnt that the bust reproduced on the stamps had been executed by an Austrian'.[26] Possibly in his disappointment, the King instructed that a new frame be prepared, with the head image that had been used in the Transvaal stamp. In October 1902, a die proof was produced and various colour trials were printed of the ONE PENNY value but the whole project was abandoned on the 'score of expense'.

Great Britain: 1902 ONE PENNY black. The head in this proof was taken from the Transvaal stamps which the King preferred.

The Prince of Wales had not finished with his paper. He went on to detail such specifics as the Levant overprints on Edward VII stamps with Turkish paras and piastres and the various 'official' stamps, overprints of various departments of state – the ADMIRALTY, the BOARD OF EDUCATION, and the ROYAL HOUSEHOLD. His knowledge was exhaustive, detailing the dates of registration and minutiae of overprints of the ARMY OFFICIAL, the INLAND REVENUE (IR), GOVERNMENT PARCELS, and the OFFICE OF WORKS (OW) used on Queen Victoria stamps. Mention, too, was made of the ARMY TELEGRAPHS overprint. As before, these officials were all illustrated with prime examples from his own, particularly strong collection.

Having dealt with adhesive stamps, the Prince of Wales moved on to another area well represented in the Collection: 'the stamps embossed or printed on envelopes, wrappers, post cards, letter cards and telegraph forms'.[27] Before he ended, he made mention that a differently laid out plate of the ONE PENNY stamp was registered in October 1903. This was because the Post Office was about to issue 'small books, containing twenty-four stamps of this value, to be sold at the price of 2s. ½d'. The books contained four pages of six stamps, in two horizontal rows of three, each interleaved with waxed paper and bound between red cardboard with wire staples. As the margin was needed for the binding, the stamps were specially printed in four panes of sixty each, in vertical columns of ten, with columns one to three upright, four to six inverted so that when guillotined in panes of six and bound, the books opened the same way with all the stamps upright. The Prince of Wales's own half sheet of these stamps, with the third and fourth stamp in each column a tête-bêche (in which one stamp is inverted in two adjoining stamps), was examined with especial interest as it was unique in private hands. It is still in the Collection.

The paper, obviously written by the Prince of Wales himself, was born of

Great Britain: 1902–10 ONE PENNY red. This rare sheet with rows of tête-bêche was specially printed for booklets. That way, with every fourth, fifth and sixth column inverted, the books opened the same way.

his intensive study of his own collection. In his modest way, he 'did not claim for these notes the importance of a philatelic paper, but that all the information and dates given may be relied upon as authentic'.[28] He described himself as 'a prentice hand', but his paper was a true service to philately. The Prince can only have been on a considerable high having delivered his paper himself, for when the meeting broke up he repaired to the Marlborough Club in Piccadilly with one of his equerries, the Viscount Crichton, to play bridge.

There was one further treat for the sixty members who had turned out to hear their President, for he had brought with him the two rarest and most prized stamps in his collection that had very recently come into his possession: the two 'Post Office' Mauritius.

★ ★ ★

As the Duke and Duchess of York had mounted the steps of Le Réduit, Government House in Mauritius, to stay on 5 August 1901 during their tour, the Duke might have been thinking of the ball held in that residence fifty-three years before, that is synonymous with two of the most famous stamps in philatelic history; the POST OFFICE Mauritius 1847 ONE PENNY and TWO

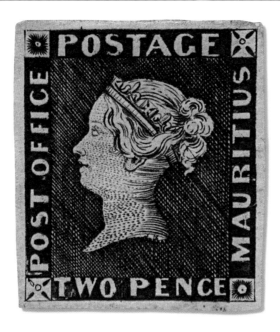

Mauritius: 1847 TWO PENCE deep blue, unused. When the Prince of Wales bought the TWO PENCE
Post Office Mauritius in 1904, it was the highest price ever paid for a single stamp.

PENCE. Then, a little over two years after his return, came the moment he had longed for: to buy not only the Mauritius TWO PENCE but the ONE PENNY (on cover) as well.

On Mauritius, the mail charge had been collected on delivery, until a government order (no. 13) decreed that from 1 January 1847, all letters, newspapers and parcels posted within the island with previously unused stamps 'shall pass by the Post free of Postage'.[29] To this end, J. Stuart Brownrigg, the Colonial Postmaster initially asked the miniaturist and engraver (also variously described as a watch-maker, watch-mender, jeweller, planter and printer) Joseph Osmond Barnard to estimate the price for engraving a plate and supplying the stamps for the new service. Barnard, who had arrived at Port Louis some years before as a stowaway, quoted £10 for the plate, and ten shillings per thousand for the stamps. In the end, the estimate (dated 12 November 1846 now in the Tapling Collection in the British Library) was revised to £10 for both the engraving and the stamps.

It was a protracted affair. Barnard used the same plate to engrave both the ONE PENNY and TWO PENCE values. For the image, he clearly copied the William Wyon head of Queen Victoria that he had seen on the Great Britain issues, adding his initials JB to the neck, the lettering for POSTAGE at the top, and ONE PENNY or TWO PENCE at the bottom. On the right side is engraved MAURITIUS, on the left, POST OFFICE. When this was corrected to POST PAID in 1848, it was assumed that Barnard had made a mistake, but he was merely following the current postmark 'MAURITIUS / POST OFFICE'. It was also rumoured that Barnard had forgotten the exact wording agreed on, only to be reminded, wrongly as it turned out, when he passed the General Post Office on his way home. He then printed the stamps, the ONE PENNY in orange red, the TWO PENCE in deep blue. The island postmaster confirmed that 700 had been prepared, (there were 500 of each value in the end) and were ready for purchase the next day, 20 September 1847, making them the earliest Colonial postage stamps.

The issue was ready in time to send out the invitations to a ball at Government House the next day, given by Lady Gomm, wife of the Governor, Sir William Gomm, to foster relations between the French and British planters on the island. Of Barnard's original printing of the 1847 issue, only twenty-seven are known to survive: fifteen of the ONE PENNY and twelve of the TWO PENCE, and one of these, unquestionably the finest of the four unused, is in the Royal Philatelic Collection. This famous stamp had belonged to the schoolboy collection of James Bonar, who had been brought up in Scotland but moved to London in adulthood. There, he worked for the Civil Service Commission and was living in Hampstead, north London, when he came across the pocketbook that had served as his stamp album. He was about to give it to his grandson when a friend, a Miss D. Thomas, came to dine. Aware of her interest in philately, Bonar showed her the pocketbook. She flicked through the pages and found nothing of much interest until she came to Mauritius. There, to her amazement, was a perfect example of an unused TWO PENCE stuck in the middle of the page. Miss Thomas advised her host to take advice, and Bonar sent for Nevile Lacy Stocken of the stamp auctioneers, Puttick and Simpson.

Stocken pronounced the stamp genuine, and worth at least a thousand pounds. His next move was to remove it from the page, no easy matter as the gum had soaked into the porous paper of the stamp. He boiled the stamp for a few minutes, a brave act with something so valuable – the page floated away and the gum was lost, but the appearance of the stamp may have been somewhat enhanced. To much publicity, the MAURITIUS POST OFFICE was entered for auction on 13 January 1904 at Puttick and Simpson's London galleries, 47 Leicester Square. It was then that the Prince of Wales and Tilleard heard about the stamp.

The Prince was determined to possess it, at almost any cost. He began by sending Tilleard to offer James Bonar £1,200 to withdraw the stamp from auction and sell it to him privately. The next day, 24 December 1903, Bonar wrote to Tilleard:

> After you left me, I at once wrote to Puttick and Simpson conveying your offer, very much in the terms you suggested. However, they are against it, not only because they expect a higher sum than £1,200 will be reached, but also because the acceptance of a private offer would be a breach of faith.'[30]

Royal muscle held no sway.

The Prince of Wales was disappointed, but not surprised. The stamp had been widely advertised for sale by auction without the disclaimer 'unless previously sold by private treaty'. Had it been withdrawn, the auctioneers and Bonar would have been liable for the expenses of all interested parties – many from abroad. The Prince replied to Tilleard from York Cottage:

> I return you Mr Bonar's letter. I am sorry that I cannot buy this Mauritius stamp direct from him, but I understand the reasons given by Messrs Puttick and Simpson. I am still very anxious to have the stamp and now authorise you or an agent to bid for it at the auction up to £1,550 inclusive. I am particularly keen to buy the stamp although it does seem a great deal of money to give for it. I suppose of course you have seen the stamp & can guarantee that it is genuine. I hope your prophecy that it will only fetch just over £1,000 will be correct & Puttick & Simpson will be wrong. You better see Sir William Carington & show him this letter & ask him to give you the sum I have named. When does

the sale take place, sometime in January I understand.

I hope we shall be successful,

Believe me

very sincerely yours,

George

The Prince had intended to go to £1,550 'inclusive' of agent's fee. The closer the date of the sale, the more agitated he became. He could not bear to lose a stamp he had not even seen. He fired off another letter to Tilleard on 4 January, a week before the sale:

Many thanks for your letter & for sending me the Catalogue of the sale with which I was much interested. I see there are some other rather nice Mauritius stamps besides the 'Post Office' to be sold. You might send me another catalogue after the sale with the sums that each stamp fetched written against them which would be very interesting.

I feel just as keen about possessing this stamp as I did before and wish you every success. I shall be waiting anxiously after the 13th to hear what you were able to do.

Believe me

very sincerely yours,

George

As the excitement mounted he wrote again to Tilleard:

… I hear from Sir W. Carington that he has given you the money I named, & armed with that, I wish you every success & trust you may be able to obtain the stamp for £1,200. I entirely approve of your getting any other of the Mauritius stamps you can at the sale, providing they go fairly cheap, I agree with you in thinking that it would be a pity to miss this opportunity of securing some of these good stamps. I see there are as many as 38 lots all Mauritius. I hope you will not forget to send me a catalogue after the sale, with price put against each lot & marked with a X the ones you bought for me, it would interest me very much to see what they fetched. I also see there are two rather fine Newfoundland stamps in same sale, in fact, I leave it to you to bid for whatever you think I most want.

You can send me a telegram here [York Cottage] on Wednesday if you have secured the 'Post Office'. Better say merely 'Stamp is yours' & write later full particulars.

Wishing you good luck

Believe me

very sincerely yours

George

The last line 'Better say merely 'Stamp is yours' and write later full particulars' perhaps reveals that he did not want his wife or father to know what he had paid for it: telegrams, like postcards, were considered fair game for prying eyes and gossips.

On the day of the sale it was very cold and a bye-day at the Sandringham shoot in Norfolk. The Prince, normally an exceptional shot, performed badly, his mind elsewhere. Meanwhile in London, the saleroom of Puttick and Simpson was packed. Collectors and their agents from all over the world had gathered to witness the sale of the great rarity. At last it was the turn of Lot 301, the TWO PENCE POST OFFICE MAURITIUS. The bidding opened at £500, and rose quickly in £100 increments to £700, then to £1,000 with a new bidder. C. J. Phillips, the dealer acting on behalf of the *Reichpost Museum* (the German Postal Museum) in Berlin was the underbidder at £1,400 when the German dealer Philipp Kosack advanced the bidding to £1,420. He dropped out with the new bidder, J. Crawford, the Prince's agent acting anonymously, securing the lot with the final bid of £1,450, just within his brief from Tilleard. As the Prince of Wales entered in his diary the next day, 'About the rarest stamp in the world & this is a record price'.[31] It was a record price, for any stamp.

The sale was widely reported in the press and the Prince of Wales was mooted as the possible buyer. This gives less credence to the account given by the Assistant Private Secretary and equerry to Edward VII, Captain Frederick Ponsonby (later Lord Sysonby) in his autobiography. His fellow equerry, Arthur Davidson, 'had occasion to telephone to the Prince of Wales about something, and having finished he added: "I know how interested Your Royal

Highness is in stamps. Did you happen to see in the newspapers that some damned fool had given as much as £1,400 [*sic*] for one stamp?" A quiet, restrained voice answered: "I was the damned fool."[32] Sir John Wilson, former Keeper of the Royal Philatelic Collection, repeated the story, adding that the Prince of Wales often retold it 'accompanied by a hearty laugh'.[33] The expression 'damned fool' was very much part of the vocabulary of the Royal Family – Princess Victoria would greet her brother every day on the telephone with 'Hallo you damned old fool'[34] with the same response. The Prince of Wales was fond of telling another version of the same story. He once asked Commander Godfrey-Faussett, himself a philatelist, what he thought of a 'chap who paid £1,400 for a stamp',[35] The wretched equerry replied: 'I would call him a silly ass, sir.'

When the Prince of Wales heard that he had been successful, he wrote to Tilleard from York Cottage – addressing him, for the first time as '"My" Dear Mr Tilleard':

> I was much interested by reading your long letter received this morning, telling me of all that took place at the auction yesterday. I hasten to send you my warmest thanks for all the trouble you have taken about it. I know that I should never have been able to have bought the stamp without your kind assistance & I am sure that I am most grateful. ... £1450 is certainly a great deal of money to give for a stamp, & it is no doubt a record price, but in spite of that I am very pleased to have it in my collection as I believe it is such a fine copy; & I am also very glad that I have kept it in England & prevented it going to Germany. I am glad that the Public are not aware who the purchaser was, although the Times says that they <u>believe</u> it was bought for me. I quite approve of the £10.10 [10 guineas] expenses for agent for expenses et. et, & call it very reasonable. I am glad you were able to buy 3 other Mauritius stamps & hope also the Newfoundland & British Guiana. Please keep the balance whatever it may be of the £1550 and please put it as you suggest to the credit of other purchases already made or to be made. I quite agree that you ought at once to increase the fire insurance on the collection. No, please keep the 'Post Office' locked up in your safe in your office in the City, until I come to London, which will be at the beginning of February, when I hope you will bring it to Marlborough House to show me, I will

let you know later which day. You might ascertain quietly the price of the 1d. Post Office which belonged to Lord Kintore, although I do not think that I shall be able to buy it now. ...[36]

But buy it he did, later in the same year. It was attached to the envelope of an invitation to Lady Gomm's ball, addressed to Ed.[mond] Duvivier Esq., and bore the ONE PENNY orange-red stamp cancelled with a large, double-lined MAURITIUS POST OFFICE postmark, dated 21 September 1847. Also stamped on the envelope is PENNY POST in a rectangle. While the invitation itself would have been given up at the door, the envelope, one of three known extant, was kept as a souvenir of the evening. It came to light fifty years on when Madame Duvivier was going through her papers prior to moving house. It was then sold on 30 March 1898, for £600 to the London stamp dealer W. H. Peckitt, who entered it for auction later in the year. He withdrew the cover before the sale, and sold it privately to the Earl of Kintore for £850

Mauritius: 1847 ONE PENNY orange-red, used on cover, known as 'The one penny Post Office'. The envelope, addressed to a Mr Duvivier, contained an invitation to Lady Gomm's ball.

that year. In 1904, it passed to the Prince of Wales by private treaty. However, the Prince used the past tense 'belonged' in his letter to Tilleard, which suggests that there might have been another link in the chain of ownership between him and the Earl.

Almost six years later the Prince of Wales was offered another ONE PENNY Post Office Mauritius through Tilleard. He wrote back to him:

> Your letter just received, after reading it I at once came to the conclusion that £2,000 was a ridiculous price to ask for the 1 d Post Office Mauritius, especially as one could not swear that it was an unused one & I have a genuine used one on the envelope. They are quite welcome to it in America. I am sure you will agree that I was right, with the same sum we can get a great many good stamps which will be much more useful to my collection'.[37]

But the fascinating story of the Post Office Mauritius does not end in Puttick and Simpson's saleroom as far as the Royal Philatelic Collection is concerned. In 1912 the original Barnard printing plate came to light, apparently among Sir William Gomm's papers at Drummond's Bank, Charing Cross, London. It was 'found' by Colonel Dominic Colnaghi, who claimed to be the governor's grandson. The Gomms were childless, although Colnaghi might have been the son of an adopted heir or a secretary who had 'acquired' the plate. The plot thickens in that there is no record of a package being withdrawn from Drummond's at that time. The Mauritius Government set up an enquiry to look into 'the theft of the engraved plate Mauritius Stamp 1847'.[38] Wherever it had come from, the plate was bought by Nevile Stocken, who offered it first to Henry Duveen, then to the Earl of Crawford, both of whom turned it down. The Prince of Wales, by then King George V, was not interested either, possibly because of its dubious provenance. The plate passed to a dealer David Field who had it for sale on his stall at the 1912 Jubilee Exhibition in London. Later, it turned up in Paris where some reprints were taken, but only after certain minute changes were made to distinguish the reprints from the original. The Collection has a 'Complete set of reprints taken from the engraved copperplate, the 2d. left of the 1d., in black, blue and orange-red.'[39] Both the blue and orange-red imitations are marked on the back 'reproductions *d'après l'original* No. 15'. Photographs of the plate, dated 1913, are also in the Collection. The whereabouts of the plate itself is not known.

Although they do not have the romance of the POST OFFICE MAURITIUS, the second issue, the POST PAID MAURITIUS is no less fascinating. As the 'only objection' to the original Barnard plate was that 'there was only one impression of each label, [so] too much time would be occupied in working off any large number',[40] Barnard was commissioned to engrave two more plates, of twelve stamps arranged in four rows of three. For these he worked on a palimpsest, the backs having been used to print handbills advertising the Grand Hôtel d'Europe, Port Louis, in French and English, the French version for the ONE PENNY, the English for the TWO PENCE. They were similar to the previous issue save that POST OFFICE became POST PAID along with such details as the shading on and around the Queen's head. As Barnard had no means of replicating a single stamp, he engraved each of the twelve stamps singly, as close to the original engraving as possible. Thus, through these slight differences, the position of each stamp on the plate can easily be identified (plated). Further, when engraving the seventh stamp on the TWO PENCE, Barnard failed to cut enough of the surface around the O away, leaving the C of PENCE as an O; this stamp is known as the 'PENOE error'.

The Collection holds several excellent examples of this issue. From the earliest impression, on greyish white wove paper, there is a single TWO PENCE in indigo-blue, the sixth stamp on the sheet of twelve. There is also an unused single copy of the orange (no.7) as well as an unused pair (nos. 11 and 12) and

Mauritius: 1848–59 TWO PENCE blue, early impression. It is known as the 'PENOE error' after Barnard, the engraver, slipped up on the seventh stamp making the C of PENCE an O.

Mauritius: 1848–59 ONE PENNY orange-vermilion, earliest impression, an unused horizontal pair. Known as the 'Post Paid Mauritius', it was engraved on the reverse of a copper plate formerly used to produce handbills for the Grand Hotel, Port Louis.

four other used copies (4, 5, 6, and 11). From early impressions there are four ONE PENNY vermilion used (nos. 2, 3, 5, and 6): of the TWO PENCE blue nos. 1, 5 and 7 (the 'penoe error') unused and no. 3 used.

Like all respected, wealthy collectors, the Prince of Wales was continually being offered stamps that dealers knew he would like, filtered to him through Tilleard. While he was at York Cottage for the partridge shooting at Sandringham, he received a parcel and letter from Tilleard on 23 October 1904. He replied,

> I shall certainly take the 4 small books from Russia which you have sent me to look at … They seem to me to be extremely cheap … & I am sure they will be very useful for my collection. Some of the Australians are very good, especially Western Australia & Queensland. With regard to the three unused 2d. Post paid Mauritius stamps, I think they are very fine & it would be a pity to miss the chance of getting them … I will certainly take the error Penoe & one of the others, I thought perhaps it was hardly necessary to have both, but if you advised it, or it would make a difference in the price of the other two, I am quite ready to take all three, perhaps you would let me know what you suggest. I am returning them by registered letter. …

While the Australian stamps will remain unidentified, the three Mauritius certainly came from the dealer B. Gordon Jones. While Jones was passing through Calcutta, he was offered a packet of fifteen Mauritius stamps that had been sent from the island to a sugar broker in the city's Burra Bazaar.

C. F. Lamour, the leading Calcutta philatelist, stated that they were as fine as anything in the Tapling Collection. The stamps, nos. 1, 5, and no. 7, the PENOE error, in unused condition, were thought to have been on envelopes but had escaped the postmark. That the Prince of Wales bought all three is a prime example of just how fortunate he was in having Tilleard as his adviser. The Prince appreciated the fact too. Two days later he wrote twice to Tilleard, once confirming his purchase, adding 'As you say, it might be a very long time before an opportunity of getting such fine ones occurs again. And I am sure we have got them very cheap' and again enclosing the cheque with a note to say 'Perhaps soon you will have enough to start Mauritius in a book.'

If the Prince of Wales did not have 'enough' Mauritius, it was not long before he did, with such rarities as the prize block of five TWO PENCE deep blue, from the intermediate print, with a PENOE error beside nos. 8, 9, 11 and 12, bought from a French collection by a dealer and sold to him in 1910.

Barnard had been printing between a thousand and fifteen hundred stamps an hour, and by 1858 after ten years, the unhardened plates had worn so badly as to render the last impression little more than a blur of ink. Robert Sherwin, Keeper of the Prison, who had done some departmental engraving, was asked to repair the TWO PENCE plate, but returned it, unfinished, a fortnight later. Then Jules Lapirot, an actor-cum-engraver, pronounced it 'too far gone to produce a good impression', [41] and offered to engrave an entirely new plate for £10. It was delivered in February 1859. The resulting stamps have been described as 'the greatest libel on Queen Victoria ever perpetrated on a postage stamp', while in Mauritius, it was known as the 'TWO PENCE Mozambique'.[42] The Collection holds a few of these 'less than brilliant unused' Lapirot TWO PENCE in various shades of blue, together with four used no. 8, with the N of PENCE reversed.

Such was the demand for stamps in the Colony that the unfinished plates Sherwin had worked on were found and reworked, possibly by Sherwin himself. For some reason, only the TWO PENCE plate was used, and the result-ing stamps issued in October 1859. The Collection has two of these deep blue stamps, 'Large Fillet' bluish paper, imperforate, no. 5 and no. 9, unused together with a pair of used (nos. 3 and 6) purchased in 1931 from Sir Alexander Cardew and now part of a reconstructed plate. In 1878, Major

Mauritius: 1859 (March–November)
TWO PENCE deep blue, early impression, unused
engraved by Jules Lapirot. The result known as
'the TWO PENCE Mozambique', was described
as 'the greatest libel on Queen Victoria ever
perpetrated on a postage stamp'.

Mauritius: 1859 (October) TWO PENCE
deep blue, unused. Barnard's original worn
TWO PENCE plate was re-engraved by Robert
Sherwin, Keeper of the Prison and
sometime engraver.

Mauritius: 1848–59 ONE PENNY colour worn
impression, unused. After 10 years, the plates of
both the ONE PENNY and the TWO PENCE wore
out to render the stamps virtually
unrecognisable.

Mauritius: 1859 (December) ONE PENNY deep
red, unused. This lithographed issue by Louis
Dardenne was the last of the Mauritius locally
printed stamps.

E. B. Evans RA (the expert on the Mulready letter sheet and envelope) was
stationed on the island and arranged for a few impressions to be taken from
the reworked ONE PENNY plate, one of which is in the Collection. In 1911, the
plates were discovered in the basement of a government office in Port Louis,
and were rescued by the then Governor, Sir Cavendish Boyle. He brought
them to England and contacted Tilleard, who in turn wrote to Sir Arthur
Bigge (who later became Lord Stamfordham), the King's Private Secretary:

> I saw today Sir Cavendish Boyle the Governor of Mauritius. He has brought
> home with him two of the original small copper plates used for printing the
> 12 types of stamps used in Mauritius in 1859. These I believe it is his intention

to offer them to His Majesty, and you will no doubt hear from Sir Cavendish Boyle on the subject. The plates are of the greatest Philatelic interest and should be in safe keeping.[43]

Tilleard suggested that they be defaced, and that if the King, as the Prince now was, did not want them, they should be donated to the Royal Philatelic Society, London. The plates were indeed defaced by vertical lines (and they are now in the museum of the Royal Philatelic Society London). A few pulls, however, were taken on proof paper then mounted on card to be included in the Collection.

The last locally printed stamps of Mauritius were lithographed by Louis Dardenne, the ONE PENNY and TWO PENCE in various shades of red and blue, and are well represented in the Collection, both unused and used, some on cover. The next year, 1860, a new supply of De La Rue stamps arrived from England, which ended an unparalleled colonial philatelic era.

For the Prince of Wales, the meeting of The Elder Brethren of Trinity House, (the maritime body responsible for coastal navigation), on 23 May 1906 took precedence over his preferred engagement, which had been to open the International Philatelic Exhibition of which he was patron. However, he managed a short preview, as he recorded in his diary: 'At 10.0 went to see the Philatelic Exhibition held in Horticultural Hall, Westminster. Lord Crawford, Tilleard & all the members of the committee received me & showed me round. The finest lot of stamps ever got together before valued at between £400,000 & £500,000. I showed my Mauritius, Hong Kong & King's Head English stamps. Stopped there till 12.0.'[44] Then he had dashed off to lunch with the Elder Brethren. His place at the rostrum was taken by the Earl of Crawford.

Even with his overweening sense of duty, it must have been torture for the Prince of Wales to drag himself away from so rich an exhibition, with superb entries from all over the world. The Earl of Crawford won the championship cup for his Great Britain entry, one of exceptional quality; as the Prince admired the many rarities, a microcosm of British philately, all beautifully arranged and written up, he could not have contemplated that one day he would have the chance to acquire such important material. However, the

Great Britain Official Inland Revenue: 1902–04
SIX PENCE pale dull purple, a horizontal pair.
These are considered to be amongst the rarest
of all normal British stamps.

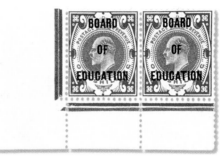

Great Britain BOARD OF EDUCATION: 1902–04
ONE SHILLING dull green and carmine,
a horizontal corner pair.

sight of the bronze medal, which bore his image, placed beneath his own exhibit *Great Britain Postage Stamps, including Official Stamps and Fiscals Available for Postage (Unused only)* must have afforded him great pleasure. He had merely reassembled all the material that he had used to illustrate his paper '*Notes on the Issues of the United Kingdom During the Present Reign*', given to the Society two years before, with a few fiscals and official stamps recently acquired of which he was particularly proud. These included such rarities as the 1902–04 I.R. OFFICIAL SIX PENCE, 'probably the rarest of all normal British stamps, and little more than a dozen specimens are known; a mint pair and a single [the one shown] are in The Royal Philatelic Collection'.[45] Its rarity stems from the fact that it was issued on 14 March 1904, two months before it was withdrawn and stocks destroyed. Another very rare stamp exhibited was the 1902–04 official ONE SHILLING with Edward VII head, overprinted BOARD OF EDUCATION. A schoolboy found one in a penny packet of stamps, which he sold for £375. There is no way of telling whether the Prince of Wales had been the purchaser.

Moving on, the Prince of Wales paused to examine his display of Mauritius, entered in Class II, where naturally his two POST OFFICE and the PENOE error attracted the most attention (see Appendix II, page 317). For this display, he won a silver medal against stiff opposition although H. J. Duveen's equally fine Mauritius exhibit was displayed but not entered for competition. The Prince of Wales also won silver for Hong Kong, a strong entry, 'practically complete in single specimens, and also exceedingly strong in pairs and mint blocks of four. The single stamps include not only the postage stamps with all the rare varieties, but also the postal fiscals that were authorised for postage use.'[46] His existing collection had been bulked out when he 'bought a beautiful collection of unused stamps of Hong Kong'[47] through Tilleard the year before. Part of this purchase made up the competition entry, along with the famous Hong Kong 1863–71 96 CENT olive-bistre, from his uncle the Duke of Edinburgh's collection. The set of Trinidad 1891 overprinted 9^d in black to commemorate his visit in HMS *Thrush* was admired, but received no award in a strong class.

The covertly competitive side of his nature, which surfaced when he applied himself to any of his chosen pastimes, drove the Prince of Wales to match his collection of stamps against the world's finest. His two silver medals and the bronze must have delighted him: tangible recognition of his collection from the most respected philatelic body in the world. However, despite the awards, the time, effort and money that he put into his collection, the presentation and some of the content of his exhibit let him and Tilleard down. As can be seen from the illustration of the Prince's Mauritius entry in Stanley Gibbons' *Monthly Journal*, the display was a mess. It was not written up with even a single note, and the stamps crowded the page. Some of the used examples were heavily cancelled, spoiling the appearance of the rest of the matched series – later they were all replaced with unused examples. The Prince's display was at odds with one of the new criteria for exhibiting: 'The seal of fashion in specialised collections has been set as upon *well-described written up and scientifically arranged* [author's italics] collections.'[48] Yet it won the silver medal. His Hong Kong entry was better: 'The condition of the stamps in this exhibit is faultless, and among the exhibits of the smaller colonies it may rank with Mr Tompson's Barbados and St Vincent as being unsurpassed'.[49]

Despite the dismal presentation of the Mauritius exhibit, the judges had gauged accurately the Prince of Wales's measure as a collector. Marcellus Purnell Castle, a member of the judging committee, noted that 'The general character of the exhibits concerning condition, scientific arrangement and philatelic knowledge and completeness was far above any other exhibition that had ever been held.'[50] Although much had been spent on the two POST

OFFICE MAURITIUS, the other stamps had been accumulated piecemeal, bought when available for 'completeness' – hence the clumsy used varieties – rather than rarity. In that, the Prince was one of 'that larger class of collectors who have to rely rather upon philatelic knowledge and patient collecting, than upon their financial powers of acquisition'.[51] Although he frequently showed parts of his collection in exhibitions and at meetings of the now Royal Philatelic Society, London, he was never again to exhibit competitively.

It is not surprising that after the International Exhibition of 1906, the Prince of Wales decided to drop the foreign issues within his collection to concentrate on Great Britain and her Empire. What is surprising is that he took so long to come to that decision. He was not lessening his area of study by much, for along with the Empire, there were the protectorates and other countries, such as Morocco, where the Post Office of Great Britain had the postal agency. Then there were the services and private telegraph-company stamps, and later airmail stamps. Although by then he was devoting up to three full afternoons a week to his collection when in London, with such a wide field it was virtually impossible for him to become more than a gifted amateur; had he concentrated on one or two countries, he would certainly have become an expert. But he was content with his choice, and at his death, he passed on a collection of Great Britain, the Dominions and Colonial territories that is virtually complete in every issue. Certainly it will never be rivalled in content, or uniqueness. The sale of all his foreign stamps, of which there is no record, must have gone a long way in financing the future acquisitions in his chosen field. Perhaps his decision to concentrate on Great Britain and the Empire might have been influenced by the thought that, one day, his own head would grace their stamps.

CHAPTER FOUR

Throughout his life, the Prince of Wales, later King George V, was an inveterate letter writer, a habit born partially through communicating with his mother who was deaf. For him, it had always been a comforting form of communication, and even with the advent of the telephone he preferred to write. Of all his correspondents, John Tilleard was one of the most regular, and usually responded in person. The Prince of Wales had long trusted his philatelic adviser, and his confidence in him was not misplaced. One letter, however, is more telling than any other that was written by the Prince of Wales to Tilleard. It reveals their relationship but, more importantly, shows his aspirations with regard to his collection. It is dated 19 February 1908, from Marlborough House, London, some time after Tilleard had negotiated the private purchase of parts (mainly Barbados) of the A. S. Tompson West Indies Collection:

> I quite approve of everything you have done & propose to do with regard to the Barbados stamps. *But remember I wish to have <u>the</u> best collection & not one of the best collections in England, therefore if you think that there are a few more stamps required to make it so don't hesitate to take them, now that you have got the chance* [author's italics]. I think I ought to have one or two of the 1d on half of five s, as I may have great difficulty in getting them again. …

The Tompson collection of Barbados was the first really important study collection Tilleard bought for the Prince of Wales. Much of it had been exhibited at the International Exhibition of 1906, where it had won a gold medal and even more admiration for its 'beauty of specimens, completeness, and choiceness of exhibit' and 'stood second to none in the exhibition'.[1] Tompson's West Indies collection was sold in its entirety for £6,800 after the exhibition, but it is not known how much of the Barbados material passed into the Royal Philatelic Collection. In his diary, the Prince of Wales refers to buying 'a small collection of Barbados', but that was in December 1906, and 'a quantity of Barbados stamps' in February 1908, Tilleard and he mounted them in a brand new album, rather than adding to the existing album as was their normal practice.

On 5 March 1908, the Prince of Wales 'presided at a meeting of the Royal Philatelic Society in Southampton Row, over 30 members were present' where he showed them his 'collection of Barbados, which is really very fine now'.[2] Tilleard read his paper 'On the Occasion of a Display of the Stamps of Barbados from the Collection of His Royal Highness the President'.[3] He could hardly have had better material to illustrate it, for with the Prince of Wales's original holdings, and the recently acquired Tompson material (see Appendix III, page 318) he had, at his disposal, the basis of one of the finest collections of Barbados at that time. By matching Tilleard's paper with the items named in the Exhibition Catalogue of 1906, it is possible to identify the provenance of some choice rarities, shades, bisects and varieties that were shown to the members that night.

Tilleard spoke of the 1855–58 deep blue ONE PENNY stamp 'bisected vertically joined to a whole stamp on part of a newspaper, which bears the "1" numerical cancellation and is dated OC 21, 1857'.[4] Another exciting stamp was a double print HALFPENNY in deep green of 1861, one of two then known, along with a double print ONE PENNY blue and the unique double print ONE SHILLING black, of 1861–70. Also shown from the Tompson collection was the pair of ONE SHILLING black imperforate, again very rare and much admired. He produced a block of four of the rose-red SIX PENCE, likewise of the 1861–70 issue, to show how it could be confused with an imperforate copy of a 'later perforated issue of this value in colour very similar to the first 6d. stamp'.[5] Like the 1860 'pin-perforated' stamps he spoke of next, these were all ex-Tompson, as was the ONE PENNY blue (one of three) all rare unused, and therefore highly desirable. But the single most thrilling stamp from

Barbados:
1861–70
ONE SHILLING
error of colour
that came from
the Tompson
Collection.

Barbados: 1856 deep blue ONE PENNY stamp bisected vertically and
joined to a whole stamp on piece.

that source was the Britannia ONE SHILLING error blue of the 1861–70 issue.

The 'Britannia design' for the original 1852 die for the Barbados stamps had been commissioned by Perkins, Bacon and Petch from the watercolour by Henry Corbould. It was originally intended for the Mauritius issue of 1848, but was not used there until 1858 when it variously replaced the locally printed stamps. It was first utilised in the first issue for Trinidad in 1851. Corbould's watercolour, stamp size on card, is finely executed. It shows Frances Teresa Stewart, the celebrated Restoration beauty (see Appendix IV, page 319) as Britannia, holding a spear in her right hand, while her other arm rests lightly on a shield emblazoned with the Union Flag. She is seated on bags of raw sugar, the chief export of both Mauritius and the islands of the West Indies. A full-rigged ship, sailing to the Motherland, is on the horizon. On the bottom of the card, in pencil, Corbould has written 'The Engraver, with a magnifying glass, (such as I have not) can finish the toenails rather more',[6] and 'Mauritius' below the image. Some time after the dies had been made, the original Corbould sketch disappeared. It turned up in an auction house in

Chancery Lane, London in July 1919, and was bought for the Royal Philatelic Collection. These very early island stamps were prepared through the Crown Agents, with the brief that 'It would be desirable that the stamp for Colonial use be so different from that employed by the General Post Office at home that it may be easily distinguishable.'[7]

From the beginning, (15 April 1852) Barbados was well served by the Perkins, Bacon and Petch printings. By 1861 higher denominations were called for and, among others, a ONE SHILLING, in brownish-black, was produced. When the stock dwindled, they were reordered and the new supply of 50,000

Henry Corbould's original watercolour of Britannia. Originally intended for use in Mauritius, it was first used for Barbados and Trinidad. On the bottom of the card, Corbould has written in pencil, 'Mauritius', then 'The Engraver, with a magnifying glass, (such as I have not) can finish the toenails rather more.'

Enlargement of the watercolour.

ONE SHILLING was sent to the Colony, leaving the Port of London on 28 April 1863. For some inexplicable reason, they were all printed in blue, the exact shade of the ONE PENNY value. The error was only discovered after they had been landed at Bridgetown. There was great consternation as to what to do. Clearly, they could not be issued, nor were they, as the blue ONE SHILLING would be confused with the ONE PENNY. An alternative was to reprint the ONE PENNY, but as Perkins, Bacon – the Petch was dropped in 1853 – wrote to the Colonial Secretary, 'the mode you suggest, i.e., to send you stamps of the value of 1d. with a white ground and the figure of Britannia in Blue would not only involve the expense of a new Die & Plate but could not in fact be engraved without sacrificing the security of the background... Under the circumstances, we await your orders as to the 1d. stamps, & are quite ready to forward with them a fresh supply of the Brown 1/- labels at the earliest period after receiving your reply'.[8] In the end, an entirely new stock of ONE SHILLING, this time in brown (although brown-black is a more accurate description) was sent out to Barbados, 'in place of those sent out by mistake which will be returned to you, if you desire it, only a few having been disposed of for a postage label album'. The stock of 50,000 redundant ONE SHILLING stamps was destroyed on the island save for those few in the 'postage label album'. They were supposed to have been cancelled by pen with a diagonal cross but have long since been cleaned. Only a dozen are known to exist now, one in the Royal Philatelic Collection and another in the Tapling Collection.

With such material from the Royal Philatelic Collection to work on, Tilleard was in his element. His paper continued with 'the most interesting of the stamps of Barbados, the provisional made in 1878 by overprinting the value of 1d. on each of the two halves of the 5s. stamp, which was perforated down the centre for division so as to form two stamps of the new denomination, the original value being cut off'[9] – the very stamps mentioned in the Prince of Wales's letter that February (see page 97), which had been exhibited by Tompson in 1906. The

Barbados: 1878 provisional overprint 1d. on each of the two halves of the 5s. perforated down the centre, a present from Queen Mary to George V.

overprinting was carried out by the West Indian Press. However, as a great number of this FIVE SHILLING dull rose issue was used for the provisionals, they became extremely rare unused. There are two unused severed pairs in the Collection, one a present to the King from Queen Mary in 1917.

With the difficulties of delivery, overprints in all the Colonies were common. Again, the West Indian Press overprinted HALF-PENNY on the FOUR PENCE deep brown stamp of 1892. The first overprint was ordered in red, but the Colonial Postmaster considered them indistinct, so returned the pane with instructions to print the rest in black. As every stamp had to be accounted for, the trial red pane was included with the others and printed in black. Examples in the Collection of these double surcharges in black and red, a vertical pair with no hyphen on the lower stamp, also came from Tompson. Tilleard ended his paper with a word on the Kingston Relief Fund issue of 1907, ONE PENNY on TWO PENCE slate-black and orange. It was produced to raise money for the victims of an earthquake in Jamaica, and became interesting to philatelists through a series of errors in the overprinting. There are several such errors in the Collection, and this is a prime example of how the Prince of Wales kept abreast of every issue of interest, and made sure that his collection was up to date. Finally, Tilleard and the Prince of Wales were thanked by M. P. Castle, editor of the *London Philatelist*, where it was said that the Prince's specialised collection was 'shown in great strength and profusion, pairs and blocks of scarce unused varieties abounding, and even the rarest varieties being frequently numerously shown in several shades. In fact, the collection fully attains the twentieth-century high-water mark of specialised Philately, being undoubtedly the finest lot of Barbados stamps ever collected'.[10] A week later, the Prince exhibited the same collection of Barbados stamps, and 'took Bertie [Prince Albert, later Duke of York, then King George VI] to Caxton Hall to see a Philatelic Exhibition got up by the Junior Philatelic Society of London'.[11]

Barbados: 1892 HALF PENNY on FOUR PENCE deep brown, vertical pair. The surcharge was doubly printed, first in red, afterwards in black.

The purchase of the Tompson study collection of Barbados put the Prince of Wales on a new philatelic

John A Tilleard MVO, the first philatelic advisor to George V as Duke of York and Prince of Wales. He was appointed in 1893.

footing. At that time, he decided that he would concentrate on unused corner blocks of four, wherever possible, much in the manner of his mentor Lord Crawford. In his quest 'to have the best collection, and not just one of the best collections in England' he was ideally placed. Tilleard was a positive conduit from the dealers, private collectors and acquaintances, and as 'His Royal Highness the President' of the Royal Philatelic Society, London, he was always notified of anything interesting. More often than not he was given first refusal, often at a favourable price. In addition, he was completely *au fait* with the current market value of stamps. A letter from the price-conscious Prince to Tilleard shows his delight in his success and friendly rivalry: 'I am glad you have secured the stamp for £20 especially as it was offered to Lord Crawford for £50.'[12] Wisely he took the view that when something he needed was on the market, it should be bought there and then. His letters to Tilleard are littered with instructions to buy as 'it would be a pity to miss the opportunity', or (referring to an army official error stamp), 'It is absolutely necessary I should have one in my collection & it might be some time before one got the chance of getting one again & the price named is not a very high one considering the rareness of the stamp'.[13] But he would not buy at any price, and was shrewd enough not to become over-excited with what was on offer, but to trust his advisor. One example of many is his letter to Tilleard:

> I see that Stanley & Gibbons [sic] have just bought the whole of Mr [M. P.] Castle's Australian collection [he originally sold it in 1895]. I suppose it will be broken up & each stamp sold separately. I see there are some very fine ones amongst them. The worst of it is I fear he will ask a very large price for them. There are 25 unused Sydney Views, what would he ask for them do you suppose; then there is the 4d. blue error of South Australia, which I see he considers one of the rarest stamps in the world. No doubt for our purposes, Stanley & Gibbons are not good people to buy from, but at the same time when one sees such a fine collection as these, one does not like to pass them over. Perhaps you would let me know, what your views are on the subject, & if you thought it worthwhile to try & get any of them & which ones.[14]

It is not known whether the Prince of Wales succumbed to any of these particular temptations, but New South Wales, especially the Sydney Views and South Australia, are virtually complete within the Collection, with many proofs and essays. The 1868–79 FOUR PENCE deep ultramarine of South Australia that escaped the surcharge mentioned in the letter is in the Collection, both a used and an unused example. The unused one, possibly ex-Castle, has its original gum, and only 'one other unused specimen is known, which was originally joined to this one'.[15] Certainly, by this time it can be assumed that the Prince of Wales knew exactly what he wanted, and bought solely in relation to his areas of study.

However, some countries gave him more pleasure than others, and harking back to his days in HMS *Thrush*, his first love was always the West Indies. He had bought a small collection of Grenada in 1904, which 'added to the stamps I already possess of Grenada ought to make a very fine lot indeed'.[16] Later, in 1908, he wrote to Tilleard: 'I certainly approve of your getting any stamps of the Turk's [*sic*] Islands collection which you spoke to me about in London the other day. I agree with you in thinking that the opportunity ought not to be lost of making my collection as perfect as possible.'[17] Again, neither the vendor nor the description survives. However, the content of the W. B. Avery Collection of Nevis stamps that Tilleard bought for him in its entirety the next year can be deduced. The Prince had been greatly impressed when he first saw it at the exhibition of West Indian Stamps (where he was the only exhibitor of Turks Islands stamps) back in 1893. Even then he had noted 'Mr Avery's [collection of] Nevis ... for completeness and perfection of specimens, must take very high place, the unused plates of all the issues, and the inclusion of all the rarities, leaving scarce anything to be desired'.[18] The Prince must have been delighted with his purchase, which 'is about the best known'.[19] He invited Tilleard to Marlborough House, asking him to bring 'the Avery collection of Nevis stamps and also my collection so that I could compare the two together'. [20]

The amalgam of the two collections was shown to members of the Royal Philatelic Society, London in 1913. Then the collection filled two volumes, and 'everything that is known to exist in the stamps of "Nevis" is comprised in the collection'.[21] In keeping with his predilection for the French school of collecting, the King, as he now was, showed an impressive array of proofs and colour proofs, including the proof in black on card of the very first ONE PENNY stamp of 1861 'before the corner stars were completed'.[22] Also shown were the 'fine set of proofs on card taken from the plates of the twelve types of each value engraved for the first issue [1861]' with two complete sets of colour trials (see Appendix V, page 319). A feature of the Royal Philatelic Collection is that it never fails to delight, not only for its completeness but for the unexpected rarities. With Nevis that night, the members were shown a used ONE SHILLING yellow-green on laid paper 1866–76, and a hitherto unknown vertical strip of three lithographed ONE SHILLING deep green stamps 1876–78.

Browsing through the two albums of Nevis stamps, the members could not fail to notice the many examples of the retouches, the ONE PENNY vermilion of 1876–78. The study of retouches seems to have been an abiding interest of George V, as Prince of Wales and as King, and there are many examples throughout the Collection. The Nevis retouches were all lithographed and were easily, if somewhat carelessly, judging by the errors, corrected.

Part of the Nevis collection was exhibited at the International Philatelic Exhibition in Berne in 1910. The President, Baron de Reuterskiöld, was well known to the Prince of Wales through their shared interest in the Turks Islands, and it was he who persuaded him (by then King George V) to send the exhibit. It was the only time that he ever exhibited abroad. In general, he disliked lending his collection to anyone other than the Royal Philatelic Society, London, or to exhibitions organised by them. In the past he had had a bad experience when his displays were exposed to direct sunlight, the stamps fading and having to be replaced. In the early days, the leaves were pinned to boards, which meant that the stamps had to be remounted and written up. And, of course, there were no polyester protectors to keep the pages clean and flat.

Condition was becoming more and more important to the Prince, hence his preference for unused specimens. He was, of course, following the current fashion, and influenced by the great collectors Phillip Ferrari, George H. Worthington, Henry J. Duveen and, of course, the Earl of Crawford, all of whom, despite their vast wealth had 'difficulty of forming an unused collection, but difficulty is always an inducement to the big collector'.[23] Although used specimens were always taken if an unused one was unavailable, the study of postmarks was then not fashionable. Tilleard was never very interested in them, and neither was the Prince of Wales. But later, when, as King, his own image was cancelled with heavy ink, he held 'no childish views such as King Ferdinand II of Sicily, known as Bomba, who considered postmarks as a defacement of his own portrait'.[24] Not so the present Earl of Wessex, who as a boy at Gordonstoun writing home, pressed down the stamp bearing the image of his mother, Queen Elizabeth II on his letter home with the cry 'Sorry Mama!'[25] Another advantage of concentrating on unused stamps was that, unlike those on piece, they needed less space to store, and were easier to manage by a single curator. However, some areas, like the Ionian Islands and Heligoland, are considered better collected used on covers than unused.

The United States of Ionia, ΙΟΝΙΚΟΝ ΚΡΑΤΟΣ (made up of Corfu, Paxos, Levkas, Cephalonia, Zante, Ithaca and sundry islets) were ceded to Britain in 1815, and returned to Greece in 1864. The first and only issue (from Perkins, Bacon) of British Protectorate stamps were issued in 1859, and the Collection holds several examples of each of the three denominations ½d., 1d., and 2d., including unused multiples, and three covers with examples of island hand stamps or manuscript cancellations.

Heligoland, a small island in the North Sea, came under British rule in 1814, then was ceded to Germany in 1890 in return for German recognition of the British Protectorate of Zanzibar and Pemba – a somewhat unequal deal that Henry Morton Stanley, the explorer of Africa, described as 'giving a new suit in exchange for a trouser button'.[26] The issues of Heligoland were exactly the kind of philatelic challenge that the Prince of Wales probably relished. Until 1867, the Free City of Hamburg was responsible for the island's postal service when its stamps were replaced with Heligoland stamps, typographed by the Imperial Printing Works of Berlin. Some bore the image of Queen Victoria, while all had the denomination in schillings. There were later reprints from Berlin, Leipzig and Hamburg. Later, in 1919 as King, he attended a meeting of the Royal Philatelic Society, London, and showed his collection of Heligoland to the members. 'He thought that Collectors were apt to magnify the difficulties of separating the reprints from the issued stamps and considered that these obstacles could readily be overcome by any philatelist who was willing to devote a little time to the study of the subject.'[27] That night, the members could see from the used and unused specimens from his collection just how he had mastered the difficult question of the vagaries of the various printings and reprintings, proof, if proof was needed, that he 'had become a really good judge of stamps and an experienced philatelist'.[28] But however much the Prince of Wales perfected his own collection, the Great Britain stamps of his father's reign were in need of attention.

By about 1908, it had been decided to replace Great Britain bi-coloured stamps with single colours on the grounds of expense, and De La Rue were commissioned to come up with improved designs. The 4[d] kept its original design but was printed in a single colour, orange, and issued on 1 November 1909. The 2[d] value had a completely new design, and from that essays

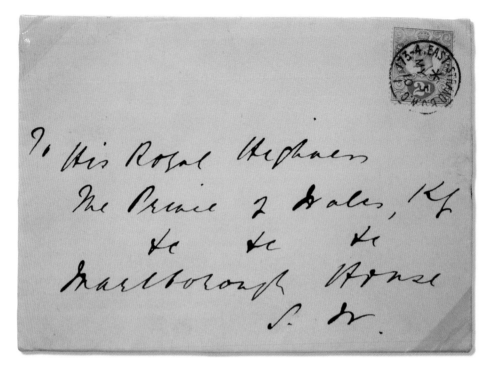

Great Britain: 1910 (May) 2d 'Tyrian Plum', used on cover. The only used example of this issue,
it was sent to the Prince of Wales, and arrived 6 May 1910, the day Edward VII died.
The issue was subsequently never released to the public.

and proofs were prepared, some now in the Collection. Then there were colour trials made on 'wmk perf. in pale sage-green, orange and lilac',[29] and many colours not in the Collection. Of the three, the last (more a shade of purple) was chosen – again a single and south-west corner pair, unused, were in the Royal Philatelic Collection though the single was sold in 2001. The stamp was soon dubbed the 'Tyrian Plum' from its colour, which was entirely appropriate for a Sovereign on whose Empire the sun never set, for the colour is also known as 'Royal Purple' (see Appendix VI, page 319).

The stamp was put into production and 100,000 sheets were printed for issue in early May 1910. A friendly dealer or a thoughtful philatelist at Somerset House (some say the Prince engineered it) sent a letter to the

Prince of Wales bearing the 'Tyrian Plum' to arrive on 6 May 1910, the seventieth anniversary of the Penny Post. But the Prince had more pressing matters on his mind, for the King, as the bulletin from Buckingham Palace announced, was suffering 'from bronchitis and his condition causes some anxiety'.[30] That evening, Edward VII died peacefully. His valet always reported that His Majesty said he would die on a Friday, and he did. With his death, the whole stock of the 2^d 'Tyrian Plum' issue was destroyed, although some unused examples survived. The used 2^d 'Tyrian Plum' on the corner of an envelope addressed to 'His Royal Highness The Prince of Wales, KG etc, etc, etc, Marlborough House, SW [London]', is the only known example of the stamp to have gone through the postal system.

And so, for the final time in his life, the position and name of His Royal Highness, the Prince of Wales changed, for he was now His Majesty King George V.

CHAPTER FIVE

❖❖❖

Balmoral Castle

September 21 1910

My dear Mr Tilleard,

I am commanded by the King to say that their Majesties hope that you will be able to pay them a visit here this month and that you will stay for three or four days. Any day would be convenient to their Majesties for you to arrive and if you will be so good as to telegraph to me at once which day you would like to come a carriage will meet you at Ballater Station, the train arriving there at 5pm. If you were here for a Sunday, perhaps you would bring a frock coat and top hat. Dress for dinner is evening dress, black waistcoat. Trousers. [Rather than the knee breeches and stockings worn with evening dress in London and Windsor].

    I am very truly Yours

    (Signed) Harry Verney

    Deputy Master of the Household

Exactly a week later, on 28 September, John Tilleard was at Ballater station, and indeed Henry Verney and a brougham were there to meet him. For Tilleard, it was a pleasant drive as the carriage sped along the ten miles to Balmoral Castle, followed by a dogcart with his luggage. The road hugged the Dee, with its dramatic falls and shaded pools, but the river was noticeably down after the heatwave of a fortnight before. The thick canopy of the trees shaded the open carriage from the autumn sun. The King merely recorded that 'Mr Tilleard arrived & we talked about the designs for the new stamps.'[1]

For George V Balmoral, with its grouse moors, stalking, and miles of fishing on the Dee and its tributaries, can only have been a foretaste of Heaven. But despite the sporting delights of his private estate, the King was concerned by the pressing problem of the new stamps of his reign. The issue was not proceeding as he had planned.

Towards the end of June 1910, not two months into his reign, the Postmaster General wrote to George V:

> Mr Herbert Samuel, with his humble duty to Your Majesty, begs to submit in the accompanying memorandum the particulars relative to the designs for the frames to the new postage stamps which he proposes, should they meet with Your Majesty's approval, to embody in his invitations to the artists selected to compete for this work.
>
> After consultation with the President of the Royal Academy and with others, he would submit that the invitations should be addressed to Mr C. W. Sherborn, Mr G. W. Eve and Mr Garth Jones, all of them designers of repute of book plates and title pages and specially qualified therefore for this work, which is of a somewhat analogous kind.[2]

The general guidelines set out in the memorandum included such stipulations that at least one of the designs should have a lion *couchant* at the foot of the stamp.

Once again, George V knew that he could rely on Tilleard for help and advice for his own stamps. As Prince of Wales, he had been absent for the design stage of the Great Britain issue at the outset of his father's reign, but he and Tilleard were invited in 1903 by the Government of Canada to design their Edward VII stamps. The idea had been first put forward during his visit in HMS *Ophir* two years before, and he and Tilleard produced a perfectly acceptable stamp. They chose to portray Edward VII three-quarter face, closely cropped by an oval, with the value wedged into the bottom corners.

This experience could well have led to George V's decision to go for a three-quarter face portrait for his own issue. For this, he chose a photograph of himself (in full dress uniform), taken by the court photographers W. and D. Downey, one that he and Queen Mary particularly liked. Although he was adamant that this image would work on his stamp, he was disappointed with all the designs for the frame submitted by the three chosen artists, the Royal Mint and sundry others. He discussed the question with Tilleard at Balmoral, and decided to invite his friend, Bertram Mackennal, a sculptor who was already designing the coinage for the Royal Mint, to tender a design for a whole new stamp. Mackennal refused to compete with the others, but later, for a fee, produced designs that, with minor alterations, were acceptable. G. W. Eve's submissions for the higher values were also successful, and the Royal Philatelic Collection holds Mackennal's drawings, the original Downey photographs and examples of all these drawings, water-colours and essays.

All should have been well for the complete set of the lower values to be issued before the Coronation on 22 June 1911, but by a series of circumstances that might well have been avoided, only the HALFPENNY and ONE PENNY values were issued in time. And they were dreadful stamps. The catalogue of disasters began when De La Rue's contract to print postage and revenue stamps came up for renewal at the end of 1910. They had been printing Great Britain stamps continuously since 1855, and had all the skills, expertise and machinery to produce first-rate stamps, in quantity and on time. Their contract had, in fact, expired in 1900, but was extended for ten years.

In a bid to retain the contract, De La Rue produced an unsolicited essay, which they presented to the King on 26 May 1910. Like their contract, the essay was rejected. George V, a friend for many years of Sir Evelyn De la Rue, must have been devastated when the printing contract was finally awarded to Harrison and Son, 'despite their lack of experience in printing stamps and use of fugitive inks'.[3]

Unlike De La Rue, Harrison and Son had no experience either in engraving or plate making – they were, after all, merely the printers of the *London Gazette*. The Royal Mint, with equal lack of expertise, stepped in to provide the finished plates. For this, they hired a freelance engraver, J. A. C. Harrison (no relation to the printer), to make the dies using the designs of Mackennal and Eve for the frames, surrounding what has famously become known as

Canada: 1903–12
Edward VII issue, stamps
designed by Prince of Wales
and John Tilleard for
Government of Canada.

Original drawing by Bertram Mackennal.
This was approved and adopted for the
ONE PENNY value, December 1910.

Photographs of Bertram Mackennal's designs that were not used, September 1910.

'the Downey Head'. J. A. C. Harrison had no experience of engraving for typography, just as the Royal Mint did not have the facilities, experience or equipment to manufacture the plates. In the end, specialised machinery had to be imported from the United States. Nor does the story end there. Part of the blame lay with Mackennal's design. As a sculptor, he had never before designed a stamp. Neither was the King blameless: his choice of a three-quarter face was difficult to reproduce convincingly and anyway 'The use of a photograph was not compatible with the typographic process',[4] although it was used successfully by De la Rue for National Savings Stamps. The net result was a disaster.

The King was deeply disappointed. When the Harrison proofs of the new stamps arrived, he summoned Sir Evelyn De la Rue to the Royal Yacht, then moored off Cowes, Isle of Wight, and remonstrated with his friend. 'Make me look like a stuffed monkey, don't they?'[5] he cried. Sir Evelyn had to admit that indeed they did, but there was nothing he could do about it. The King might have remembered another vilified stamp, the Lapirot engraving of the 1859 issue of Mauritius where Queen Victoria's head was likened by the French to *une tête de singe* (see page 91). As such a keen philatelist, he must have been hurt, too, by the universal criticism. For a start, the British public was not used to the revolutionary three-quarter face head on a stamp as for seventy years, profiles were all they had ever known. Further criticism appeared in the press: 'Philatelists and the general public wondered, once more, why a great country like Britain should have to use stamps that would disgrace the most insignificant republic of Central America.'[6]

The King, too, made his feelings known: On 28 June 1911, shortly after his Coronation, Sir Frederick Ponsonby, his Assistant Private Secretary wrote to the Secretary to the Post Office, Sir Matthew Nathan:

> The King desires me to ask you to tell the Postmaster General that it was a great disappointment to him to find that the new Stamps have been such a failure.
>
> His Majesty, who as you know has always taken a great interest in Philately, had looked forward to producing a Stamp that would rank as one of the finest in Europe, but although infinite trouble was taken over the design the result can hardly be considered satisfactory.

This new Stamp, much to The King's regret, has been received with loud abuse in the United Kingdom and judging by the letters addressed to His Majesty with contempt abroad.

The King quite understands that any extravagance in the production of Stamps should be avoided, but considers that in the laudable desire of economy the other extreme has been reached and a Stamp totally unworthy of this country has been produced.

His Majesty wishes to know what the cost of producing a new Stamp would be with the same process that is used in the larger Countries of Europe.[7]

The response from abroad must have been rapid, as only six days had passed since the issue of the stamps. Not surprisingly, the Downeys were also stung by the criticism, and they commissioned an engraver to produce a die from their work. This they used on their trade card – a mistake as it was even worse than the original Harrison engraving. Perkins, Bacon also produced a die to show what an experienced stamp printer could achieve from a photograph. Impressions from these dies are, of course, in the Collection.

However, if the King was embarrassed by his stamps at home, he was determined not to proliferate the disaster in the Dominions and Colonies. South Africa, whose stamps had always appealed to him, produced the first issue of his reign to bear his image. It was printed by De La Rue in time for the opening of the Union Parliament on 4 November 1910 (the Collection holds

South Africa: 1910 2½d blue. Printed by De La Rue, this was the first Dominion issue of George V's reign along with the die proof.

not only a die proof and a plate proof of this 2½ᵈ blue stamp, but also many examples of shades on bluish paper and two overprinted specimens). But South Africa had jumped the gun, for the King 'expressed the wish that the Colonies would adopt the same head as designed for the English stamps'.[8]

Once again, Tilleard was brought in to advise. Sir Frederick Ponsonby wrote to him on 2 September 1911, prompted by the South African Parliament's proposal for a new issue:

> His Majesty however was horrified to think that the mess there has been with the English stamp would be reproduced in South Africa. The King therefore wishes to produce a really good head and at his own expense. He hopes that when this has been adopted in South Africa, the Post Master General will be able to see the difference and so the English stamps will eventually be copied from them.[9]

The Downeys were asked for further copies of the two photographs of the King taken in 1910, one in profile, the other three-quarters face. Tilleard was then asked to 'get the best engraver' he knew 'and have a really good engraving of the profile head done and sent to His Majesty at Balmoral'. Tilleard took the photographs to 'Messrs de la Rue & Co ... that firm being, in my opinion by far the best for such work', and preparation of the dies, using the profile head, was put in hand immediately. Four days later Tilleard went to inspect the proof and made certain suggestions. Just a few days after receiving his instructions, Sir Evelyn De la Rue wrote to Tilleard:

> ... Lastly there is a new impression in which the changes you recommended have been carried out. This is printed on a perfect oblong card. I think you will agree that the changes effected give the head a better appearance as well as an improvement in the portrait, though neither is an exact reproduction of the photographic proof originally approved. We could by putting a new die in hand make a line for line copy & the effect produced by a die thus cut would be almost indistinguishable from the photographic proof, though it might not print so well on the machine as the die at present in existence.[10]

Tilleard wrote to George V's Assistant Private Secretary, Major Clive Wigram, enclosing examples of the De La Rue dies for the King's approval:

> …it has occurred to me that the result of the head being satisfactory it might be submitted to the Cape authorities without having another one prepared as at first proposed there wd no doubt be a great advantage in the same head being used for South African stamps as that for the other Colonies whose stamps are prepared here and there could perhaps be more chance of the same being ultimately adopted for the stamps of the Mother Country.[11]

The King was delighted with the amended De La Rue die proofs, and insisted that he send them himself to the Colonial Office. That De La Rue produced the dies so quickly, and from a photograph, was a measure of their professionalism and an obvious snub to Harrison and Son. Much of the material connected with the many and varied attempts to replace the Downey Head is in the Collection.

Meanwhile, the work to replace the Downey Head on the stamps of the 'Mother Country' was well in hand. Again, Bertram Mackennal was commissioned to produce what became known as 'the Profile Head'. There were, in fact, two heads, one taken from the designs he had prepared for the coinage to be used for the HALFPENNY to the FOUR PENCE values, except for the ONE PENNY and TWO PENCE HALFPENNY values, which were taken from the designs for the Coronation Medal (later used for the General Service Medal) and became known as the large 'Medal Head'. An intermediate version of the 'Medal Head' appeared on the FIVE PENCE to ONE SHILLING values, while an even smaller version was used for fiscal stamps. Mackennal and Eve shared the design of the frames, Mackennal working up his complete stamp in clay. These were then photographed, and the Collection holds a 'bromide' (as the prints were then called after the paper used) approved by the King with his initials. Also prominent in the Collection are the eight colour-trial sheets for the ONE PENNY stamps, the King's preference initialled by him.

With the poor quality printing and subsequent errors, the frequent re-working of the dies with the resulting proofs and trials, along with the essays

Great Britain: The photograph of the sculpture, together with the original photograph from which Bertram Mackennal produced the 'Profile Head' and 'Medal Head'. The approved design is signed by George V.

for all the new stamps, there was a vast amount of philatelic material, all of which makes fascinating study for the specialist. But for George V it can only have been torture to see the one thing, his own stamp, he had looked forward to for so many years being ridiculed. Notwithstanding these early disappointments his collection for the whole of his reign is remarkably complete with all the issues – the Commissioners for the Inland Revenue were still supplying him with proofs and corner blocks of four – and well bears comparison with any other part of the Collection, excepting possibly the 1839–41 material.

At last, in 1913, there was an issue of stamps that should have given George V great pleasure and one of which he could be justly proud, the 'sea-horses' design for the higher denominations of HALF CROWN, FIVE SHILLINGS,

TEN SHILLINGS and ONE POUND. Once again, Bertram Mackennal designed the stamp and it was engraved by J. A. C. Harrison. It is, indeed, truly handsome. There is a classical feel about it, with Mackennal's profile head of George V set in a wreath of laurel leaves, suspended from garlands. Three seahorses, pawing the waves, draw a chariot bearing a defiant Britannia, trident at the ready, her shield emblazoned with the Union Flag. It is full of movement and worthy of Great Britain's role as ruler of the Empire. Further, they were line-engraved and thus a better impression was achieved. But there was a problem. Mackennal had included an extra horizontal line in the St Andrew's Cross.

Like his father, George V was a stickler for correct dress and ceremonial accuracy in keeping with his position as King Emperor, and such an error would have been an anathema to him. However, as each value was engraved separately, the corrected flag was applied at the same time as the denomina-

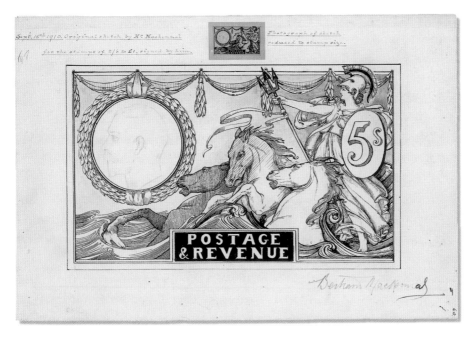

Great Britain: 1910 artwork for 'sea-horses' design submitted by Bertram Mackennal for the higher values. George V was particularly pleased with them.

tion; consequently, the shield of each value differs slightly one from another. No further printings of the ONE POUND value were required after 1913/14. There were three different printers throughout the life of this stamp: Waterlow, De La Rue and Bradbury Wilkinson. The Collection holds an excellent record of the issue, which includes the two fine drawings by Bertram Mackennal, die proofs, colour trials and imprimatur blocks of four of each value from Waterlow's registration sheets.

Notwithstanding the problems with the new stamps for his reign, George V and Tilleard continued as ardently as ever with the collection – in virtually his first act on becoming King he became Patron of The Royal Philatelic Society, London, handing over the presidency to the Earl of Crawford, and reverting to ordinary membership at two guineas per year. Both Tilleard and Marcellus Castle, editor of the *London Philatelist*, were created MVO (Member of the Victorian Order, an honour in the gift of the Sovereign) in the Coronation Honours List for services to the King and to philately.

Just two days before he acceded to the throne, 4 May 1910, he had written as Prince of Wales to Tilleard: 'I am glad that my offer of £500 for the New Brunswick and Nova Scotia stamps has been accepted and I enclose a cheque for that amount.'[12] Again, it cannot be deduced as to exactly what he bought or from whom, but two years later, on 23 May 1912 he showed a fine collection of New Brunswick and Nova Scotia stamps to the autumn meeting of the Royal Philatelic Society, London. There were some particularly choice items among the New Brunswick display, not least an unused block of nine dull-red THREE PENCE of 1851, four of the yellow (shades) SIX PENCE and two mauve (shades) ONE SHILLING, all in the attractive Royal Crown and Heraldic Flowers series printed by Perkins, Bacon. Many examples of the next issue (1860–63) were shown that night, and what particularly excited the members were two examples of the famous brown FIVE CENTS Connell issue.

In 1859, the Hon. Charles Connell was appointed Postmaster General of New Brunswick, a Colony in its own right since it had broken from Nova Scotia in June 1784. It was an important post as it held Council Rank and a salary of £600 a year. Soon after his appointment, the Council decided that New Brunswick should switch from sterling, with pounds, shillings and pence, to dollars and cents in line with the United States. Thus, a whole new currency and stamp issue were required, and the new Postmaster General, was detailed to produce the stamps. Perkins, Bacon had printed their first issue, but Connell approached the American Bank Note Company of New York (which at that time was also printing the stamps of Canada) and negotiated an advantageous contract for printing the new stamps. The order was originally for ONE, FIVE, TEN and TWELVE & HALF CENTS values, but at the last minute, Connell realised that a SEVENTEEN CENTS stamp was needed to cover the postage to Great Britain, via New York. Connell himself had chosen the designs for low values – a train, Queen Victoria's head, the paddle steamer

New Brunswick: 1851 THREE PENCE dull-red, unused block of nine. This particularly fine series, printed by Perkins, Bacon, is known as the 'Royal Crown and Heraldic Flowers'.

Washington, and the Prince of Wales (Edward VII) in Highland dress. This left one design or image short for the fifth value, that, for some unexplained reason, was the FIVE CENTS.

Charles Connell was at his country house at Woodstock, sixty miles from the capital Fredericton, when the new stamps arrived from New York. As they were being unpacked, Mr Hale, the Secretary to the Post Office, was aghast when he reached the 50,000 sheets of 100 stamps of the FIVE CENTS denomination. Staring up at him was not the portrait of a member of the Royal Family, or indeed anything pertinent to the Colony, but 'the even features, a good, generous mouth, well-set eyes and a firm jaw'[13] of a man he recognised only too well: it was a full-face portrait of Charles Connell. Consternation followed, as the issue was due for imminent release. The Provincial Secretary, S. L. Tilley, sent a telegram to Connell informing him of the Governor's veto of the stamp. When the Council met, it was decided that the Queen should replace Connell for the FIVE CENTS stamp, and by then there was a new Postmaster General.

New Brunswick: 1860–63 FIVE CENTS brown.
The head of Charles Connell, Postmaster
General, mysteriously appeared in the centre,
hence the stamp is popularly known
as the 'Connell'.

There are various theories as to how Connell's portrait appeared on the stamp that now bears his name. Most likely, as the choice of design was his, he chose it either for vanity or, as some would have it, to please his daughter. Alternatively, as the extra image was required after the SEVENTEEN CENTS was added to the order, Connell's secretary provided a photograph of him, thinking the Postmaster General an appropriate subject.

Whatever the reason, the whole issue was acquired by Connell from the American Bank Note Company for £56 15s and it was delivered to his house at Woodstock. Two days later, he burned every sheet on a bonfire in the garden – all except a few that he kept as souvenirs. There is some conjecture as to how many were kept back and how they came on to the market. Some were used to decorate the menus for a banquet Connell gave; the guests kept the cards and later steamed off the stamps. One known example was given by Connell to Francis C. Foster who requested one, enclosing a current FIVE CENTS stamp to cover the return postage. The two Connell daughters, Ella and Alice, were each given a sheet. Alice was frequently approached by collectors for a 'Connell', but always refused on the grounds that she did not think anyone should profit by 'something that had caused their father such mental anguish',[14] and burned her sheet. If Ella had been the reason that the stamp was created in the first place, it is most likely that she kept hers intact. A unique and perfect vertical pair was found by a local doctor in a book bought from the late Charles Connell's estate. There are many known examples: all of the major collections have several, but the die proofs, plate proofs and specimens are more rare – the Collection holds examples of each on a variety of papers and in several colours.

If the New Brunswick rarities were not enough for the 1912 autumn meeting of the Royal Philatelic Society, London, there were also the delights of those from Nova Scotia. Through Tilleard, the King exhibited such rarities as all these stamps in all three shades – cold violet, purple and deep purple – unused of the famous ONE SHILLING of the 1851–57 issue (the plate proof in black on white card was also shown), and from the same Perkins, Bacon issue, three of each of the desirable unused yellow-green and the dark green SIX PENCE. But the real gems of the evening were the two bisects (where a stamp is cut in half, usually diagonally, when half of its value is required and no issued stamp is available). That night, the members marvelled at a cover with sevenpence halfpenny's worth of stamps of the 1851–57 issue, the half-ounce postal rate to the West Indies. The charge was made up of the 'Crown and Mayflower of Nova Scotia' stamps, a SIX PENCE dark-green, and a pair of red-brown ONE PENNY, the left hand one bisected diagonally. This is the only known example, and it was displayed from the Collection that night in 1912 – yet Edward Bacon, Tilleard's successor, published his account of acquiring it for the Collection in September 1923:

an interesting envelope bearing a bisected One Penny stamp of 1853, which I have not previously seen recorded. The envelope was sent from Annapolis,

Nova Scotia, to St John, Antigua, and was franked with a specimen of Nova Scotia Six Pence dark green, one of the One Penny value and the upper half of a One Penny stamp cut diagonally from the left top to the right lower corner, thus making up the postal rate of 7½d.

The dated postmarks are, on the front: 'Annapolis, N.S. Ja 26, 1860'; and the back: 'N. Ja. 27, 1860, N.S.' in a transverse oval; 'St. Georges, Bermuda, Fe. 15, 1860'; 'Antigua, Mr. 5, 60'; and another postmark which is indecipherable.[15]

According to the minutes, Bacon was not present at the meeting in 1912 and, clearly, this is the same cover that he said he bought for the Collection in 1923. The most likely explanation is that the cover was 'borrowed' for the evening, and whoever owned it then, sold it later to the King. Perhaps he took eleven years to pay? Like much in philately, the true answer will probably never be known.

There was no doubt, however, about the other equally exciting bisect that made up the 1s. 10½d postal rate using a purple ONE SHILLING, a SIX PENCE deep green, and pair of pale blue THREE PENCE, the left hand stamp bisected diagonally, on piece. These stamps would most likely have been used on a parcel, Nova Scotia being one of the earliest Colonies to offer parcel posts, or a heavy letter to England sent via New York. Nova Scotia adopted dollars and cents at the same time as New Brunswick, and on that night in May 1912 the King displayed the complete issue of the new stamps.

Nova Scotia: 1851–57 ONE SHILLING purple, SIX PENCE deep green, and THREE PENCE pale blue, pair (left hand bisected diagonally) on piece. The combination of stamps, 1s. 10½d was for an internal parcel or a heavy letter to England via New York.

As much as members of the Royal Philatelic Society, London, enjoyed the displays that came from the Collection, so the King and Tilleard found it equally useful to sound them out on new purchases. Consequently, when they bought a new collection, the choice items were often displayed shortly after at the Society. At the 1913 opening meeting, George V sent a display from his recent acquisition: the Thomas Hall Collection of Fiji, which had been added to by Charles Phillips while he was compiling his handbook on the island's stamps. The collection 'which is probably the best collection of issues of this colony in existence'[16] was presented in two large volumes 'and is practically complete, nearly everything being represented, both in unused and used condition'. The members pored over the *Fiji Times* Express stamps, including the reconstructed sheet on *quadrillé* paper with only one stamp missing, and another on laid *bâttonné* paper complete, some of which could well have come from the King's wedding present (see pages 42–47).

Before 1870, settlers in Fiji were ill served by the postal service run by the British Consul. All letters to the island went to him and remained there until collected by the recipient or went 'yellow with age or were devoured by rats',[17] there being no system in place or, indeed, staff to distribute them. Enter G. L. Griffiths, the proprietor of The *Fiji Times*, the local newspaper based in Levuka, on the island of Ovalau. No doubt as a means to improve distribution of his newspaper, he came up with the idea of an internal post to deliver mail throughout the islands. On 24 September 1870, he and his partner, a Mr Hobson placed a notice in their paper announcing the *Fiji Times* EXPRESS and to say that from 1 November they would establish 'a complete postal system throughout the "Fiji Group" combined with an insular parcel delivery. No pains will be spared to render the undertaking a benefit and a convenience to every resident in the islands'.[18] The proprietors built depots and promised 'as far as possible to conduct the mode of delivery and transmission of letters on a plan similar to that adopted by Government Post Offices'; letters could even be registered. A scale of charges was published in the next edition, followed by the announcement that they intended to issue stamps to prepay carriage.

The stamps, 1 PENNY, 3 PENCE, 6 PENCE and 1 SHILLING, were printed on their own presses. There were twenty-four stamps (four rows of six) on each

Fiji: 1870 *Fiji Times* Express stamp, a remarkable reconstruction of a sheet with 1 PENNY, 3 PENCE, 6 PENCE, and 1 SHILLING.

sheet, each bearing all four denominations set out with 6 PENCE at the top, then 1 SHILLING; 1 PENNY came on the third row, with 3 PENCE at the bottom. The first printing of about five hundred sheets on *quadrillé* paper, pale rose, could not have been simpler. The words FIJI, TIMES, EXPRESS and value were printed around the outside with the number denoting the value in the middle, with printed lines bordering the stamp. There was an attempt at printed rouletting, but this did not really work, so the sheets were generally divided by scissors. The second printing, of around 3,500 sheets, used the same format, but was on laid *bâttonné* paper and the last three 3 PENCE stamps were changed to 9 PENCE for the revised postal rate. The cancellation was all done by hand with a cross, occasionally a double cross like today's hash sign.

Apparently the system worked well, and there was general consternation when a government Postmaster General was appointed the next year and postal rates rose by threepence a letter to pay his salary.

It was not long before collectors heard of the locally printed issue and wrote to Griffiths for copies of his stamps. Too late: all had been issued. So as not to disappoint (or to miss out on lucrative sales) he printed some *imitation* stamps, as distinct from reprints, this time with five rows of eight in each denomination on pale pink paper, some even pin-perforated. They were so popular that more were printed – five rows of six stamps printed on deep rose paper, followed by a third printing. As the Royal Philatelic Society, London saw that night, the Collection holds not only the issued *Fiji Times* Express stamps, but a good number of the imitation stamps as well. Interestingly, also in the Collection are 'Proof impressions on yellow wove paper (used pair)' and a '(vertical strip severed and rejoined) 6d over 1s, over 1d over 3d',[19] said to be unique, which came from the Ferrari Collection. The impression on the yellow paper is now thought to have been 'made by Griffiths to oblige a friend who collected stamps'[20] rather than a genuine proof copy.

At the end of the evening, the vote of thanks to the King was seconded by T. W. Hall, who moved that the Society's 'respectful congratulations be offered to His Majesty on being the possessor of the most complete and perfect collection of Fiji stamps known to the Society',[21] the very collection founded by Hall himself.

But the Hall-Phillips Collection of Fiji was not the only one that George V was interested in at that time. In January 1913, the Earl of Crawford died and the King lost a great friend and mentor. Before his death, Crawford had already begun to dispose of parts of his great collection through the dealer W. H. Peckitt. It would appear that the King was given the chance to cherry-pick the part of the collection where Crawford was particularly strong, St Helena and South Australia, for in a letter to Tilleard of 1 March 1912 he wrote:

> I have carefully considered all you tell me in your letter received this morning and I find it difficult to make up my mind. If it was not troubling you too much, I hope that you will come and see me Sunday evening next at 5.30 and you might bring with you the collection of South Australia and St Helena and any others I have not seen. After I have seen them and talked the matter over with you I will be able to come to a decision easier.[22]

The King was undecided until he had compared what was on offer with his own collection. Evidently what he saw appealed to him, as it is known that he purchased a collection of St Helena shortly after, and probably bought a few of the South Australia as well. Typical are the essays, the blocks and the surcharges, including the 1864–80 'thick bar ONE SHILLING vertical strip, the fifth row double, the bottom row unsurcharged (on six pence yellow-green)'[23] of which only one other example is known.

When these important new purchases, Fiji, St Helena, and South Australia (a disparate grouping with the time of their purchase the only link) had 'shaken down', a selection of each was shown at the Royal Philatelic Society, London, at their first meeting in 1913. The King might have shown some particularly choice items that he had bought from the Crawford Collection, like a small group of St Vincent stamps, characteristically 'superb, the condition being brilliant'. And brilliant the items still are, with the wonderful 1881 strip of three surcharged 4d on ONE SHILLING vermilion, and the pair of the ONE SHILLING lilac-rose of 1873 all unused.

But however much scholarship and money are lavished on a collection, mistakes are made. For George V, his was a collection of the Bahamas bought some time in 1913 from an unknown source. In it, there were a few examples of *passant pour neuf* – passed for new – where a stamp is purportedly unused. A prime example in the Collection is 'the first stamp of the Bahamas, the penny imperforate in the warm rose [reddish-lake] shade on thick paper',[24] where the manuscript or cancellation mark has undoubtedly been cleaned off. Other suspect unused stamps, inevitably sprinkled lightly throughout the Collection, have in fact been attached to letters, gone through the post but missed cancellation and the stamp steamed off the envelope to pass as unused. But the King was loath to pass on anything of whatever quality, particularly the *passant pour neuf*, and they would remain in his collection

These fine purchases from the Crawford Collection
are typical being characteristically 'superb,
the condition ... brilliant'.

St Vincent: 1872–75
ONE SHILLING
lilac-rose, pair.

St Helena: 1864–80
ONE SHILLING yellow-green,
a block of 20 (2 × 10) surcharge
omitted from bottom row.

St Vincent: 1881
4d on ONE SHILLING
bright vermilion.

until a prime example was found to replace them. Then the two stamps would be invariably mounted side by side for comparison. In the days before scientific aids to detect cleaning, the collector – even the royal collector – was prey to such practices.

The world over, George V was known as an ardent philatelist. As King he received dozens of unsolicited gifts, including many of stamps which he made a point of not accepting unless he knew the donor or the gift was an official one. However, if the gift was something that he particularly wanted, he would make an exception. For example, he had few qualms about accepting two blocks of four stamps each of the blue ONE PENNY and the violet SIX PENCE 'stamps issued by the St Lucia Steam Conveyance Company about the year 1869'[25] (actually 1873). The gift came from a Mr H. de Vaux of St Lucia through the Colonial Office. Mr E. B. Boyd replied that although His Majesty did not normally accept gifts, in this case he would make an exception. If the donor was slightly known to the King, accepting a choice gift was made all the easier. A St Vincent collector, C. M. Wells, wrote to Frank Mitchell, Assistant Private Secretary to the King: 'If I remember rightly, His Majesty has not in his St Vincent book a copy of the [1881] ½d surcharged in red on 6d green bar missing used. There cannot be more than 2 or 3 in existence & luckily I possess one: it may perhaps be unique'.[26] The stamp was accepted, and is in the Collection, along with a block of twelve of the ½d on SIX PENCE bright green, one with the fraction bar omitted.

If friends or acquaintances offered something the King wanted, they were usually given a 'swap' – an item of equal value. When the King bought entire collections, he found in them many duplicates of stamps he already had and this was an admirable way of realising their value without having to dispose of them through a dealer or at auction. If the gift was official, of course, 'swaps' were not appropriate.

On the morning of 29 May 1912, Tilleard received a letter from Sir Frederick Ponsonby, George V's Assistant Private Secretary, to say that he had received some blocks of Canadian stamps from Donald A. King, who hoped that they might be 'of interest, and lacking in the [King's] collection'.[27] They contained blocks of an 'error or rarity of the current [1911–22] 2@ [cents] with hair lines across face of stamp – this occurs on plate 4 only … a very

St Vincent: 1881 ½ d on SIX PENCE bright green, block of 12 from bottom of sheet, one error fraction bar omitted.

decided rarity of colour in the same value, on plate 6 only'.[28] The rose-red TWO CENTS were highly desirable indeed, and Tilleard was delighted to inform Ponsonby that they 'may certainly be accepted' and that Mr King was 'a well known Canadian Philatelist and holding an official position in the Canadian Post Office. Anything offered by him is more or less of an official nature'.[29] Ponsonby wrote to King accepting the stamps on behalf of George V, and Tilleard absorbed them into the Collection. After that, Ponsonby, arranged for Tilleard to deal with all stamps offered for sale and to advise on what gifts could or could not be accepted.

But Tilleard was not to enjoy his position of increased 'responsibility' for long, for on 22 September 1913, at the age of sixty-three, he died after a short illness caused through 'strain and overwork'.[30] George V had given him the title of 'Philatelist to the King' on 15 August 1910 and a salary of £150 a year backdated to 7 May, the day after his accession.

There is no doubt that John Tilleard MVO was exactly the right man to advise the King throughout the twenty years he spent at his side. He had superior, although not expert, knowledge. His advice, and not just in the purchase of stamps, was invaluable, and the King was always first to acknowledge it. Above all, he had the contacts to buy really first rate stamps. Where he fell down, however, was in mounting the collection. With his solicitor's practice, he did not have enough time to devote to it. The King mourned his death, and he sent one of his gentleman ushers to represent him at the private funeral at Golders Green, North London. When he died in 1913, the President of the Royal Philatelic Society, London – the pre-fix Royal being added in 1906, largely through Tilleard's energies and legal advice – received a letter written on behalf of the King: 'His Majesty mourns his death not only as one of our leading philatelists, but as a personal friend for whose advice on the question of stamps His Majesty always entertained the highest respect.'[31]

With the death of John Tilleard, the King's Collection entered another new era.

CHAPTER SIX

⚜ ⚜ ⚜

A career in the Royal Navy on its own might not have been the best grounding for kingship, but it makes for an ordered, methodical, disciplined mind, a useful trait in a serious philatelist, to whom a problem is a challenge to be taken to its logical conclusion. The navy had also given George V a liking for routine and punctuality – like his father, he kept the clocks at Sandringham half an hour fast. On three afternoons a week, when he was in London, the King would rise from his lunch, which had begun at precisely one-thirty, and make his way down from his private apartments in Buckingham Palace to the Stamp Room. He could either take the rickety lift to the ground floor or use the stairs. Either way it was a short step along the passage towards the Marble Hall, past the billiard room and left into the Stamp Room. He walked in as the clock on the marble chimneypiece chimed half past two.

The room that George V had chosen as his Stamp Room was bright and airy, the light flooding in through the full-length sash window from the large inner quadrangle. An oak bookcase, the shelves specially adapted to take the bound volumes, dominated one side of the room, and a square table stood in the centre. Apart from a few portraits on the walls, the room was spartan – exactly the environment that suited George V.

The new curator of the King's Philatelic Collection, Edward Bacon, would stand as the King entered the room. They would exchange greetings, the King looking directly at Bacon, speaking clearly, for Bacon was fast losing his hearing. The King knew how to cope with such an affliction, for as long as he could remember his mother, Queen Alexandra, had been profoundly deaf. Once the door had closed, the King and Bacon were in a world of their own. By that time, the Collection had become 'a ritual, compulsive in nature and addictive in quality'[1], and satisfied the King's need for order in a changing world. The footmen, who normally attended the King outside the door, were invariably dismissed, and only twice in twenty-two years were they recalled. When he was within the sanctuary of the Stamp Room, no one was allowed to disturb him except of course in a dire emergency, and since his only companion was Edward Bacon, 'it represented a comforting return to the peaceful, quiet period of his life when little or nothing was expected of him'.[2]

George V's ability to retreat to this all-absorbing world of stamps was, 'as he used to declare', that which 'saved his life in the War [the First World War]; for during such intervals as he could spare from his constant and anxious duties he would obtain complete relaxation poring over some rare issue with a magnifying glass'.[3] The said magnifying glass is in fact a 'gallery' glass, really for looking at pictures, and it is still kept in the Stamp Room. It is used on rare occasions by the Queen to inspect her stamps. The lens is large, a little over four inches across, and banded in silver; the handle is covered in shagreen, ribbed with thin strips of ivory.

Gallery glass used by George V. The large magnifying glass
is banded in silver with a shagreen and ivory handle.

Opposite: Sir Edward Denny Bacon, KCVO, Curator of the King's Collection and friend for over 25 years.
[Photo: RPSL]

By the summer of 1913, it had become obvious to George V that Tilleard would not resume his duties as Philatelist to the King after his convalescence and he realised how important it was to look for a replacement immediately. One candidate stood out far and above all others. His credentials could not have been bettered, and as an expert he had few equals. Furthermore, he was available. His name was Edward Denny Bacon.

The son of a City malt factor, whose firm he later joined, Bacon had begun collecting by 1880 at the age of twenty, the year he joined the Philatelic Society, London. In his lifetime, he held every office in the Society, 'from honorary assistant secretary, through librarian and treasurer to the Presidency'.[4] But when the family firm was wound up in 1895, Bacon retired, aged thirty-five, and devoted the rest of his life to philately. He had formed two important collections of his own, one of Japan, which became part of the Ferrari Collection, and another of postal stationery which was incorporated into the Tapling Collection. Three smaller collections followed, Nyasaland, Antioquia and the Pacific Steam Navigation Stamps (see page 47), but what truly distinguished him as a philatelist was his contribution to the important collections of others. He began by assisting his friend Thomas Tapling, 'founder of the great general collection bequeathed to the British Museum which at the time was regarded as the second collection of the world'.[5] When Tapling died in 1891, Bacon mounted, arranged and wrote up the collection for display in the British Museum. As Duke of York, George V had seen it before the exhibition opened, as his characteristically succinct diary entry reveals: 'At 12.0 went with Tilleard to the British Museum to see Mr Tapling's collection of stamps,'[6] with no further comment.

From there, Bacon moved on to Henry J. Duveen, whom he not only advised on the purchase of the major part of his collection, but also mounted and wrote it up. The motto of the collection, 'the best and nothing but the best', well suited Bacon's exacting standards. The Earl of Crawford also called on his expertise, partially in buying for his collection but, more importantly, for work on the Crawford Philatelic Library, now in the British Library. By 1912 'philatelic literature ... claims the lion's share of Mr Bacon's time and attention. For years he has been associated with the great library formed by Lord Crawford, and last year [1911] we were given monumental evidence of his labours in the shape of the *Catalogue of the Philatelic Library of the Earl of Crawford, K.T.*, – a work which richly deserves the large gold medal conferred upon it at the Vienna Exhibition last autumn, to say nothing of the plaudits of the whole philatelic world'.[7] With the completion of that great work, Bacon was without a major project – until he received a letter from Sir Frederick Ponsonby, Assistant Private Secretary to the King.

It was delivered to The Gables, Croham Park Avenue, Edward Bacon's home in South Croydon. Ponsonby wrote on 29 September 1913: 'I am writing privately to you to ascertain whether you would be willing to undertake the supervision of His Majesty's Collection of stamps ... The King knows the great reputation you enjoy as a Philatelist & feels that no one would be better fitted than you to do this.'[8] Bacon could not have been surprised by the content of the letter merely its timing, for Tilleard had just died. He replied on 2 October, a respectable two weeks later. 'I shall feel greatly honoured & proud,' he wrote 'to undertake the supervision of the King's collection of stamps, if His Majesty is pleased to offer me the post'.[9] He had intended going to the New York International Philatelic Exhibition as one of the jurors, but cancelled his trip. On 11 October 1913, Bacon had an audience with the King and was formally appointed Curator of HM the King's Philatelic Collection the next day. Captain L. B. Wildman, the Reverend Earée, Mr H. E. Haworth and Mr J. R. Taylor, all of whom had sent unsolicited applications for the post, were informed that it was no longer vacant.

The change of title from 'Philatelist to the King' to 'Curator of the King's Philatelic Collection' was the least of the changes that took place with Bacon's arrival. For a start, he told the King that he would prefer to work at Buckingham Palace, rather than the haphazard arrangement the King had had with Tilleard, who worked on the Collection at his home and kept various stamps in the safe at his office. The new arrangement suited the King well. Just ten days after accepting the post, Bacon was in harness, and remained in royal service for twenty-five years. He received a small salary of £150, which rose to £250 during the war years and remained at that level for the rest of his life. He began by informing Lord Stamfordham, Private Secretary to the King, that he was going 'to do the mounting and arranging of the collection at Buckingham Palace and His Majesty has given me a room next to the Billiard Room, where I shall be two days & sometimes three days a week'.[10] For virtually the rest of his life, he took the same train from Croydon to Victoria station (his expenses, such as his train fare from Croydon, came out of the stamp fund), arriving at the Stamp Room at exactly the same time. Such an invariable routine found favour with the King.

Bacon was renowned for his 'quite extraordinary accuracy'.[11] He relished the challenge of reorganising the Collection, as did George V the idea of seeing his ambition fulfilled to have 'the best collection'. First Bacon had to tie up a few loose ends Tilleard had left. A Mrs Kamilla Winter of Vienna, for example, had sent the King 'a stamp of Great Britain, issued from 1855/57, 4 pence, unused, rose colour on bluish paper'.[12] It was a desirable item from the first De La Rue surface printing, but Tilleard had mislaid it. Mrs Winter did not want to sell, but to exchange it for something of the same value, around 400 marks, included in her 'manco liste'. The stamp was never found, although there are several examples in the Collection, but after much correspondence, she was eventually sent nine stamps from her extensive list. Various other items were also discovered to be missing, like some Queensland proofs that were eventually found – at the King's suggestion – in Tilleard's pocketbook.

The first entry that Bacon made as curator in his account book detailed a payment made to Stanley Gibbons, Strand, London, for basic stock philatelic items '500 leaves for albums, hinges, tweezers, benzene, peroxide of hydrogen'.[13] From there on, every single penny he spent on behalf of the King's Collection he accounted for, and balanced the book every quarter. He was scrupulously honest when dealing with the King's affairs. When he sold the King his collection of 'the cheque stamps of the March 1893 issue of Nyasaland, which in those days was known as British Central Africa. He must have told the King he proposed to sell him the stamps at cost because the account book shows that he drew a cheque on the stamp account in his own favour for £283 4s 11d'. Sir John Wilson, author of *The Royal Philatelic Collection*, goes on to add that 'it is unlikely that any other collector would have done this'.[14]

Bacon was certainly a 'new broom'. He asked Lord Stamfordham to write to 'the controller of Stamps at Somerset House & the Crown Agents for the Colonies to forward all stamps to me addressed to the Palace. May

I ask you to be so good as to direct the India Office to follow the same arrangements'.[15] Three days later he went to Somerset House to see the Mint authorities 'from whom he will obtain all the proof impressions they have of the various dies, etc., used in the production of the postage stamps with His Majesty's portrait'.[16]

It is strange that such visits by Bacon should have been necessary. Perhaps the system set up by Edward VII for his son to receive the proofs, essays and corner blocks of four had broken down. Bacon was also in touch with Bertram Mackennal who 'promised to try & obtain from the engravers some further sketches & proofs of the stamps [the Profile Head issue] which he hopes to forward to His Majesty before long';[17] in the past it would automatically have been sent to the King.

With his new leaves and hinges, Bacon set about rearranging the Collection from scratch, mounting everything and writing it up. It was an enormous task, as at that time there was certainly no uniformity to the Collection: it was made up of different-sized albums that had been added to, alongside albums from as far back as the days of HMS *Bacchante*. Through Ponsonby, he asked permission from the King to make a start on the Straits Settlements, Natal, and St Helena, followed by the West Indian colonies. 'I have picked out the two first,' he wrote, 'as the stamps of these countries are in a terrible muddle at present.'[18] If Bacon had a fault, it was in his method of mounting. Throughout his life he used the large sized stamp hinge and when he placed a stamp on a page, it was to stay there for ever. Having moistened the hinge thoroughly, he 'pressed it home with such finality'[19] that it became virtually impossible to remove. But the real flaw in Bacon's mounting methods was that he never removed old hinges from the back of a stamp before applying his new large one. A pair or block of four were given two hinges. Although Bacon believed that this did the stamp no harm, the pressure of the album could cause a ridge to form round the over-proud pile of hinges. This was worse on the delicate, surface printed stamps that De La Rue prepared for the British and Colonial issues than on the engraved stamps on the thicker good quality paper. In mounting some of the rarities in the Royal Philatelic Collection that he had mounted first in the Duveen Collection, there were often two Bacon hinges as well as any others he had failed to remove. Such a basic error of judgement in one so punctilious is hard to reconcile. George V did not have time to mount his collection himself and left it all to Bacon – had he done some of it he might have been more censorious of his Curator's methods.

Writing up, however, was Bacon's forte. From years of experience, he had developed a precise, neat hand, quite different from the King's, which was rounded and had developed little from the schoolroom. Although Bacon's writing has the appearance of script, each letter is in fact printed separately, often with the whole sentence underlined. There is exactly the right amount of information on each page – the printer, the paper and watermark, the number of the plate and the state of the plate (before or after hardening, retouched) and, of course, the stamps themselves. It was Bacon, who had worked with Crawford, who set out each page with such precision and thought (in the French method of collecting) with the development of a stamp from the original artwork right through to the first printing with essays and colour trials, proofs and examples of the stamp itself. A month after he had taken office, Major Wigram wrote to him: 'The King... desires me to tell you how pleased he is at the progress you have made with his Stamp Collection.'[20]

In the past, Bacon had advised three very rich men. Tapling was a carpet manufacturer with virtually limitless resources to spend on his collection. Crawford's wealth came from coalmines, and Duveen was the foremost art dealer in Britain. With the King, Bacon, always cautious, wanted to know exactly where he stood with regard to buying material. He wrote to Wigram: 'Will you please let me know what His Majesty's wishes are as to my purchasing stamps. The course I propose if I may make the suggestion is that when I start to arrange a country, I shall get from the three principal London dealers selections, or what they term "stock books", of the country. Then after comparing the prices select the cheapest of any varieties that are wanting.'[21] He needed this confirmation as he had heard through the 'philatelic grapevine' that the stamp merchants Edwin Healey and Co. had purchased all but the United States and Great Britain of the Crawford Collection for a Mr R. B. Sparrow of Talybont-on-Usk, for what was believed to be £20,000, then the highest price ever paid for a collection. At this time Bacon's contact with the King was through his private secretaries, so it was Wigram who passed on Bacon's high hopes that Sparrow was an amateur and that it would be broken up.

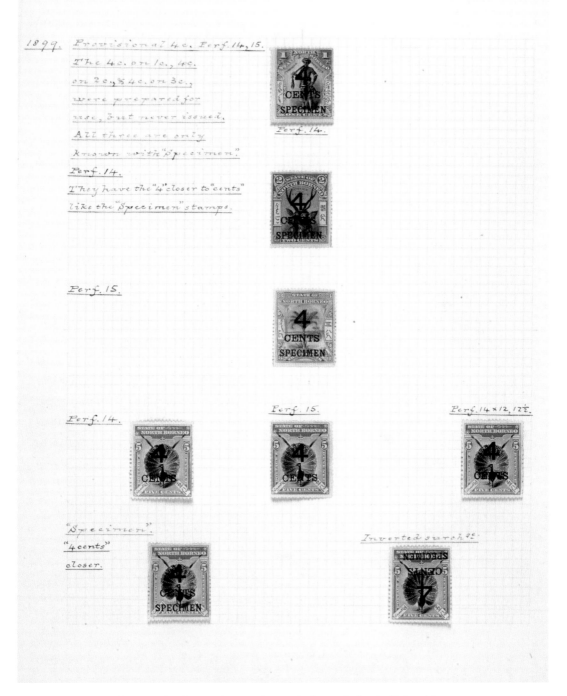

1899. Provisional 4c. Perf. 14, 15.
The 4c. on 1c., 4c.
on 2c., & 4c. on 3c.,
were prepared for
use, but never issued.
All three are only
known with "Specimen".
Perf. 14.
They have the "4" closer to "cents"
like the "Specimen" stamps.

Perf. 15.

Perf. 14.   Perf. 15.   Perf. 14 × 12, 12½.

"Specimen".   Inverted surch.
"4 cents"
closer.

A fine example of a typical page written up in the precise hand of Edward Bacon.

Bacon's 'high hopes' were realised. 'I have heard from Mr Sparrow ... [who] ... has bought the collection to break up and sell in detail. He has promised to let me have the first look through it for His Majesty and he wants me to go to Talybont-on-Usk where he lives as soon as he has the collection priced up which will be about the end of this week. I have written to say that I will go to see him.'[22] Bacon was too old and experienced a hand to succumb to arbitrary pricing, 'If the prices are too high I do not propose to buy anything', and he again asked Wigram for clarification of the King's wishes: 'I shall be glad to know what His Majesty's wishes are regarding my purchasing from the collection and to what extent he would like me to go if the prices are suitable.'[23] Within three months Bacon was making his mark, but he was not given *carte blanche* to purchase. Through Wigram the King urged caution: 'His Majesty is gratified to think that you have obtained the first refusal of any stamp. The King thinks that it would be best if you inspected the collection making a note of any stamps with their prices that you think His Majesty might purchase, and submitting your suggestions to him. Perhaps it might be possible for the King to see the stamps which you would propose for him to purchase.'[24]

Having spent so much time with Lord Crawford's collection, Bacon knew that his visit to South Wales would be fruitful. The Earl had been interested in the Great Britain telegraphs stamps, and his collection was particularly strong in this area, although at that time it was less well represented in the Royal Philatelic Collection, even though the stamps had long held a

Great Britain:
Government Telegraphs
1876 THREE PENCE carmine.

Great Britain: Government Telegraphs
1877 FIVE POUNDS orange.

fascination for the King. Telegraphs stamps were either adhesives or imprinted stamps designed to prepay 'telegraphic communications and usually attached to, or forming part of, the message form'.[25] Both Government telegraphs or private companies issued their own stamps. There were military telegraphs too, either as Government Telegraphs stamps overprinted 'Army Telegraphs' or produced in their own right.

With the purchase of the Crawford collection of telegraphs and assiduous purchases on his own account, the King's collection of telegraphs 'has no equal'. It is a difficult area to collect, as either the stamp is readily available (but never dismissed on that account) or it is virtually 'unprocurable'. With the government telegraphs there are fewer rarities, but those in the Collection – such as the 1876 THREE PENCE carmine, (Plate 4), the 1881 THREE SHILLINGS slate blue and FIVE SHILLINGS rose and the 1877 FIVE POUNDS orange – are either unique, or are one of no more than a very few other known examples.

With so many private telegraph companies each with their own issue, there are many rarities among these stamps and the Collection holds examples of those issued by the evocatively named Bonelli's Electric Telegraph Company, or the British and Irish Magnetic Telegraph Company. Then there are the issues of the Electric Telegraph Company, whose 'franked message paper coloured wove paper Wmk [watermarked with the] name of company, embossed design 1s blue on pink'[26] of 1851 is the earliest example. There are errors too, like their director's message on blue paper, 'lettered for LORD ALERED PAGET in error for Alfred'.[27]

Great Britain: Government Telegraphs 1881 FIVE SHILLINGS rose.

Great Britain: The Electric Telegraph Company 1861 FIVE SHILLINGS purple unused.

Great Britain: The Electric Telegraph Company 1864, 'Director's Message' error ALERED for ALFRED.

In a matter of only a few weeks, Bacon had proved himself indispensable. He had asked Bertram Mackennal for the 'return' of the two fine drawings for the 'seahorse' issue, and was able to report to Wigram that he now had 'the original sketches for the stamps he promised to try & obtain from the engraver. These sketches form some of the most valuable and interesting links in the production of the stamps that it is possible to have and they will be a great ornament to His Majesty's collection'.[28] He did not stop there. He called on a Mr Edward Rigg, the Superintendent of the Operative Department in the Royal Mint who

> has superintended the manufacture of the plates for the stamp [1911 PENNY and HALF PENNY]. I obtained some useful information from him and a number of highly important specimens. Mr Rigg has several small drawers full of essays and proofs connected with the stamps and is most anxious to let His Majesty have everything he wishes. I made out a list of specimens from the reference collection Mr Rigg has and he has promised to see if duplicates of these can be found. I have arranged to see him again on 20th inst and to then go through some of the drawers I had not time to see yesterday.[29]

Not everything went to plan. On looking at the Crawford collection of telegraphs he had purchased for the King, Bacon noticed that a 'message form used by the Electric Telegraph Company, inscribed "Free Message Paper. Price two shillings and sixpence"'[30] was not amongst it. Accordingly, it was arranged for Major Wigram to approach C. E. Hobhouse, the Postmaster General, for a copy of the form. Wigram wrote to Hobhouse that 'His Majesty has heard from a friend that there existed in the Record Room at the General Post Office, a volume or portfolio of odd papers among which there was a message form printed on blue paper and bears the control number 2824 in black' which the King wanted 'to add to his interesting collection of message forms issued by Telegraph Companies'.[31] Hobhouse's reply was disappointing. Although he naturally wanted to comply with His Majesty's wishes, he did 'not think it would be possible for the Post Office to spoil its collection'. He went on to say that even if they had a duplicate, they still could not let him have it as the records 'belong to the Master of the Rolls, as Keeper of the Records'.[32]

More successful was an approach concerning the collections of Universal Postal Union (UPU) specimens held by two or three Colonies – certainly St Vincent and Grenada – which had been sent to London. The idea was that every member of the UPU received five (later three) specimens of every stamp issued by all the other UPU members so that post offices could identify fraudulent stamps on incoming mail from abroad. For some unexplained reason, these Colonies forwarded their UPU collections to the General Post Office, London who anyway held their own specimens from the UPU head-quarters in Berne. For some time it had been arranged that the King would receive one copy of every stamp received from the UPU at the General Post Office, and that arrangement was reconfirmed in 1914. However, it would appear that the arrangement did not include the earlier specimens, particu-larly those from the Victorian era. Thus it was just possible that the stamps that had been returned from some of the Colonies could well be highly desirable. And so it proved. In reply to the question as to the nature of the stamps, Sir Alexander King, Secretary to the Post Office, wrote to Ponsonby: '... we know that we shall not find any complete sheets.... There may be strips of five or three specimens.... When the collections have been exam-ined, we will gladly allow any one you may send to inspect the specimens; and we will place at his disposal for the King's collection any of them which may not be represented in that collection'.[33] Bacon made at least three visits, the last in early July, and selected 'some hundreds of specimens'.

While all this was going on, it appears that Bacon asked Ponsonby to write to Sir Alexander King on another matter – postal stationery:

The King desires me to tell you that he is now including in his collection speci-mens of the stamps embossed on envelopes and telegraph forms, and of those printed on wrappers and postcards. His Majesty will be glad, therefore, if you will give instructions to have sent to Mr E.D. Bacon a specimen of each die in the colour of the issue, at the time it is approved and registered. The King would also like to have specimens of all the present and past dies with his head and also of those with the head of King Edward that can be furnished....[34]

Sir Alexander was very cooperative, and the Collection is consequently well represented in this area.

Another rich source to enter the Royal Philatelic Collection in May 1914 was the Agar collection of Great Britain. Once more there is no record as to what it contained.

Even after four years as King, George V was loath to make his first state visit to France, a republic, when there were monarchies that should have taken precedence. But he and Queen Mary went to Paris in April 1914. The visit was a great success and did much to foster Anglo-French amity with the First World War looming not far distant. The French took the King and Queen to their hearts, overcoming their republican sentiments to shout '*Vive la reine.*' Even on such a visit, the King was never far from the philatelic world, as described in a contemporary account of an eye witness.

> I was indebted to M. Th. Lemaire for a kind invitation to see the Royal and Presidential procession from one of the windows of M. Lemaire's spacious premises in the Avenue de l'Opera. On nearing my destination I perceived a large crowd in front of the premises, and was speedily made aware that it was the sumptuous decorations of the façade of M. Lemaire's premises which was inciting so much astonishment and curiosity. These decorations consisted of six immense panels, each representing one of the stamps issued during King George's reign: viz. the 25 rupees of India with a portrait of the Emperor of India; 5s Rhodesia with double effigies of King George and his gracious Queen Mary; the 1d of Great Britain; the 2 cents of Canada, the 4s of Nyasaland and the 2½ d of the Union of South Africa. The panels were surrounded by garlands of foliage, multicoloured electric lamps, with inscriptions of welcome and numerous English and French flags.'[35]

Naturally the *roi-philateliste* was delighted. As his carriage, led by the Garde Republicaine and surrounded by a squadron of cuirassiers, passed the house, the King leant forward and gave three waves in recognition of the honour at the sight of 'these immense stamps which could not fail to evoke in the Royal mind a souvenir of his well-loved Collection'. It was indeed a colourful display, with the orange and blue Indian TWENTY FIVE RUPEES, the scarlet and yellow-green of the Rhodesia FIVE SHILLINGS, and the bright scarlet of the Great Britain ONE PENNY. The other three were just as colourful, with the deep rose-red of the TWO CENTS Canada, the carmine and black of the Nyasaland FOUR SHILLINGS and the bright blue of the 2½ᵈ Union of South Africa. All of these, of course, are represented in the Collection, often as single examples, sometimes in blocks of four.

Throughout his life, George V was somewhat of an enigma. To his mother, he was her 'Darling Georgie' until the day she died; yet his own children were terrified of him. His Private Secretaries served him loyally, yet his temper and rages were legendary. He appeared divorced from the world outside, yet his acts of kindness and thoughtfulness to others were legion. But to the philatelic world, a place where he felt completely at home and comfortable, he was invariably charming and generous, both of himself and his collection. As with his other great passion, shooting, at which he was acknowledged as exceptional, the King took on a different persona. A stickler for rank and etiquette at Court, on the shooting field and in the stamp room he was classless: skill and knowledge were all that counted. He admired one of his tenant farmers at Sandringham who was a better partridge-shot than himself, just as he bowed to philatelists like Bacon and M. P. Castle for their superior knowledge. Fellow members of the Royal Philatelic Society, London were always welcome to inspect the Collection, and he himself often showed self-invited guests what they had come to see.

In anything to do with stamps, George V was invariably polite. In the early days, he received a letter from a boy in France who sent him some stamps, and wanted 'some British ones in exchange'. He asked Tilleard to 'kindly return them and thank him for sending them,[36] but to decline the offer. He corresponded at length with American collectors like C. L. Pack (from whom he had bought the New Brunswick Collection) on their mutual interest in Victoria (Australia), and Arthur Hind, often loaning him stamps for comparison. He was easily moved by the plight of fellow collectors. A Mrs Sawyer wrote telling of the 'sad plight of a sailor [Daniel M. Chandler] who had fallen down a gangway and was seriously injured'[37] and asked if the King would give him some stamps. At the King's direction, Wigram sent him a selection, and received a touching reply from Chandler. Six months later Mrs Sawyer wrote to say 'that the lad had died but that the stamps His Majesty sent brightened his last days'.[38] The King would have been greatly moved by such an expression of loyalty. He also encouraged the young, as when, according to a diary entry, he 'Showed Gerald Crutchley Lady Katty's grandson some of my stamps, he is a very keen collector.'[39] He also tried to interest his sons in philately – he took his second son, Prince Albert, the future George VI, 'to Caxton Hall to see a Philatelic Exhibition [1908] got up by the Junior Philatelic Society of London'[40] where he showed his collection of Barbados. There are diary entries, too, reporting that he had shown his eldest son Prince Edward (known as David by his family) and his tutor, Hansell, part of the Collection after tea to discuss their mutual interest in stamps.

Sir Frederick Ponsonby told of how a widow had written to the King, as Prince of Wales, asking his opinion of a stamp album left by her husband. The local dealer had offered £50 for it but her doctor had advised her to take advice. The widow had no one to consult, so turned to the Prince, 'of whose collection she had read in the newspapers'.[41] Even a cursory glance showed him that it was a very valuable collection, including a 2½ PENCE Bahamas, which apparently he badly needed. Derek Keppel, his equerry, was told to reply saying that the album should be sent to Puttick and Simpson, the London auctioneers and that the Prince would pay £10 towards advertising the sale. According to Ponsonby, Tilleard was ordered to buy the stamp at 'any price'. The collection made £7,000 and the Bahamas stamp made £1,400. Here the story falls down, as there is no stamp that fits the description at that price in the Collection or indeed, elsewhere. There is an example in the collection of an 1862 SIX PENCE lavender grey, which might have commanded such a price but apocryphal or just slightly inaccurate, such an action was in keeping with the King's sense of fair play.

George V was truly competitive with his stamps. Bacon would warn exhibitors 'of one very human foible; he did not very much like seeing stamps which he did not own himself and which he could not acquire'.[42] Sir John Wilson, a later Keeper, thought that this was due to the King's wish 'that the owners might be saved from embarrassment if he revealed how much he would like to have a particular stamp'. Some claim that he was quite ruthless, and warned of the dangers of 'letting George V near an imperforate sheet of stamps with a pair of scissors'.[43] During the great Coronation Durbar in Delhi of 1911, the King was asked if there was anything he would particularly like as a reminder of his visit. It was a rash offer, as the new King said that he would like to see the archives of the Postal Department. He spent much time there, with a pair of scissors, to the embarrassment and consternation of the postal authorities. Consequently, there are specimens 'in the Royal Collection that are not represented in Delhi'.[44]

Others accuse him of using the same subtle subterfuge as Queen Mary, who spirited away numerous pieces by admiring them to the luckless owners: if that failed, she would offer to buy them – an offer not to be refused. Such behaviour was out of character with the King – but even an obsessed collector, however royal may act out of character.

The tie beween the Royal Philatelic Collection and the Royal Philatelic Society, London had always been strong and was, if anything, strengthened by Bacon's appointment. While he was still finding his way in his post, he wrote to Ponsonby asking for permission to exhibit a selection of errors from the Collection at the early 1914 meeting. He chose the used and unused PENOE error of Mauritius, 'some excessively rare [double strip] St Helena'[45] (see page 130) and a number of other Colonial errors, including 'some fine Sydney Views'.

The 'Sydney Views' of New South Wales had long been a favourite of George V and he added steadily to his collection. He had acquired a few examples at the very beginning – he had, after all, been there on the *Bacchante* in 1881– and several more with his wedding present (see pages 42–47). When he returned to Sydney in HMS *Ophir,* members of the Sydney Philatelic Club donated more, namely the '1d., Plate II., pair and single on blue wove paper; 2d., Plate II., on yellowish wove; 3d., on blue wove paper'.[46] Then there were the twenty-five unused 'Views' that he bought from Stanley Gibbons, formerly in the M. P. Castle Collection. By the end of his life, George V's collection of Sydney Views, Laureates, and Diadems, the early New South Wales issues, was virtually complete, with examples of every issue, all the plates and retouches, along with most of the essays and proofs.

In 1849, Robert Clayton, a local engraver, had been commissioned by the Postmaster General for New South Wales, James Raymond, to design the essays for stamps to replace the then current prepaid letter sheets – embossed with the royal coat of arms on the seal of the Colony, surmounted by GENERAL POST OFFICE, sold at twopence each or 1s. 3d. per dozen. The initial designs, like those of Mauritius, were based on the ONE PENNY and TWO PENCE of Great Britain, but were rejected in favour of something more pertinent to the Colony. Clayton then took as his theme the obverse of the third Great Seal of New South Wales by Thomas Wyon, which in turn was based on the first seal by His Majesty's Engraver, Thomas Major. This showed 'convicts landing at Botany Bay; their fetters taken off and received by Industry sitting on a bale of goods, with her attributes, the distaff, beehive, pick-axe, and spade, pointing to oxen ploughing, the rising habitations, and a church on a hill at a distance, with a fort for their defence'.[47] Wyon had substituted Britannia for Industry and some rather smug settlers for the deportees, and it was this image that was translated to the stamp – the first Colonial issue not to bear the portrait of Queen Victoria.

New South Wales: 1850 TWO PENCE blue, essay. Edward Bacon identified it in the Avery Collection as the companion to the ONE PENNY and THREE PENCE essays of the first Sydney Views design in the Tapling Collection. It passed to the Royal Philatelic Collection from the Hausburg Collection in 1917.

Bacon's article, in the *London Philatelist*, on the subject hinged around the essays of the ONE PENNY and THREE PENCE values of the 'Views of Sydney' attached to an intriguing piece of paper in the Tapling Collection. A manuscript note below the stamps, in the hand of the Colonial Secretary, Sir Edward Deas Thompson, reads: 'The form and colours are approved, but the execution is very far from satisfactory, and must be greatly improved before the contract can be sanctioned.'[48] What was interesting was that the third essay, doubtless the TWO PENCE, had been in the middle but had been removed at some stage, its whereabouts unknown. But that was before Bacon had identified it in the Avery Collection. 'The colour is deep blue,' he wrote, 'and it is printed on thin, white, wove paper. Like the One Penny and Three Pence values, it has the frame printed from an engraved wood-block, and the centre from the same engraved copper plate as was used for the other two values … As regards the central portion of all three essays, it is curious to notice that the engraver committed no less than two errors in inscribing the motto "SIC FORTIS ETRURIA CREVIT" [thus Etruria grew strong] the word FORTIS being misspelt PORTIS while the word ETRURIA is rendered as ETTRURIA.'[49]

It would appear that Sir William Avery had obtained the essay in 1892 when he bought the New South Wales collection of a Mr A. J. Bulloch of Sydney. It had come to Bulloch from a Count Primoli, a kinsman of Napoleon III, who added to his collection of stamps by exploiting his royal connections. In 1909 Avery's collection passed for a staggering £24,500 to W. H. Peckitt, who passed it on to L. L. Hausburg. Bacon had written about it in a 1909 article in the *London Philatelist*, titled 'A Remarkable Find in New South Wales Essays'. This TWO PENCE essay was the gem of the Hausburg Collection of New South Wales proofs that George V subsequently bought in 1917.

Two more collections were put up for sale in the early part of 1914, the Peltzer Collection of British Central Africa and the Pelham Collection. It would appear that the King selected the best from them rather than purchasing them outright, and again there is no way of knowing exactly what he bought. But at that time stamps did not entirely occupy his mind: Europe was in turmoil. The Archduke Franz Ferdinand, heir to the Austrian throne, was assassinated in Sarajevo on 28 June 1914, and all of the major powers were drawn into what became known as the First World War.

CHAPTER SEVEN

❖❖❖

As far as Edward Denny Bacon was concerned, the war 'that would be over by Christmas' made little difference to his daily routine as he continued to travel on the same train from Croydon, three days a week to care for the Royal Philatelic Collection. As the war dragged on, so the King became increasingly reliant for peace of mind on the study of and additions to his Collection. Bacon scoured the dealers' catalogues to fill the 'wants list' drawn up at the beginning of each year, and the Stamp Room account book for 1915 shows mostly unspecified single purchases, with the occasional major one, when the King acquired a collection, or bought parts of others, like the famous Mann Collection.

William Woodham Mann was a noted, very private collector. As he rarely (if ever) exhibited and was not a member of any of the philatelic societies, it is difficult to gauge exactly what the King might have taken from his collection. Mann 'was a collector of the first magnitude'[1] who, like the King, concentrated on British Colonial issues. He was particularly strong in New Zealand and New South Wales, which were sold intact on his death, but the King, on Bacon's advice, filled much of his 'wants list' with stamps of Cape Bechuanaland, St Vincent, Newfoundland, Hong Kong, Trinidad and, surprisingly, Egypt, a new departure for him.

The war brought him no stamp bargains. In 1915, an article appeared in the *London Philatelist*: 'Despite the welter of misery caused by insensate ambitions of Germany, our pursuit still fortunately holds up its head, but with little decrease of vitality.'[2] It was thought that the heavy taxation would curb the 'middle class spending' and thereby affect 'all luxuries', but the stamp market was in fact more buoyant then than it had been in peacetime. Those who made fortunes from and during the war, and rich collectors in North and South America who continued to collect avidly, kept prices high, as did the ever-decreasing supply of better class stamps. The King could not afford to relax his buying programme against such competition and odds. He had to buy when material became available, as with the Luff Collection of Samoan Express Post.

This was a highly specialised, plated collection, not for the amateur. Like the *Fiji Times* EXPRESS stamps (see pages 127–129), they had been principally designed for the distribution of the local newspaper, the *Samoan Times*. In 1876 Mr H. H. Glover, chief artist and manager of the printing firm of S. T. Leigh and Co., Sydney, submitted the designs for the 'Express' issue, so called because the word EXPRESS appears across the centre of the stamp. The design, 'if not very beautiful, is at least quaint, while the colours of the different values [1d. to 5/-] are clear and good'.[3] However, this comparatively dull stamp gave 'the research-seeking collector a chance to use his natural faculties and abilities to advantage' in deciphering the complicated, and therefore irregular, lithographic transfers. Bacon was an authority on the 'Express' stamps and they would have afforded the King hours of study and debate in the three afternoons a week they spent closeted together. The same went for the specialised Yardley Collection of Griqualand West (a separate Crown Colony to the north of Cape Colony, South Africa) bought a year later.

The demands on George V throughout the war were especially heavy. His role as King Emperor had widened into that of a respected figurehead, the leader of the free world pitted against the German aggressor, a position that became even more crucial as the war progressed. But just as his image on the stamps of Great Britain and the Empire gave him the reassurance he needed in time of peace, so the provisionals, overprints and surcharged stamps for British Protectorates and occupied territories rubber-stamped his authority in time of war. To him they became souvenirs of British success, of the valour of the forces he notionally commanded, and a record of enemy reverses. Thus an overprint, such as 'G. R. Mafia' on German East African fiscal stamps meant a great deal more to him than to ordinary collectors.

Among many other examples, there is a complete set of Mafia overprints in the Collection. The island lies in the Rufiji River, Zanzibar, and formed part of

German East Africa until its capture by the British on 12 January 1915. The first military governor, Lieutenant Colonel Mackay, had each denomination, 2½, 4, 7½, 15, 20, 30, and 45 heller (there were 100 heller to 1 rupee) of the current German Colonial issue, depicting the Kaiser's yacht, SMY *Hohenzollern*, which had escorted Queen Victoria's coffin from the Isle of Wight, overprinted G. R. MAFIA. The King's set with overprint in black was a gift from the Countess of Bradford, Extra Lady of the Bedchamber to Queen Mary, who had been sent them by her son, Commander the Hon. Richard Bridgeman R.N., who spearheaded the invasion force on the island.

British East Africa: The overprinting of the current German Colonial issues (generally depicting the Kaiser's yacht, SMY *Hohenzollern*) was an effective propaganda tool. A complete set of G. R. Mafia overprints came from the Countess of Bradford, whose son, Commander the Hon. Richard Bridgeman R.N., had spearheaded the invasion of the island in 1915.

The British Expeditionary Force's successes throughout the First World War provided George V with a host of new areas to collect, particularly in Africa and the Near East. Part I orders for any occupying commanding officer, or their civil authority counterpart, was 'to collect and surcharge [all] the foreign issues available in the post office for use by the occupying authorities and by the local population'.[4] The propaganda value of marking the change of sovereignty was inestimable, just as the enemy fully recognised the value of such a simple and immediate act. Invariably, the defeated tried

Part of the Red Collection housed in the vault of the Stamp Room, St James's Palace.

to destroy their stocks before surrender, so limiting the number of stamps available for the British occupation forces to surcharge. But this only increased their later interest and value to collectors. Along with the orders to overprint, there were instructions from the King to his commander or first administrator to send back as much philatelic material as possible. Sir Percy Cox, for example, the chief political officer for Bushire, the port on the Persian Gulf, was punctilious in sending the King examples of both the Persian Coronation and the portrait issues overprinted 'Bushire Under British Occupation', and the King formed his collection around these early 'gifts'.

British commanders were well aware of George V's philatelic interests, and as they reported back to him through his Private Secretary, Lord Stamford-ham, it was not difficult to indulge him. Colonel Edward Northey, writing from New Langenburg in the former German East Africa, enclosed 'some stamps which The King may like to have, as also those on the envelope. They are Nyasaland stamps surcharged **N.F.** (Nyasaland Field Force) for use in German conquered Territory on this side. So far, only the ½d and 1d values have been sent to me'.[5] Two months later, he sent

> sheets of the only stamps here at present ½, 1d, 3d, and 1/- Nyasaland surcharged **n.f.** This **n.f.** has a rather curious history: it might stand for Nyasa Forces, Northern Force or Northey's Force; the Rhodesian forces are called in Rhodesia 'Northern Force'. But as a matter of fact it was intended to be N.F.F. = "Nyasaland Field force". But in a telegram I sent to Sir George Smith, a telegraphist omitted the second "F." and the stamps were overprinted "NF"
>
>   There are slight errors in some of the printings, viz: (a) on some half sheets in the 6th stamp from the top, and 5th from the left the full stop after 'F' is scarcely visible.
>
>   (b) The N on the left hand bottom stamp is misprinted.
>
> I hope before long to have sheets of 4d and 6d up here surcharged, which I will send.[6]

Northey added a sheet of FOUR PENCE NF overprints 'for His Majesty's Collection',[7] all of which can be identified in the Royal Philatelic Collection, under Tanganyika.

With Bacon's expert advice, his meticulous mounting and writing up, there was less of a challenge for George V in merely filling the gaps in his collection than there was in collecting a major new country or district. The theatres of war and the Allied successes, particularly in Africa, resulted in whole new areas for him to embark on. And he was not alone in this: he soon found himself competing against such collectors as the 4th Marquess of Bute who, with his legendary wealth from South Wales coal mines, formed an unrivalled collection of war memorabilia, especially stamps. If the King did not buy a rarity immediately, the chances were that Bute would snap it up. However, the King had first refusal of the Block Collection of war stamps.

As with the stamps of Mafia, the Kaiser's SMY *Hohenzollern* was depicted on all of Germany's Colonies, and it was these stamps that were overprinted after their surrender. A typical example in the Royal Philatelic Collection are those of the Cameroons. The German Protectorate of Kamerun was taken by the Cameroons Expeditionary Force in 1915. The entire stock of stamps was overprinted c.e.f. with the new value, such as ½d. on 3 pfennigs brown, or 1d. on 10 pfennigs red on pale blue. But it was not enough for the King to have just straightforward examples of all the surcharges: besides 'the reference collection of the German Colonial stamps used before the occupation of the Cameroons Expeditionary Force',[8] he had thirty of the most

Togoland: 1914 example
of overprinted TOGO
Anglo-French Occupation.

significant errors as well. Togoland, another West African German colony, represented an early British success. Again, there is a reference collection of the original German Colonial stamps, forty-one in number, and examples of each value overprinted TOGO Anglo-French Occupation, some surcharged, some not. When the Togo stamps ran out, they were replaced with those of the neighbouring Gold Coast, overprinted locally as before. But by April 1916 these had been superseded by London overprints, the corner blocks of four and specimens, from ½d green to the £1 purple and black on red being sent to the King direct from the printers. The Kaiser's yacht stamps were even used in Germany's Pacific Colony of Western Samoa and, again, these were over-printed, G.R.I. – Georgius Rex Imperator – and the new value in sterling when the island was taken by the New Zealand Expeditionary Force in August 1914.

Although there had been a British presence in Egypt since 1882, it was not until 18 December 1914 that it was declared a British protectorate, which provided the King with a reason to include the country's stamps in the Collection (hence the unprecedented Egypt purchase from the Mann Collection). Once again, he was not alone in his new interest. British collectors have always paid more attention (and money) to those countries' stamps that were in the Stanley Gibbons catalogue Part I (today Great Britain and the Commonwealth). In 1915 when they announced they had transferred Egypt to Part I, the demand for Egyptian stamps increased. Stanley Gibbons had bought the Earl of Crawford's Egypt collection, added further material to it, and George V bought it in its entirety, thereby pre-empting the expected rise in prices. It 'contained some very fine material in large blocks and sheets and is therefore mounted in a special large-sized album'.[9] When Egypt and the Canal Zone were declared a kingdom in 1922, once again their stamps fell outside the scope of the King's Collection, eventually almost all were sold at Spink on 17 May 2001.

The last part of the fabulous Crawford Collection to be purchased by George V was some time in early 1915. It contained the greatest assortment of Treasury essays ever put together, unequalled when combined with the King's own important collection. Such large, diverse collections were of particular interest to him and afforded him hours of enjoyable work and study.

Throughout the war, George V did not neglect The Royal Philatelic Society, London, and continued to provide displays chosen by himself and Bacon. As President of the Sixth Philatelic Congress in 1914, he sent along 'a marvellous array of well-known Mafeking' siege stamps to show to the delegates at the opening reception and soirée. 'Nearly 150 in number [which] ... is without doubt the most comprehensive collection known in this provisional issue'.[10]

Mafeking was the capital of the North West Administrative Province (formerly British Bechuanaland, now Botswana), and was the scene of the first engagement of the South African war fought between Britain (with her Empire) and the two Dutch Boer Republics of the Transvaal and the Orange Free State. On 13 October 1899, just two days into the war, the Boer commander General Piet Cronje, with a vastly superior force, besieged Mafeking under the command of the then Colonel Robert Baden-Powell. The town was small (named after the Tswana word meaning 'place of stones') with a population of seven thousand Africans (mostly from the Barolong tribe) and one thousand whites, some of whom made up the defence force of the 1,231 troops and police, all that Baden-Powell had to defend the town, forts and strategic outposts.

By 1895, Bechuanaland had been annexed to the Cape Colony, and when the country's own stamps were exhausted in 1897, they were replaced by Cape stamps overprinted 'British Bechuanaland'. Later, in October 1897, the stamps of Great Britain were overprinted 'Bechuanaland Protectorate'. But during the siege there was little possibility of sending out any external mail (although some did get through enemy lines) so the only postage was within the town itself and between the outlying forts. As Baden-Powell needed every able-bodied man to fight, he looked to his chief-of-staff, Major Lord Edward Cecil, who had been in Mafeking marginally longer than himself, for an alternative to free up the postmen for active duty. It was Cecil's idea to use the cadet corps, which had been formed on 1 December 1898, to deliver messages and the internal mail. It consisted of eighteen (later expanded to almost forty) able-bodied boys, all over the age of nine, who were delighted at the prospect of such an important role. The troop was under the leadership of Cadet Sergeant Major Warner Goodyear, then aged twelve. Each boy was given a khaki uniform with either a forage cap or a wide-brimmed hat pinned up at one side, with a yellow 'puragee' (a cockade), and a dispatch pouch for the letters.

As no civilian was allowed to visit the outposts, and no soldier defending the outposts was allowed back into town, the only way of communicating was by letter, so Goodyear and his fellow cadets were kept busy. At first they rode donkeys between the forts, but one by one the donkeys were requisitioned to feed the army. The mane and tail went to stuff mattresses at the Victoria Hospital, the shoes were melted down and used in the making of mortar shells, the flesh was turned into sausages, while the rest of the carcass was boiled down to make a kind of brawn. When the last donkey had disappeared, the Donkey Corps became the Bicycle Corps.

The Boer siege of Mafeking tied up a large number of troops and guns, and was effective, but gradually their forces were diverted south to Kimberley, which made it easier for mail carried by native runners to pass through the blockade. But by 22 March 1900, the military had taken charge of the post office, and batches of letters were smuggled through the Boer lines a few times a week. Letters carried north to Bulawayo were charged one shilling per half ounce, and south, towards Kimberley, for just sixpence. As the dangers increased, so did the price, which rose to £25 a run. Many of the Mafeking stamps that later came on to the market had been torn off letters when the runners had been captured, and often killed, by the Boers.

With the post office under military organisation, the army acquired the entire stock of 42,850 stamps at face value and, under the direction of J. V. Howat, staff-postmaster to Baden-Powell, overprinted them with the words 'MAFEKING', and 'BESIEGED', with the relevant surcharge between the two words, printed locally by Townshend and Co. Sixteen surcharges were printed between 23 March and 28 April 1900, some on the then current Cape stamps, Hope either seated – 1d. on HALFPENNY green, and 6d. on THREE PENCE magenta, and 1/- on FOUR PENCE sage-green – or Hope standing, with 1d. on HALFPENNY green and 3d. on ONE PENNY carmine. The last two are rare, and there are several examples of these provisionals in the Collection, used, unused, and on covers. Any printed stamp would do for the surcharges, and a cache of both the 'Bechuanaland Protectorate' and the 'British Bechuanaland' overprints, five years out of date, was found in the vault of the local post office. Again, they were printed with surcharges, great care being taken not to interfere with the original overprint. The Collection contains several items of both types of overprints, including an example of the rare used 1/- on SIX PENCE, purple on red rose on British Bechuanaland on an envelope addressed to Cape Town.

The lower values, ONE PENNY and THREE PENCE, of the surcharged stamps for the internal mails were running out by March, and needed to be replaced. Ingenious to the end, the besieged set about printing a complete issue. For the THREE PENCE, a photograph of Baden-Powell was specially taken for the stamp by David Taylor (thereby disproving that the stamps were produced without his knowledge), while Cadet Sergeant Major Warner Goodyear with his bicycle, was a good choice for the ONE PENNY. When Taylor was on the point of taking the photograph of Goodyear, a shell landed nearby blowing them off their feet – the town was shelled daily, except on Sundays and Christmas Day. Undaunted, the pair picked themselves up, brushed off the dust, and resumed the session. The photograph, four inches by three inches, was printed on blue ferro-prussiate paper, the type used by architects, laid horizontally. It is now in the Collection, with another from which the background has been cut out. In these photographs, it is possible to see just how young Goodyear was, and the large stone under the pedal to keep his feet off the ground to give the appearance that he is in motion.

The ONE PENNY stamp was designed by a medical officer on Baden-Powell's staff, Dr Will A. Hayes, and again the Collection holds a photograph of the first design he drew, along with copies of the proposed stamp. It is indeed a handsome one, landscape with Goodyear on his bicycle with an ornamental border and the inscription V.R., SIEGE OF MAFEKING 1899–1900 LOCAL POST, ONE PENNY. There is also a complete imperforate proof sheet of twelve stamps, with notes in Dr Hayes's handwriting giving the reasons why he was dissatisfied with the first design in the margin: 'Proof of the new 1d. I am doing another as this is not clear enough. W. A. Hayes, P.M.O., Siege of Mafeking.' The third and final design was approved, and the Collection also has the essay marked 'The 3rd is the final one. I did the design. W. A. Hayes P.M.O., Siege of Mafeking.' It is portrait shape with ground removed to the level of the pedals.

David Taylor produced the stamps photographically from the three glass negative plates printing on horizontally laid paper (originally destined for legal documents), with a very small part of the sheet watermarked *Oceana Fine*. As the stamps were printed by the same process as was used in making draughtsmen's blueprint plans, they were blue. The slight colour variation that occurred was due to the uneven mixture of the two chemicals, ferric salt and potassium ferricyanide, used in the printing. The Collection holds several examples of all shades, used and unused, singles and in blocks. In all, 9,476 'Bicycle' stamps were printed and issued.

Cape of Good Hope: Mafeking 1900 (7–11 April) ONE PENNY. Photograph of Cadet Sergeant Major Warner Goodyear on ferro-prussiate paper.

Cape of Good Hope: Mafeking 1900 (7–11 April).

Photograph of
first proposed design.

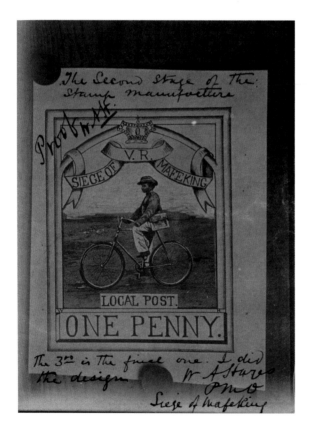

ONE PENNY
blue on blue,
unused.

ONE PENNY
second design,
proof.

The paymaster, Captain H. Greener, designed the THREE PENCE Baden-Powell stamp. They were printed in two sizes, 6,072 of the smaller, 3,036 of the larger, in exactly the same way as the ONE PENNY. The Collection holds several examples, including a sheet of twelve with margins, and, bought much later (1947), a used pair of imperforate dated 2 May [1900]. But the real Mafeking rarity in the Collection is the THREE PENCE reverse design (6–11 April 1900). Only twelve were printed on a single sheet, of which ten are known. The error occurred, apparently, when 'Mrs Taylor, the photographer's wife, who assisted in the preparation of the stamps – which, as is well known, were produced by photographic process – explained to my informant [Arthur Stamford] that the negative was turned the wrong way, and as all the paper issued had to be accounted for and returned, it was necessary to hand in the spoilt sheet along with the rest.'[11] Of these, only three are unused and the Royal Collection formerly held one unused, and three used, but today it has just one of each.

THREE PENCE
blue on blue, error
reversed design, unused.

After 217 days, the Siege of Mafeking was raised on 17 May 1900 by British forces commanded by Colonel Bryan T. Mahon. A native runner had taken a coded message to Baden-Powell: 'Our numbers are Naval and Military Club multiplied by ten [94 Piccadilly × 10 = 940], our guns the number of sons in the Ward family [the Earl of Dudley and his five brothers = six guns]; our supplies, the officer commanding the 9th Lancers [Lieutenant Colonel Little = few].'[12] When the news of the Relief of Mafeking reached Britain, it caused uproar – the immense celebrations at the news resulting in the coining of a new verb, *to maffick*: 'a journalistic word used to designate the extravagant behaviour of the London crowds on the Relief of Mafeking'.[13] It was always said that Baden-Powell 'incurred the Queen's displeasure' that he had put his own image and not hers on the Mafeking stamps, but at the news of the end of the siege, she immediately sent a telegram to Lord Roberts

ONE PENNY
first proposed design
as stamp.

Proof of the new 1ᵈ. I am doing another as this is not clean enough. W. A. Hayes PMO.

W. A. Hayes. PMO. Siege of Mafeking

with her congratulations, and specific instructions that Baden-Powell be promoted to Major General, hardly the action of an aggrieved Sovereign. Baden-Powell had been impressed by the deeds and discipline of the cadet corps, under the leadership of Warner Goodyear, throughout the siege and it was this that inspired him to found the Boy Scout movement in 1907.

Throughout the whole of the South African war, towns surcharged and overprinted their stamps when, like Mafeking, they were besieged or occupied by the Boers, or the British occupied Boer towns. The overprints and surcharges, often with errors, became an intense area of study for George V. A prime example is Vryburg. The town was occupied by the Boers in October 1899, and the Cape of Good Hope stamps were surcharged and overprinted ZAR. (Zuid Africaansche Republiek); the Collection is strong on all the surcharges and errors. One particular item of interest, bought from the Ferrari Collection (see page 221), is the HALFPENNY green Cape of Good Hope (seated figure) overprinted ZAR in black in sans-serif letters 4 mm high, dated 'No.[vember] 22, '99' on piece. This is attached to a telegraph form bearing the inscription: 'The stamp marked Z. A. R. and date stamped Vryburg B.B. was surcharged by the Boers when they captured Vryburg. I took a letter of a dead Boer (shot) with two of these stamps on the letter. One stamp I sold for £2 to a Capt. Gillespie.'[14] Vryburg was evacuated by the Boers on 7 May 1900, and Cape of Good Hope stamps were endorsed in manuscript with the initials C. St. Q., Mr C. St Quinton, the military magistrate, 'owing to the date obliterator being missing'.[15] Again the Collection holds two covers, one HALFPENNY with a figure of Hope (seated), the other ONE PENNY of Hope (standing) so obliterated. The stamps of Transvaal came with the British reoccupation, and the Collection includes two other great rarities: the 2 PENCE brown and green, and the TWO PENCE dull blue and green, overprinted V. R. SPECIAL POST, only one other example of each is known.

Opposite:

Cape of Good Hope: Mafeking 1900 (7–11 April).

Top: THREE PENCE blue on blue, unused, a rare sheet of twelve.

Bottom: ONE PENNY first proposed design as stamp in a proof sheet of 12, annotated by W. A. Hayes.

With the rest of Britain, the then Duke of York followed the news of the South African war as it unfolded in the daily papers and magazines such as the *Illustrated London News*. He began collecting immediately, and added steadily over the years. Consequently, that part of the Collection reads like a philatelic history of the war, with near complete examples of such places as Schweizer Renecke, the town near the Bechuanaland border under siege from the Boer forces between 1 August 1900 and 19 January 1901. There the garrison commander authorised the overprinting of the word BESIEGED on both the Cape of Good Hope and Transvaal stamps, again examples of each are in the Collection. There is also a good showing of other local issues produced during the war, from such places as Lindenburg, Rustenburg, and the over-printed fiscal stamps of Volksrust – although the Duke considered the stamps of Pietersburg 'too dull to collect on his usual scale'.[16]

Although George V bought most of his stamps, he continued to receive unsolicited gifts. Some, like that from a Captain Alfred D. Fripp, came with a piece of interesting postal history. Fripp, a doctor at the Imperial Yeomanry Hospital wrote from the Mount Nelson Hotel, Cape Town, to the King enclosing a surcharged stamp from Bloemfontein. His letter contained an account of life in the military hospital, but his real 'object in sending this short note was to enclose to your Royal Highness the above stamp. I believe they will become extremely rare for very few stamps were found in the Post Office at Bloemfontein when the town surrendered – and those few were as you see on the above specimen surcharged VR 1d by Lord Roberts. They were all bought up in a few minutes – and already they are fetching 10/- each

Cape of Good Hope: Vryburg, 1900, 2 PENCE brown and green and the 2½ PENNY blue and green, overprinted V. R. SPECIAL POST, on piece with only one other known example.

Opposite: Cape of Good Hope: Vryburg, 1900. *Top:* HALFPENNY with a figure of Hope (seated), on cover. *Bottom:* ONE PENNY of Hope (standing). They are cancelled with the postmaster's initials, the date plugs having gone missing.

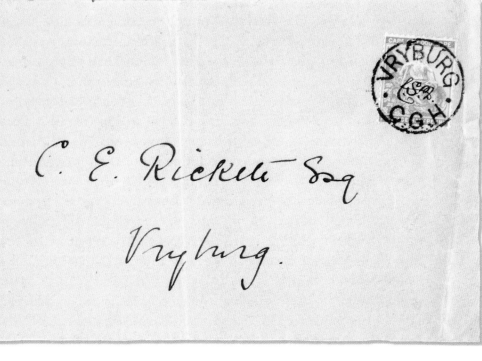

C. E. Rickett Esq

Vryburg.

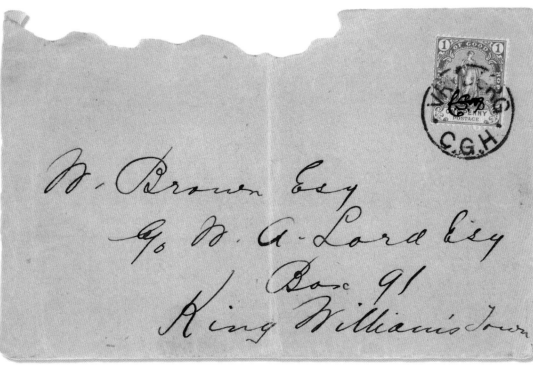

W. Brown Esy
C/o W. A. Lord Esy
Box 91
King Williamstown

out here. Knowing the interest taken by you in the collection of stamps, I thought I would send one'.[17] There is no way of knowing exactly what Fripp sent, but it is probable that it was an example of 1d on ONE PENNY Orange Free State, 1900 of the British Occupation overprints. It was issued after the fall of Bloemfontein on 13 March 1900, where doubtless Fripp was attached to Lord Roberts's army. It was a kind thought, but he had paid an inflated price unless there was some error in the Curling & Co. printing of the surcharge. Two months later, Fripp wrote again from the Imperial Yeomanry Hospital: 'I found to my surprise when I was in Bloemfontein that there was no scarcity of the surcharged stamps there yet so I bought a lot of them – but certain ones, e.g. the "ROSE 6^d" and the 2½d and the 4^d are very difficult to obtain – costing 3/6 to 7/6 each. I shall be delighted to give your Royal Highness any that are not in your Collection.'[18] Despite Fripp's trouble, his offer was not taken up.

Just as the Prince of Wales had given a set of Trinidad (possibly the 9d. surcharges commemorating his visit on HMS *Thrush*) for the Boer War Funds, so as King he donated a very rare specimen, the NINE PENCE straw of Great Britain, for auction in aid of the National Philatelic War Funds. The stamp had come from the 1865–67 issue printed from Plate 5, registered on 24 April 1866 but never put to press. Twenty years later the Great Britain issue of 1883 was produced by De La Rue with their doubly fugitive inks as a 'safe-guard to the Revenue'.[19] This issue served both for postage and revenue and became known as the 'Unified Series'. The stamps were universally condemned, and Parliament ordered a commission of inquiry to look into the series and other related postal matters. The commission consisted of the Postmaster General, the Secretary to the Post Office, the Chairman of the Board of Inland Revenue and a 'Stamp Committee' consisting of a chairman and four members.

Great Britain: 1865–67 issue NINE PENCE straw printed from Plate 5. This 'abnormal' was donated by George V and raised £525 in the National Philatelic War Funds Auction, 1915.

The Stamp Committee sat between 1884 and 1887. One of their most notable functions was to steer the 'Jubilee Issue' (1887–1892) through its production. As a reward for their service, each member was given a memento: an album entitled *Before and After the Stamp Committee* with examples of all the issues (two of 1884 and 1887) over which they had presided. However, to make the series complete, a NINE PENCE stamp was required and the only ones available were on the imprimatur sheet of the unissued Plate 5. A total of thirty-six stamps were removed and perforated by De La Rue. Twelve were then returned to the imprimatur sheet, while twelve of the perforated stamps found their way into the presentation albums. One example, lettered K–L in the corners, was removed from an album and discovered in the Crawford Collection of Great Britain bought by the King in 1915. A *really* good present is one that the giver would rather keep, and it must have been a wrench for George V to select it as his contribution to the War Fund having so recently acquired it. Bacon mounted it on a card, inscribing it:

> This 9d. Plate 5, Gt. Britain stamp was taken from my collection and given to
> the National Philatelic War Funds Auction in September 1915
> (signed) George R.I.

At the auction, as Lot 35, the stamp was bought for £280 by Stanley Gibbons, who immediately offered it back into the room, where it made a further £245, the purchaser was Frank Godden, a well-known dealer. Some time afterwards, it passed through both the L. O. Trivett and the Arthur Hind collections, still on its original card. But the King was never able to replace it.

Towards the end of 1915, the peace of the Stamp Room was upset when Edward Bacon ruffled feathers within the Household. He was generally the mildest of men. 'He was not a great talker: an expression of a contrary opinion to that held by some colleague was often limited to a shake of the head and a smile, which sufficed to stop any further discussion'.[20] But his deafness kept him apart, and often made him appear aloof to those he did not know well, and his stiff, formal manner belied his sense of humour. In addition 'he could fall into an almost royal rage when the occasion seemed to demand it,'[21] and was too easily slighted when crossed.

Shortly after his appointment, Bacon had set up a system whereby the King automatically received from the Post Office the corner blocks of four of the registration sheets and the stamps of all new issues. The system worked well and the stamps were forwarded to Bacon in the Stamp Room. However, with his meticulous eye for detail, he noticed various omissions and sent the list to Col. Wigram, the King's Assistant Private Secretary, as it was his job to liaise between the King and the various government departments. Wigram wrote to Mr G. E. Murray, Secretary of the General Post Office:

> Some years ago the Board of Inland Revenue at Somerset House sent the King specimens cut from the series of registration sheets of Postage Stamps, which are now at the General Post Office.
>
> Since that period, sheets of a number of other stamps have been registered and His Majesty hopes that you will let him have a pair cut from one of the corners with full margins left on both sides of each of these sheets particulars of which I enclose.
>
> The King would also like to be furnished with the dates of registration in each instance and for the future to have a similar pair sent to him of each sheet registered with the date so that his collection may be kept up to date.[22]

Wigram received a polite reply from Mr Murray:

> With reference to your letter 17 instant, the registration sheets for all stamps issued in the late or in the present reign are at present complete and I think it would be a mistake to mar their completeness by detaching individual stamps. I understand that this view commends itself to the King as in your letter of the 3rd March 1914 to Sir Matthew Nathan you state "His Majesty recognises that if the sheets had never been cut it would be best to keep them entire but as several specimens have been detached at various periods one more from each sheet can make little or no difference."
>
> But there is a duplicate collection of registration sheets comprising most of the stamps in question from which we can supply the specimens His Majesty requires if this will meet his wishes.
>
> With regard to the future I think the best plan would be to have a duplicate sheet printed at the time of registration which can be sent entire to Mr Bacon for His Majesty's collection.

It is of course important that these stamps should not find their way into the hands of philatelists and I have no doubt that you would make arrangements that any specimens which are not required for His Majesty's purpose would be duly destroyed.

If these suggestions generally would meet the King's wishes I will arrange that the details shall be settled in consultation with Mr Bacon.[23]

The King agreed that this was the best solution, although he thought it would be better for the Post Office to cut off the corner block for him and for them to destroy the rest of the sheet. The plan was immediately adopted. But Bacon was not satisfied that Murray was being entirely honest over the registration sheets, and he felt sure that not all of the sheets of missing proofs were entire. He made the mistake of writing to Murray direct, then going to see him without an appointment, believing that his position, as Curator of the King's Philatelic Collection, would be enough to secure the interview. He was rebuffed, and in a fit of pique complained to the King of Murray's rudeness. Wigram – whose conversation was studded with cricketing terms – was 'put into bat again'. He went to Mr Murray 'fearing that friction was going to arise between Mr Bacon and the Post Office Secretariat, which might lead to some unpleasantness if not smoothed down'. In a secret memorandum, Wigram continued:

Mr Bacon, being an enthusiastic Philatelist, appeared to be rather grasping as regards some of his demands for stamps. Mr Bacon told His Majesty that Mr Murray had been rude to him, and that he (Mr Murray) had refused to see him when he went to the General Post Office to inspect the surplus sheets of stamps. …

I found Mr Murray most affable and obliging, and willing to help His Majesty in any way.

With regard to Mr Bacon's contention that as some of the individual sheets of the collection of sheets had been mutilated, it did not matter if the remaining whole sheets were also mutilated, Mr Murray impressed on me that the policy of the Post Office was to preserve intact as many individual sheets as possible. He considered it a slur on the Post Office that, in the past, these individual sheets had been allowed to be cut into. He explained that when once a sheet had lost one stamp off it, there was a great temptation for those connected with the Department to pick off another one until gradually the sheet diminished.

There would be no difficulty in future as a duplicate sheet could be printed especially for the King.[24]

Although officially a member of the Royal Household, Bacon had overstepped the mark by usurping the Private Secretary's Office. Later Wigram called him in and, in his gruff, forthright manner, pointed out Bacon's misdemeanour. The meeting was recorded in another private memorandum written by Wigram:

I saw Mr Bacon this morning.

About a month ago he wrote to Mr Murray Secretary, G. P. O. regarding the impression on a postmark on a letter said to have been posted during the Irish Rebellion, at the same time asking him for specimens of any new issue of stamps for His Majesty's collection.

Mr Murray had not answered Mr Bacon's letter, and on the 27th instant Mr Bacon wrote another letter to Mr Murray, as a result of which, Mr Bacon this morning had a reply from some subordinate in the Post Office, writing in Mr Murray's name.

The King had spoken to me about Mr Bacon's letter, and of the discourtesy of Mr Murray in not replying to Mr Bacon.

I explained to His Majesty that Mr Bacon had no business to write direct to Mr Murray in His Majesty's name and that Sir Frederick Ponsonby had already come to an agreement with Mr Bacon on this point.

I also reminded the King of my interview with Mr Murray in December 1915, on account of some friction having arisen between Mr Murray and Mr Bacon.

I pointed out to Mr Bacon that his writing direct to Heads of Departments placed the King in a very false position, as he really had no authority to write in the King's name. If the Head of any Department chose to ignore his letter, there were really no legitimate grounds of complaint. On the other hand, if letters were written through the Private Secretary's Office, Departments could be brought to book for not answering after a certain period of grace.

Mr Bacon said that he was sorry, but had misunderstood what the arrangement was as regards letters. He promised not to offend again in the letter writing
line, and said he would send to the Private Secretary's Office all letters for Heads
of Departments containing any request on behalf of the King.[25]

Such a mistake would have been avoided had Bacon been on more intimate
terms with the rest of the Household. Because of the nature of their positions,
senior members of the Household were particularly close, like members of
an exclusive club: they messed together in their own dining room and
followed the King from palace, to castle, to house and back again. Bacon, a
former City merchant with no service background, was not of their ranks,
and although over the years he spent more time closeted with the King at
Buckingham Palace than most of the Private Secretaries and Equerries, he
remained a stranger to them all. His deafness also contributed to his exclusion,
and throughout his time at the Palace, he preferred to lunch on his own, the
footman tipped a shilling to bring the tray to the Stamp Room.

Bacon's lack of day to day contact with the Private Secretaries meant that
although he sometimes instigated a piece of fascinating postal history, he was
not party to it as it unfolded in their offices on the other side of Buckingham
Palace. For example, after an article entitled 'War Provisionals for Salonica'
appeared in the April 1916 edition of the *London Philatelist*, readers were
informed that 'Towards the end of February a certain number of current
British stamps were overprinted at the British Army printing office in
Salonica with the word "Levant" in thick letters, but by March 9th it was
decided to withdraw the issue.'[26] On the strength of the article, Bacon wrote
to Colonel Wigram to ask him to write to the Commander-in-Chief Salonica,
Lieutenant General Sir Bryan Mahon (the same who had relieved Mafeking),
'to try to obtain for the King a corner block of four, a pair or a single specimen
of all the values of Great Britain stamps that have been overprinted with the
word "Levant"'.[27] By then Wigram had become used to the King's philatelic
needs and passed on the request, adding that 'His Majesty would also be glad
to receive specimens of any mistakes that have been made in the overprinting
– such as one row of stamps overprinted, and then a row that has missed the
overprinting'.[28] Unsure that he had written to the right person, Wigram fired

off a similar letter to H. J. Creedy, Private Secretary to the Secretary of State for War to find out exactly who was 'responsible for new issue stamps in territories under British Occupation, or the surcharging of ordinary stamps in these parts'.[29] He also enquired if the Army Postal Department 'have any say in the matter'. F. G. A. Butler, Private Secretary to Bonar Law, the Secretary of State for the Colonies, also received a letter, adding that 'His Majesty would like to receive specimens of stamps of any further issues in territories occupied by the British under the administration of the Colonial Office.' There was also a request for all war stamps, Wigram asking if 'General Smuts [was] having a new issue in East Africa, or surcharging the German Stamps?'[30] Smuts, in fact, authorised a completely new issue.

The letters went round and round. Wigram drew Creedy's attention to the article in the *London Philatelist*; Creedy replied that he had forwarded the King's request to the Post Office. F. H. Williamson of the Army Postal Service then wrote to Creedy at the War Office to say that 'the specimens of the [Levant] issues which would appear to have sold out',[31] which either meant that he had tracked them down and they really had sold out or, more likely, that he knew nothing about them. Somehow Mr Murray, Secretary of the Post Office, entered the scene having come up with the 'only denominations of which we have at present [½ – 1 – 3 – 6 written in manuscript in the margin] overprinted "Levant"'.[32] Wigram thanked him, adding that 'His Majesty hopes that you will be able to send him specimens of the other denominations, details of which appeared in the "London Philatelist" of April 1916, and will be interested to hear the circumstances in which these were produced when you have received your report.'[33] On 15 May 1916, Wigram wrote to Harold Nicolson, who had served in Constantinople and had recently joined the Eastern (Europe) Department at the Turkish desk in the Foreign Office: 'I hope that the Consul General at Salonika, to whom you have written, may be able to produce these'. [34]

Harold Nicolson cannot have relished his task, for collecting stamps was total anathema to him. Much later, in 1946, he was to launch a vicious attack on philatelists, prompted by the sale for £5,000 of the Duke of Buccleuch's block of forty-eight TWO PENCE blue and fifty-five red-brown ONE PENNY of 1841 that had been found lying in a drawer. 'What enrages me,' he wrote, is that 'there are people in the world who are prepared to pay … such immense sums of money for tiny, unusable, frail, ugly and wholly meaningless objects…' It suggested to him 'a mind which is adhesive and small'.[35] His view of the King was little better: 'For seventeen years, he did nothing at all but kill animals and stick in stamps,'[36] and that from his official biographer.

Whatever his personal feelings about the King's request taking up his valuable time during a crucial period of the war, he embraced the task and forwarded a copy of Wigram's letter to the consul general at Salonica. Meanwhile Lieutenant General Mahon wrote to Wigram from Army Head-quarters, Salonica: 'Until I received your note two days ago I had no idea that any Stamps overprinted "Levant" were in existence. Certainly none are in use by the British Army.

I am now making enquires as to whether the Navy have had stamps surcharged in this manner, and if they have and any are left of them, of course those desired by the King will be sent to you'.[37] Wigram then heard from Murray at the GPO that the stamps were overprinted for some proposed, but abandoned, naval expedition, and hoped that the Army Post Office still might come up with something. The Collection holds an 'Essay prepared for an issue of stamps prepared at Mount Athos which never took place. The designs were made by Lt. Cdr. H. Pirie-Gordon and were photographically multiplied aboard HMS *Ark Royal*',[38] doubtless to be used in connection with the abandoned naval scheme. But it gave the designer, Pirie-Gordon an idea.

Long Island: 1916 (7 May) ½ Penny on 20 pa. Turkish fiscal stamp, green and buff. Only 25 were printed by Lt. Cdr. H. Pirie-Gordon with philatelists in mind.

Meanwhile, seemingly unconnected with any of the correspondence from the Private Secretary's Office, the same Lieutenant Commander Henry Pirie-Gordon wrote to Lord Stamfordham on 7 May 1916. 'May I venture to request that you will be so kind as to submit, with my humble duty, the enclosed postage-stamps of Long Island for His Majesty's gracious acceptance. As you will perceive some of these stamps are overprinted on captured Turkish fiscal stamps, while others are

Long Island: 1916 (7 May)
HALFPENNY produced by
Pirie-Gordon on a typewriter.

typewritten.'[39] All of these stamps were gratefully received into the Collection, admissible as Pirie-Gordon, Senior Naval Officer, Long Island (the captured Turkish island of Chustan in the Gulf of Smyrna), was a serving officer. Clearly Pirie-Gordon knew exactly what he was doing in producing the surcharges, unquestionably for collectors, as he kept the numbers to a minimum. Of the ½ Penny surcharge on 20 paras green and buff with black G.R.I./ Postage overprint in red, only twenty-five stamps were printed, of which twelve examples are known today. Similarly, only twenty-five were printed of the surcharge in black of the ONE PENNY on 10 paras carmine and buff, and twenty of the TWO PENCE HALFPENNY on the 1 piastre violet and buff. To present an example of each to the King would help to authenticate the probably unauthorised printing. The other part of the gift was a quantity of stamps, from ½d to 6d. that Pirie-Gordon had produced for internal use on the island. These were typewritten on various papers, usually pale green, but also on thin carbon paper with a variety of ribbons and colours, examples of most being in the Royal Philatelic Collection. The King was delighted and asked Stamfordham to reply to Pirie-Gordon that he thought that the stamps 'have been very cleverly designed'.[40] But these flimsy typewritten stamps were still not those he had read about in the April edition of the *London Philatelist*.

The first complete set of 'Levant overprints' that George V received came through Harold Nicolson by way of Mr Wratislaw, the Consul General of Salonica. Wratislaw had managed to buy them from a local collector, and Nicolson was asked to send the Consul a signed photograph of the King for his trouble.

Meanwhile Lieutenant General Sir Bryan Mahon came up with the solution:

Full enquiries have now been made in regard to the stamps overprinted with the word "LEVANT" and I regret to find that the transaction was entirely irregular and not authorised by Admiral Sir John de Robeck or Rear Admiral Stuart Nicholson. It would appear that a certain Officer in the Royal Navy caused certain stamps to be surcharged without having previously obtained the sanction of the Admiral. The stamps therefore cannot be well treated as genuine and their value to a stamp collector is presumably nil. In any event those that are now left have been handed over to the Postmaster General's Department and if the King requires some, which however I doubt when he knows the circumstances, they can be obtained, I think in London.

The question of the culpability of the Naval Officer concerned is being dealt with by Sir John de Robeck but I do not know what decision he has arrived at.[41]

Then, as if nothing had happened, a letter from Pirie-Gordon's father-in-law arrived in the Private Secretary's Office enclosing a complete set of the over-printed stamps – fifteen in all, followed by a letter from 'Lieut Commander Harry Pirie-Gordon DSC RNVR, Senior Naval Officer, Port Laki, Eastern Mediterranean Squadron' to Lord Stamfordham: 'Not having a complete set the authorities have approached me privately, as I was, in the first instance, concerned with the overprinting of these stamps, and have asked me to supply them with the required set'.[42]

After Pirie-Gordon's scheme was unmasked, there was another 'round robin' of self-righteousness – Wigram to Mahon: 'We all thought the issue of these stamps rather fishy, and I expect the young fellow who did it made a nice sum of money out of the dealers,'[43] while G. E. Murray of the Post Office wrote, 'It is pretty clear that the issue was unauthorised':[44] Wigram wrote to Murray 'Lt Commander Pirie-Gordon seems to have cornered all the stamps – it will be interesting to hear how he explains his conduct before the Court of Enquiry.'[45] It would appear that Pirie-Gordon survived all censure as he transferred to the Army, ending up as a lieutenant colonel.

The story does not end there. An article appeared in the March 1917 edition of the *London Philatelist*, debunking the stamps as having 'no philatelic status'. However, there is in the Collection a copy of 'The Long Island Gazette (published by authority) No 1 May 16th, containing lists of postal rates and numbers

British Levant, British Field Office in Salonica: 1916. This complete set of 'Levant' overprints on cover was a present from Queen Mary to George V.

of [Long Island] stamps made',[46] produced by Pirie-Gordon to give 'his' stamps authenticity. Notwithstanding the article, and the refusal of Stanley Gibbons to include them in their catalogue at the time, Bacon steadfastly maintained that they were genuine, and therefore should be included in the Collection. He mounted them all, and wrote them up accordingly. Furthermore, he bought 'A complete set of the stamps with 'Levant' overprint used on an entire envelope, Salonica 1916'[47] for Queen Mary to give to the King in 1920.

It is indeed surprising that the King should have admired the typewritten stamps produced by Pirie-Gordon, as it was known that he 'was not interested' in such issues, generally known as 'Missionary Stamps' after those produced in Uganda. In 1894, the British Protectorate of Uganda was ratified in the former Kingdom of Buganda. But the country was in a sorry state, not least the postal system. To improve matters, George Wilson, a government official, went to see the only man to own a typewriter, the Reverend Ernest Millar from the Church Missionary Society. 'At lunch-time Wilson looked in,' reads the entry in Millar's diary, 'and wanted us to help with his idea of a postage system in Uganda. I consented to print some stamps for him and printed off a sheet of all values, from 10 to 50 shells.'[48]

The 'shells' were cowries (*Cypræa moneta*), a common form of currency on the Indian Ocean littoral. The internal postal system was announced on 16 March 1895 with strict instructions that only one letter was permitted in an envelope on pain of confiscation and that 'letters insufficiently stamped will not be posted'.[49] The Collection holds two pieces, one 30 cowries, the other 50 cowries, both stamps of the first issue, 20 March 1895. They must be the simplest ever produced for Millar had just typed UG at the top and the value in the middle. The horizontal lines were a series of hyphens, the vertical five apostrophes. The sheets, brittle *bâttonné* paper normally reserved for his sermons, were typed in black (for that was the colour of the ribbon) in thirteen rows of nine. Each row was a different value of either 5, 10, 20, 25, 30, 40, 50, or 60 cowries, with extra rows of the most common, 20 and 25 cowries.

It was a laborious process, particularly as Millar had to take out each sheet as he reached the bottom of the page and turn it round so creating a series of tête-bêche. With such repetitive work, errors naturally crept in. The cancellation was generally a stroke of the pen or a cross.

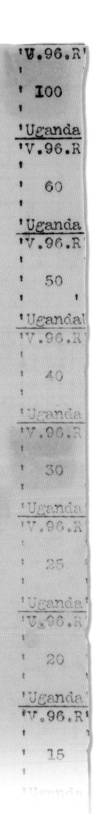

Above: Uganda: 1896 1 ANNA and 3 ANNAS on COVER.

Left: Uganda: 1896 10 to 100 violet, part of a strip of nine, unused.
These missionary stamps, known as 'Cowries', were produced
on a typewriter by the Reverend Ernest Millar.

The system worked well and further stamps were required of Millar's typewriter. These were a little narrower. Then, around the end of April, a brand new, superior typewriter was delivered from England, naturally with a new ribbon – *violet* in colour. The collection holds a violet 20 cowries, used with pen cancellation. To ring the changes, Millar changed the design in June 1896 to 'V. 96. R' at the top, Uganda at the bottom with the value in the middle. Again, the Collection holds a left hand strip of nine with all the denominations from 10 to 100 cowries. The next issue, 7 November 1896, was designed on a typewriter, then typeset. There is a good showing of it in the Collection, including the many errors.

At around the same time as the Pirie-Gordon 'issue', and in the same vein, the King received a letter from a Mr Herbert Pease (Assistant Postmaster General), 'Since the first institution of postage stamps in 1840, so far as the Post Office is aware, there has been only one case in which a postage stamp of the United Kingdom has ever been forged, and <u>successfully uttered</u>.'[50] One of these samples he enclosed was the 1867–80 ONE SHILLING green, that had been used to pay the postage on telegraph forms at the Stock Exchange, hence its name, the 'Stock Exchange Forgery'. Nor was it a very clever forgery. The stamps were blurred in appearance, they purported to be from Plates 5 and 6 and some of the corner letters were from impossible positions on the plate, but as they only went across the counter of the Stock Exchange post office and not through the mail they remained undetected until 1898. The culprits were never caught. There are examples from both Plates 5 and 6 in the Collection.

Great Britain: Forgery of 1867–80 ONE SHILLING green taken from Plates 5 and 6, no watermark. They were used to pay the telegraph fee at the Stock Exchange, hence their sobriquet 'Stock Exchange Forgery'.

Some areas of the Royal Philatelic Collection bear witness to the changes in the history of a country. Hejaz (now in Saudi Arabia) had been part of the Ottoman Empire since the sixteenth century. It was an important region, not least for the Hejaz railway that connected Damascus with Medina. When Turkey entered the war in 1914, British interests in Egypt, particularly the Suez Canal, were threatened. Backed covertly by the British, in June 1916 the Sharif of Mecca, Hussein ibn Ali revolted against the Turks on behalf of the Arabs and proclaimed himself King of Hejaz. He destroyed all symbols of Turkish occupation, starting with the stamps.

The advantage of a new issue of Hejaz stamps was twofold: first, they had to be replaced anyway, and second, as the successes of the Arab revolt were being ignored by the enemy and neutral press, Ronald Storrs, Oriental Secretary at the British Agency (later the High Commission) in Cairo, 'decided that the best proof that it [the successes] had taken place would be provided by an issue of Hejaz postage stamps, which would carry the Arab propaganda, self-paying and incontrovertible, to the four corners of the earth'.[51] He travelled to Hejaz with a young intelligence officer from Cairo, T. E. Lawrence, to arrange for the replacement issue. Lawrence had experience in surveying and the printing of military maps. It was here, as Storrs admitted in his autobiography, that Lawrence 'became known permanently as 'Lawrence of Arabia'.

The plan for Britain to produce a new Hejaz issue was adopted enthusiastically by the Foreign Office, and Storrs wrote to the Sharif. By return of post, he sent his own pencil sketch, which Storrs dubbed 'a design purporting to typify Islamic architecture, but to the layman indistinguishable from the Eddystone lighthouse'[52] – it was in fact the Jebel Abu Quedeis Mosque. This essay is in the Collection, along with a note by Storrs: 'Designed by Sherif [sic] of Mecca for Hejaz Postage 1 piastre stamp. Enclosed in letter to his agent, Elias Bey Bibbane, July 1916, and later handed to me for opinion Aug 3 1916. In view of provisional issue already prepared by the Egyptian Survey Dept. decided to wait further instructions from H.H. before proceeding further with this design.'[53]

Hejaz: 1916 (July) 1 piastre, essay drawn in pencil by Sharif of Mecca for his own postage stamp.
Ronald Storrs likened the sketch of the Jebel Abu Quedeis Mosque indistinguishable from
the Eddystone Lighthouse. It was not adopted.

Design by Sherif of Mecca for
Hijaz Postage i.P.T stamp.
Enc. in letter from him to his
Agent Elias Bey Bibbane, July 1916
& by Latter handed to me for opinion
Aug 3 1916. 
In view of
provisional issue
already prepared by Eg. Survey Dept.
decided to await further instructions
from H H before proceeding further
with this design.

RS
3 hm 16

H E shewn & informed

Storrs was unhappy with the design, as he and Lawrence had already wandered around the Cairo museum looking for 'suitable motifs in order that the design in wording, spirit and ornament, might be as far as possible representative and reminiscent of a purely Arab source of inspiration'.

They had selected the carved panels on the doors of El Salih Talayi Mosque in Cairo for the ¼ piastre green, the last page of the fourteenth century Holy Qur'an in the mosque of El Sultan Burquq, Cairo (½ piastre, scarlet), and a prayer niche from a mosque in Qus, Upper Egypt (1 piastre, blue) for the new stamps. The stamps were printed by the Survey of Egypt and issued on 20 August, Storrs remarking that 'It was quickly apparent that Lawrence already possessed or had immediately assimilated a complete working technique of philatelic and three-colour reproduction, so that he was able to supervise the issue from start to finish.'[54]

The first proof sheets fell into the hands of Brigadier General Gilbert Clayton, Director General of Military Intelligence, Cairo, who sent them on to his friend Clive Wigram:

My Dear Wigram

The Sherif [sic] of Mecca asked for some stamps to be printed for him here, and attached is a sheet of what were decided on as the most suitable. Of course no mention has been made of our doing this for him and, indeed, they will not be sent without the approval of H M Gov'. I thought you would like a sheet of the first trial issue. It would be as well to keep it quiet though, or else there will be a rush of philatelists to secure specimens, and undesirable publicity would result. It will be better to keep it quiet until the Sherif begins actually to use the stamps'.[55]

Lawrence relished his task because, as he wrote to his brother Arnold, 'one has long ideas as to what a stamp should look like, and now one can put them roughly into practice'.[56] He also mentioned to his brother that he intended to have flavoured gum 'so one can lick without unpleasantness'. His idea was to flavour the red values with strawberry essence and the green with pineapple juice. He also resisted stamp-dealers' requests to buy in bulk, writing to his brother 'You have no idea what an enormous and profitable affair the stamp trade is.'

Notwithstanding the tasty gum, the stamps were ill received by the Sharif, for his chosen mosque was rejected, as was his suggested inscription – 'The Government of the Sherifate [sic] of Holy Mecca and its Dominions'. Clearly he had territorial designs. The stamps were issued in late August, but it was not until 18 September 1916, that General Clayton wrote again to his friend, Clive Wigram, enclosing 'a complete set of the new Sheriff's [sic] stamps which are now finished and ready for use'.[57] The delay was caused by 'the whisper of a case of smallpox in the Survey Office where the stamps had been printed'.[58] A member of the staff, believing that 'the Royal tongue would moisten the mucilage of some 400 stamps', boiled the whole batch in a saucepan, so removing the gum and spoiling the stamps.

The King received examples and proofs of all the subsequent issues of Hejaz stamps from Clayton's successor, Colonel Reginald Wingate; they can all be identified in the Collection, including sheets of the 2 piastre, the ¼ piastre and the 20 paras red, which Wingate hoped would 'arrive safely, but in these days of submarine activity one can never be sure'[59] – the last mailboat had been torpedoed off Port Said. The Collection is virtually complete with the whole range of issued stamps, some in the King's chosen blocks of four with plate numbers, and essays. As with Egypt, the King stopped collecting Hejaz in 1922.

The final postscript to the colourful affair rests with the publication of the splendid work, *A Short Note on the Design and Issue of Postage Stamps Prepared by the Survey of Egypt for His Highness Husein Emir Sherif [sic] of Mecca and King of the Hejaz*. It is a remarkable piece of philatelic literature, complete with essays, stamps and details of the design and production. Two hundred copies were printed, and copy Number 3 went to the King with a suitable inscription.

CHAPTER EIGHT

The winter of 1916 was particularly severe, and December the second coldest month in the whole of the twentieth century. Austerity gripped the nation, and no more so than at Buckingham Palace. 'I cannot share your hardships,' George V told his troops, 'but my heart is with you every hour of the day.'[1] His civilian clothes were put away, and he wore only uniform of navy blue or khaki. In London, he rarely went out to dine, and never to the theatre. His only relaxation was the Stamp Room. On one particularly cold day – the coal fires were kept to a minimum – the King noticed Edward Bacon's coat hanging on the back of the door. Bacon, fragile at the best of times, suffered badly from catarrh and the King could see that this thin black garment with silk facings afforded little protection against the biting cold outside and the snow piled high in the streets.

One day a footman appeared in the Stamp Room and told Bacon that His Majesty wanted to see him upstairs in the private apartments. Bacon must have felt apprehensive at the summons and, later, puzzled by the conversation he had with the King, which could quite well have waited until their next meeting. Not long after, Bacon arrived in the stamp room to find a large brown box from Davies and Son, tailors by appointment to His Majesty at that time, with his name on it. It contained a heavy, fur-lined, black worsted coat, with a thick astrakhan collar. Bacon tried it on, and it fitted beautifully – during his audience the King had arranged for his tailor to take the measurements of the inadequate black coat. 'Bacon could never recount this incident without emotion.'[2]

The King also valued his *confrères* in the stamp world, and was saddened at their deaths. Occasionally he attended the opening meetings of the Royal Philatelic Society, London when he displayed some of his material, and would talk to the council, fellows and other members. Some he knew better than others, particularly those on the Expert Committee who came to consult Bacon, and to use the Royal Philatelic Collection for comparison. One such noted philatelist was Leslie R. Hausburg. The King and Hausburg shared an interest in plating and, in particular, in lithographic transfers. Hausburg had a brilliant mind: a noted mathematician, he was *senior optime* in the Cambridge mathematical tripos. He was also a particularly gifted ball-player, being a tennis half-blue and played at Wimbledon, where he lost in the semi-finals of the men's doubles in 1894. He also qualified for the singles in 1902, but did not play in the tournament. After a brief spell in industry, he decided that his private means were sufficient to indulge in travel and serious philately. He also served on the council of the Royal Philatelic Society, London later becoming honorary secretary.

India had always been of particular interest to the King. As early as May 1895, when Duke of York he had shown that part of his collection, the first of many such displays, to the members of The Philatelic Society, London. He had added to his collection during his tour of 1905–1906, even finding time to meet a Mr Wetherell who showed him 'his collection of stamps, which is a very fine one'[3] at the Residency at Bangalore. Shortly after he was home, 8 May 1906, he was proudly showing Tilleard 'all the stamps I brought back from India'.[4] Soon after he attended the International Philatelic Exhibition (see page 93) held that year in London, where he saw Hausburg, the co-organiser and a significant exhibitor – he was showing his collections of South Australia, New Zealand, Victoria, which won a gold medal in its class, and India. His Indian exhibit was the basis of the exceptional collection that Hausburg subsequently sold to the King in 1916.

The King was delighted with this purchase for its completeness in so many areas, and for the many rarities. He and Hausburg were fascinated by bisects, and the King must have been delighted to own the 1855 FOUR ANNA black on a cover to an address in Glasgow from Singapore, and another to Boston, with its diagonally bisected 1860 EIGHT PIES mauve with a

ONE ANNA brown, a FOUR ANNA black and a pair of EIGHT ANNA rose, both of which he remembered from Hausburg's 1906 exhibition. Another good stamp to pass into the Collection was the famous ½ ANNA red Scinde Dawk of 1 July 1852.

The history of that stamp begins in 1841 when General Sir Charles Napier led a British expedition against the province of Scinde (now Karachi, Pakistan), which, despite astounding odds, he captured at the battle of Meeanee in 1843. A classicist, Napier is said to have reported his success with the Latin word '*peccavi*' – 'I have sinned'. He resigned as Governor four years later, and was replaced by Sir Henry Bartle Frere as Chief Commissioner. Immediately Bartle Frere 'was particularly active in the development of public works',[5] like constructing the harbour, but also, by 1 July 1852, founding a postal system. He began by producing a stamp, the first to be issued in Asia. With the assistance of Mr Coffey, the new postmaster, Bartle Frere, established the *dawk*, a Hindi word for 'transport by relays of men and horses, and thence "the mail or letter post"',[6] with the prepaid rate within the province of one anna per half *tola* in weight – a tola was 180 grains troy, the weight of a rupee (quarter of an ounce or 6 grams). The only letters exempt from the charge were those from soldiers, sepoys and policemen to their commanding officers or subordinates.

There were three issues, red, white and blue, of the single design of a stylised merchant's mark of the East India Company – 'a heart-shaped device divided into three segments in each of which was one of the letters E, I, C. Above this was the figure 4, and at the foot the value ½ ANNA. The whole was enclosed in a circular garter containing the inscription SCINDE DISTRICT DAWK.'[7] The design was embossed on either a wafer, or on wove and laid paper in the three colours. The most successful was the blue, printed and embossed on nearly white paper to give a 'cameo' effect with the 'design raised in colour-less relief on a coloured ground',[8] while the other two, the white and the red, were monochrome. There is a possibility that they were produced individu-ally, as some examples have faint blue registration lines drawn on the paper, and the Collection holds an example of the ½ ANNA blue and a used pair of the ½ ANNA white and another on piece. The white was the least successful of the three as it was difficult to see on the white paper, while the rarest is the

India: 1854–55 HALF ANNA, blue with the bottom margins 'Lithographed under the Superintendence of Captain H. L. Thuillier, by H. M. Smith, Surveyor General's Office, Calcutta May 1854'.

red: it was particularly brittle and cracked in use. The stamps were finally withdrawn by order of the Governor of Bombay in October 1854.

It was soon clear from the success of the Scinde stamps that there should be a national postal system in India. In 1853, locally engraved essays were produced, some of which are in the Collection, but it was soon realised that this was not the way forward as production was so slow, and that a specialist London stamp printer should be employed for the new issue. Meanwhile, Captain Henry Landor Thuillier (amazingly named after his brother-in-law, the Welsh romantic poet Walter Savage Landor) was experimenting with printing stamps on the lithographic presses at the Surveyor General's Office in Calcutta. He was involved in the Great Survey of India, so was well practised in printing maps in colour and thus his stamps proved very successful. He started with four denominations – HALF ANNA, ONE ANNA, TWO and FOUR ANNAS. The Collection holds, among many other examples, a fine strip of sixteen of the HALF ANNA in blue with the bottom margins inscribed 'Lithographed under the Superintendence of Captain H. L. Thuillier, by H. M. Smith, at the Surveyor General's Office, Calcutta May 1854'.

In 1922, the King was awarded the Tilleard Medal by the Royal Philatelic Society, London for his display of the FOUR ANNAS.

Thuillier was certainly competent in all aspects of surveying– if he had been Surveyor General of India when the tallest mountain in the world was

India: 1854–55 FOUR ANNAS, blue and pale red on piece, error – head inverted. George V was awarded the Tilleard Medal for his display of four of this issue.

The Tilleard medal was awarded to George V in 1922.

measured, it would have been called Mount Thuillier rather than Mount Everest. Thuillier printed the three lowest denominations in a single colour, but when it came to the FOUR ANNAS, he decided to produce it in two colours. This, of course, meant two separate operations, one for the frame in one colour, and another for the head. Copper dies were engraved locally, then the images laid down on two lithographic stones by way of lithographic ink and transfer paper. There were twelve stamps to a stone, in three rows of four. As exact registration was obviously needed to place the head correctly in the centre of the frame, a series of wavy lines, with attractive rosettes where they crossed, were added, along with a similar inscription on the HALF ANNA sheet in the margin. Head, lines and inscription were printed in blue after the red ink, used to print the frame, had dried. The paper was yellowish-white, with a watermark of the arms of the East India Company.

In the main, all went well with the two printings done by hand, but occasionally the sheet was put in back to front for the second printing, which meant that the heads (not the frames) were inverted. It is known that at least four sheets of twelve 'Inverted Heads' FOUR ANNAS were printed, probably more. A pair was found in Southampton on an envelope in a bundle of miscellaneous correspondence bought by Stanley Gibbons in 1899. This FOUR ANNAS Inverted Head was cancelled with a diamond of dots obliteration. As they were printed back to front, the heads and frames obviously do not marry up numerically. This example was Frame setting position 5, Head 8. However, when no buyer for the entire cover could be found, the stamps were cut out and trimmed. One was sold to H. J. Duveen, the other bought by Hausburg, who exhibited it in the 1906 International Philatelic Exhibition. It then passed to George V with the rest of the Hausburg Indian Collection. A second Inverted Head, (Frame position 2, Head 11) passed into the Collection some time after it was shown at the Royal Jubilee Exhibition in 1935.

Over the years, Hausburg sold George V odd items for unknown sums – either the current book value or, more likely, what he had paid to a dealer when it was surplus to his exacting requirements. Ill health prompted him to disperse some of his other collections, including the New South Wales proofs, which went to the King, with selections from his Queensland and

South Australia. Hausburg died in 1917, aged just forty-five. His executors sold the remainder of his collections to Thomas William Hall – the same Hall whose Fiji collection had been bought by the King five years earlier.

Hall was a remarkable philatelist, despite poor eyesight and colour-blindness. He, too, was well known to the King, being Chairman of the Expert Committee of the Royal Philatelic Society, London (also President 1923–29) and editor of the *London Philatelist*. They often exchanged items, particularly relating to New Zealand. Hausburg always wanted George V to have his collection of Victoria, and Hall made his offer to the executors on the understanding that the King should have it. It was a truly remarkable study collection, virtually complete, and therefore an extremely good amalgam-ation, for 'its late owner had been not only a student and a master in reconstructing the settings of the lithographed and stereotyped stamps',[9] but also in the reconstruction of some of the early issues. Practically all of Hausburg's material was first rate as he 'had a more critical eye than most of his contemporaries in detecting what was really unused. There are very few specimens, which can be proved to have come from his volumes, that can be suspected of having been cleaned'.[10] The King would have known exactly what was in the Victoria collection, for over the years Hausburg had published his findings extensively, giving examples from his own material.

Although the King had a large disposable income (even after he had handed over £100,000 of his savings to the Treasury to help the war effort) he liked a bargain as well as the next collector. If he bought one stamp at its market value, and another example of the same stamp 'for a song', he had them mounted together and took great delight in telling how he had come by his bargain. On occasion, he would acquire something relatively cheaply, that later became extremely valuable. One such stamp was a great rarity, the 1847 imperforate ONE PENNY red, B-blank from Plate 77 bought from Charles Nissen, the King's favoured dealer, for just eleven guineas on 26 October 1917. This Penny

Great Britain: 1841–47 imprimatur of ONE PENNY red, registered on 12 January 1848 from Plate 77B, after the B-blank error was corrected.

Red was exactly the same design as the Penny Black – the colour was changed due to the Treasury obsession with lost revenue from cleaned stamps (see page 15). When Plate 77 was being prepared, as the 'siderographist' (literally one who engraves plates) added the check letters to the bottom left- and right-hand squares, he failed to punch in the letter A in the right-hand corner of the first stamp in the second row, that is, row B so leaving it blank; it is known as the 'B-blank error'. This error was discovered in January 1848 by Edwin Hill, inspector of postage stamps at Somerset House and brother of Rowland Hill. He immediately wrote to the printers, Bacon, Perkins and Petch, and demanded that they insert the missing letter A into the blank square. The new plate was registered on 12 January 1848 as Plate 77B. The 'B-blank' specimen in the Collection, one of no more than a score, is used, but there is also a fine unused example of the same stamp from Plate 77B.

Great Britain: 1841 ONE PENNY rose red from Plate 77. It is known as the B-blank error.

By chance, another Great Britain rarity, also in the Collection, comes from Plate 77. This one is also a ONE PENNY rose red, but from the 1858–79 issue, when it was decided that check letters should be in all four corners instead of just the lower ones. Another innovation at that time was the addition of the plate number inserted in the network at each side of the design. The original Plates 69 and 70 of that issue were faulty and discarded. The next few were

Great Britain: 1858–79 ONE PENNY rose red, Plate 77, unused.

perfect, the first, Plate 71, being registered on 14 March 1861 and the last, Plate 225, on 31 December 1878. The Collection holds two imprimaturs from each registered plate. However, Plates 75 and 77 were defective and never registered or lodged with Somerset House, although one or two sheets of Plate 77 were printed and the stamps issued in the normal way. Although no example of Plate 75 has come to light, there are nine specimens (four unused and five used) of Plate 77, unused AB is in the Collection.

The Royal Philatelic Collection contains much that is truly rare, and it is frustrating not to be able to identify their sources. One such interesting rarity is the 'OP:PC error'. In 1860, 10,000 sheets of the new THREE HALFPENCE stamp were printed for the increased postal rates for carrying newspapers. But the new rate was not sanctioned by Parliament, and the stocks were subsequently destroyed. But, as so often happens in philately, a few specimens of this rosy-mauve stamp leaked out of the system and into collectors' hands, including several to the Royal Philatelic Collection (it also holds the Perkins, Bacon essay of the stamp). Ten years later, in 1870, the same THREE HALFPENCE denomination was successfully introduced, in rose-red, using the original 1860 Plate 1, as well as the new Plate 3. It was then noticed that there was a curious error on Plate 1. The third stamp, that is C, on the 16th or P row of the block, should have been lettered CP:PC was in fact OP:PC. There has been much speculation as to how the error occurred, but most likely the siderographist first put the C in reverse, then tried to rectify his mistake by punching the square again, that time with the C the right way round but making it into an O. Apart from the two OP:PC errors, the Collection holds

Great Britain:
1873–80 2½ d
rosy-mauve error –
LH:FL as opposed
to LH:HL.

many examples of both printings, and therefore both colours as well. The rosy-mauve strip of three in the Collection was thought to be unique, but others have since come to light. Errors fascinated the King, but more for the history behind them than for their rarity value. He bought them as and when they became available, like the used and an unused examples of the LH:FL (instead of LH:HL) error on the 1873–80 rosy-mauve 2½d Plate 2 issue.

In essence, a complete collection of mid-Victorian issues of Great Britain is extremely difficult to acquire by comparison with some of the Colonial countries, for although the 'home-grown' rarities tend to lack the allure of their Empire counterparts, they are much more scarce and therefore harder to find, and thus very expensive. The most sought-after rarities of Great Britain are termed 'abnormals', and were another of George V's abiding interests and great successes. These abnormals began in the usual way with the finished plate ready for the press. First an imprimatur sheet was printed off, usually followed by five further sheets. The imprimatur sheet was then registered and kept imperforate in the archives of the Inland Revenue Stamp Office at Somerset House. Some of the five extra sheets were then perforated, and issued along with the rest of the issue.

Very occasionally the stamp was not issued – like the 1865–67 issue, NINE PENCE straw printed from Plate 5 (see page 173) – or the issue was so long delayed after registration that the original colour was changed. So if the stamps from the five sheets were the only ones to be printed from that plate, they became very rare indeed and were known as 'abnormals'. The Royal Philatelic Collection is studded with them.

Typical of the abnormals is the THREE PENCE 1862–64 rose, known as the 'threepence secret dots' from the white dots that were included in the design. One of the sheets from this faulty Plate 3 was perforated, somehow went into stock and was issued in the normal way. One of these, BF, is in the Royal Collection. From the same 1862–64 issue is the bistre 'NINEPENCE Hair Lines' from Plate 3, so called from the fine, uncoloured hair lines across the outer squares with the check letters. Of the seventy known examples, only ten are unused. One, DC, is in the Collection, along with a used example, RB. In a similar vein, the ONE SHILLING deep green, again the 1862–64 issue, also has hair lines across the outer angles of the check letter boxes, and although registered 16 June 1862 it was never perforated officially. The Collection holds a fine example, AA unofficially perforated 14, together with one imprimatur imperforate example, SF, and an imprimatur pair AK/AL, one of only two known.

A later issue, 1867–80, also contained an abnormal, the SIX PENCE mauve from Plate 10, registered 1 April 1869 but, again, never put to press. There are only ten known examples, all used, one DA being in the Collection. Then there is the FOUR PENCE vermilion, Plate 16 (1873–80), also rare, with the Collection holding one used example, EJ, of eight known, while the FOUR PENCE sage green from Plate 17, was registered on 30 July 1877 but issued three years later in grey-brown, but not before a few of the sage green had found their way onto the market, with one example, AD postmarked Bradford, in the Collection.

Just when it was thought that all the abnormals were known, another was discovered in 1915 – the ONE SHILLING green Plate 14 (1873–80). The King instructed Bacon to find it for him, and he eventually came up with a fine example, AL postmarked Greenock along with other examples of the imprimaturs. These are among the cream of the Great Britain rarities, and are

Great Britain: 1862–64 THREE PENCE rose.
An 'abnormal' known as the 'threepence
secret dots' from the white dots that
were included in the design.

Great Britain: 1867–80 SIX PENCE mauve
from Plate 10, used, registered 1 April 1869
but never put to press.

Great Britain: 1862–64 ONE SHILLING deep
green imprimatur imperforate corner pair
AK/AL, one of two known, together with a
single SF from this imprimatur sheet, and
the unofficially perforated example AA.

Great Britain: 1873–80
ONE SHILLING green,
Plate 14 AL, abnormal,
postmarked Greenock.

Great Britain: 1867–80
FOUR PENCE
vermilion, Plate 16
EJ abnormal, used.

Great Britain: 1867–80 FOUR
PENCE sage green, Plate 17, AD
abnormal, postmarked Bradford.
It was registered 30 July 1877
but not issued. Three years later
it was issued in grey-brown.

priced as such. It takes someone with great knowledge to appreciate them for their history, rather than their rarity and great price. The King was just such a collector.

In his great work *The Royal Philatelic Collection*, Sir John Wilson lists five pages of Mulready envelopes and caricatures in his catalogue. The finest extant collection put together by Major E. B. Evans was sold to George V in 1917. Evans had served in the Royal Artillery, at one stage in Mauritius, where he also researched the early issues, and Bermuda. On his retirement, he was for many years the editor of *Stanley Gibbons Monthly Journal*. He also wrote a monograph based on his collection of Mulready envelopes (see page 17) and related material, which was first published in 1891. As a collection it is second to none, with examples and errors (like the double printing of a Mulready, possibly the first ever philatelic error), used and unused material. There are also examples of its adaptation for commercial use, such as advertisements for *Whitaker's Almanack* (from 1868), and even a stamp dealer, E. A. Holton, of Boston, Massachusetts (1895).

It is surprising that the Mulready and caricature envelopes appealed so much to the King. Although the Mulreadys formed part of the history of postage stamps, the caricatures can only have distressed him. In the main, the caricatures lampooned authority, which cannot have amused him. There is an element of Whig Party caustic wit about them, explored by political satirists such as George Cruikshank, where John Bull and Britannia, symbols of authority and the nation, are ridiculed, although the target was principally the postal system rather than the nation. In one Britannia is portrayed as a scarecrow, seated on a pig; in another she is inebriated; and depicted in a third as a washerwoman sailing in a washtub drawn by ducks, while a mermaid 'cocks a snook' at her. The Evans' collection included other illustrated envelopes. Some were purely decorative, like the fine Acre envelope published by R. W. Hume of Leith, or their tourism envelope showing a map and scenes within a radius of fifty miles of Ben Nevis and Edinburgh. Some envelopes advocated free trade and a world penny post, others were used for propaganda, such as the anti-slavery movement, or the Temperance Society which graphically illustrated that 'Intemperance is the Bane of Society'.

In the final stages of the war, when the German offensive had faltered, and

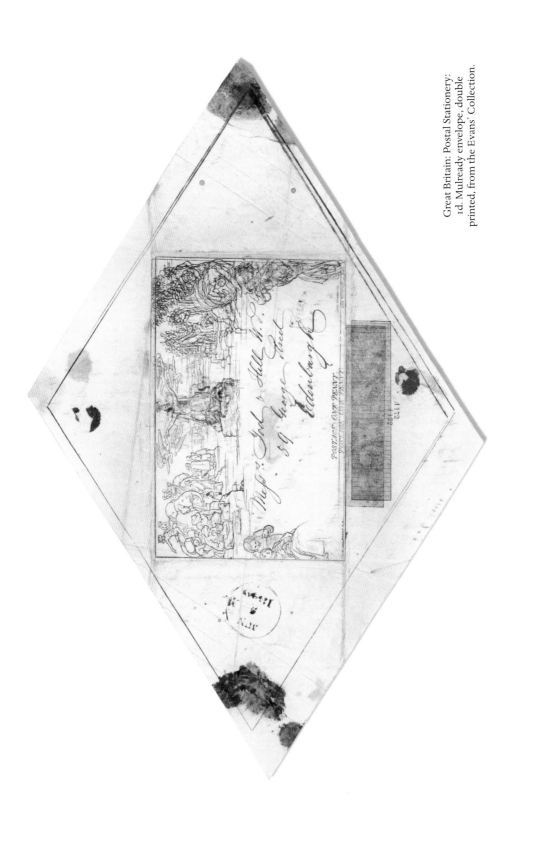

Great Britain: Postal Stationery:
1d. Mulready envelope, double
printed, from the Evans' Collection.

Caricature of the Mulready envelope with Britannia portrayed as a pig in a cover by R. W. Hume of Leith first used in May 1840.

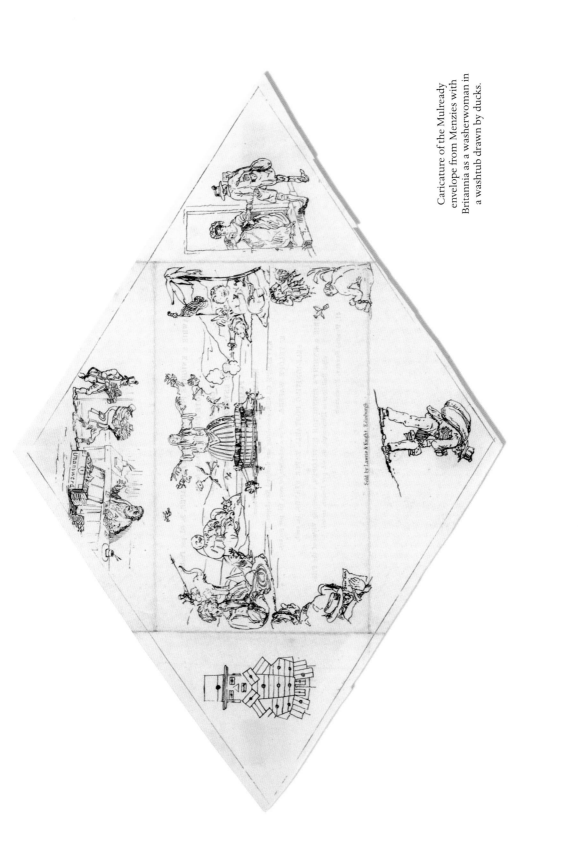

Caricature of the Mulready envelope from Menzies with Britannia as a washerwoman in a washtub drawn by ducks.

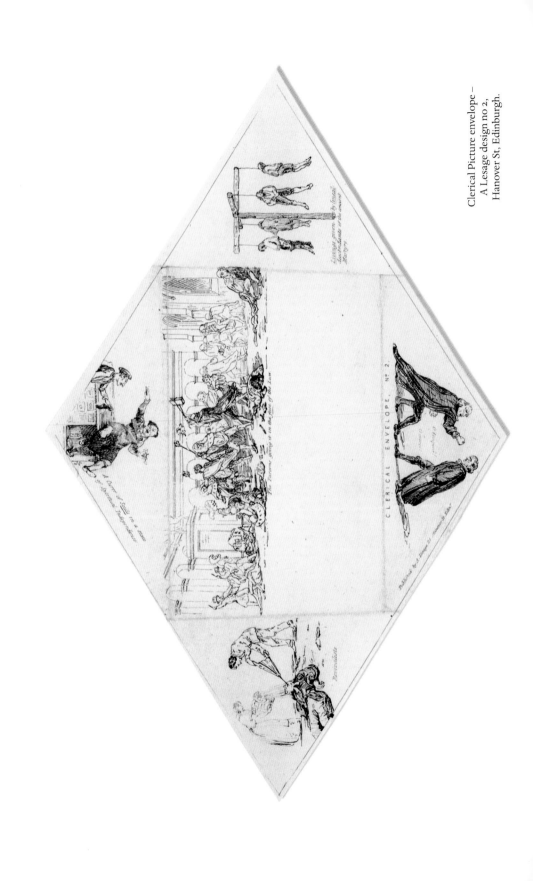

Clerical Picture envelope –
A Lesage design no 2,
Hanover St, Edinburgh.

the Allied armies under Marshal Foch had struck back, a mood of growing optimism spread through the country. Still the King needed a new challenge in the Stamp Room, and the purchase of the Daun collection of Zanzibar in July 1918 provided it. Daun had built up specialist collections of parts of Africa, the Orange River Colony, the Orange Free State and the largest and finest collection of Zanzibar. The King, when Duke of York had been fortunate to cherry pick some of the collection after Daun's death in 1901, but the collection of Zanzibar came to him, seventeen years later, in its entirety. It was quite

Illustrated envelope from the Anti-Slavery movement.

Temperance Society envelope showing that 'Intemperance is the Bane of Society'.

remarkable in its completeness, largely through Daun's work in unravelling the complexities of the overprinting of the 1895 issue of Zanzibar on the stamps of India – which gave hours of study and enjoyment to the King.

By November 1918 the war was over, and the troops began to come home. With the celebrations and the victory parades, a degree of enthusiasm developed for the new age. The War had spawned advances in technology, not least in the development of a more reliable combustion engine and in aviation. The Sopwith Aviation Company had been at the forefront of the manufacture and research of aircraft throughout the war, with such aeroplanes as the Sopwith Camel and the Sopwith Pup that had become the mainstay of the Royal Flying Corps. Sopwith's chief test pilot was a brilliant young Australian called Harry Hawker, who was credited with several design improvements and flying techniques, including how to survive a stall. The

King had personally given him the MBE in October 1918 for his services to aviation, in particular for 'his work in the development of a number of aeroplanes such as the "'1½ Strutter", the "Camel", the "Pup", the "Triplane", the "Dolphin" and the "Snipe"'.[11]

Soon after the war, Lord Northcliffe, the proprietor of the *Daily Mail*, reissued the challenge he had made on 1 April 1913:

VAST *DAILY MAIL* PRIZES

THE AIR PROBLEM

THE WATERPLANE BRITAIN'S BEST WEAPON

£5,000 PRIZE, CIRCUIT OF ENGLAND AND SCOTLAND

£10,000 FLIGHT ACROSS ATLANTIC

> We offer £10,000 to the first person who crosses the Atlantic from any point in the United States, Canada, or Newfoundland to any point in Great Britain or Ireland in seventy-two continuous hours. The flight may be made, of course, either way across the Atlantic.
>
> This prize is open to pilots of any nationality and machines of foreign as well as British construction.

Hawker already held several aviation records, including endurance records. With Thomas Sopwith's backing, a specially designed biplane was prepared with a 12-cylinder 350-horsepower Rolls Royce engine with a top speed of 118 m.p.h., appropriately called the *Atlantic*. For the flight, he had teamed up with Lieutenant Commander Kenneth Mackenzie-Grieve, RN and together with Sopwith they sailed to Newfoundland with the plane, arriving in late March 1919. They planned to take advantage of the next full moon, in mid-April, and would operate the first mail flight across the Atlantic.

Earlier in the year, on 2 January, a new Newfoundland stamp depicting a caribou was issued commemorating the actions of the Newfoundland Contingent (Regiment) during the war with each denomination inscribed with one of their battle honours. To commemorate the flight, the 3 CENT brown, inscribed GUEUDECOURT (a battle honour from the Somme) was chosen to be overprinted with five lines in black: FIRST TRANS-ATLANTIC AIR

POST April 1919. In all, just 200 stamps were overprinted locally by Robinson & Co. Ltd of the offices of the *Daily News*. Sopwith Aviation was to be paid a dollar for carrying 110 letters, ten being 'of an official nature'.[12]

Although Newfoundland was the closest point to Ireland from America, it had the great disadvantage that the weather was generally atrocious at that time of year. By mid-April it had deteriorated badly, and the flight was postponed. Two other aviators, Raynham and Morgan, had crashed on take off, and when news reached them that a US Navy seaplane had made it to the Azores, Hawker decided to leave. The following day, 18 May 1919, at 17.55 GMT, he and Mackenzie-Grieve left the Mount Pearl airfield and headed east.

Newfoundland: 1919, 3 CENTS brown, overprinted in black FIRST TRANS-ATLANTIC AIR POST April 1919. The inscription GUEUDECOURT was a battle honour of the Newfoundland Regiment from the Somme.

All went well for the first four hours. Then the weather closed in as the expected north-easterly wind came straight out of the north. Dense rain-clouds formed and visibility worsened. Disaster struck: the plane developed a fault in the cooling system, which Hawker managed to correct, but not for long. The plane spluttered on at a much-reduced speed, and when daylight came they could see how dire their situation was. They were surrounded by heavy clouds that they could neither fly round nor through. They were blown 150 miles off course: 'Fog, cloudbank and ice formation on the wings added to the dilemma of the trip.'[13] When Hawker dropped from 12,000 to 6,000 feet with no improvement, he decided to try to fly below the clouds. As the plane descended, he switched off the engine to cool it, but the icy air froze the water in the plane's radiator. He struggled to restart the engine, but to no avail. Just as the plane was about to hit the water, the engine spluttered into life and they were saved – for a time.

As they were now 800 miles from Newfoundland and with no hope of reaching Ireland with their faulty engine, Hawker decided to use the remaining power to find a passing ship and ditch the plane. After a two-and-a-half-hour search, they found the Danish tramp steamer *Mary*, bound for Pentland

Firth from the Gulf of Mexico. Hawker, an extremely fine pilot, set the *Atlantic* down on the sea about a mile in advance of the ship and awaited rescue. Pilot and navigator were both saved. But the ship was old, ill equipped, and without radio, so with no news of the ditching, it was believed that the aviators had perished in their attempt. But on the morning of 25 May, news of their rescue was sent by semaphore as the ship passed the Butt of Lewis. It was of the stuff that sells newspapers, and both men received a tumultuous welcome as they travelled south by train.

Three days later Hawker and Mackenzie-Grieve were in London at Buckingham Palace. George V wrote in his diary that he had 'receivd Mr Hawker (Australian) and Lt Comd^r Grieve who started to fly from Newfoundland to Ireland last week. They got 1100 [*sic*] miles across & then had to come down into the sea on account of feed pipe to water tank getting choked, they [were] picked up by the Danish steamer "Mary" & landed at Thurso. We had given them up as lost. I gave them each the Air Force Cross.'[14] This was a singular honour, particularly for Hawker who was a civilian. The Air Force Cross had been struck in June 1918 for 'distinguished airmanship' and courage of those not in action in the newly formed Royal Air Force so, strictly speaking, the King should not have made the awards. However, through Hawker the criterion was changed to make 'individuals not belonging to our air force (whether naval, military or civil) who rendered distinguished service to Aviation in actual flying'[15] eligible for the award. Although they did not make it, Northcliffe was so impressed with Hawker and Mackenzie-Grieve's attempt that he gave them a cheque for £5,000.

But the story does not end there. As the central section of the *Atlantic* had been fitted out like a lifeboat, the plane remained afloat long enough to be picked up by another passing freighter, the American *Lake Charlottesville* which hoisted it aboard and carried it to Falmouth, still with the mailbag. The letters had suffered from the sea-water, but not so badly that they could not be delivered. Of the 200 overprinted stamps, ninety-five were delivered through the post in the normal way. Eighteen were damaged and destroyed, while eleven unused were presented to the likes of the Governor of Newfoundland, Sopwith and George V, who had taken a keen interest in the whole proceedings. The remaining seventy-six examples were sold at twenty-five dollars each in aid of the Permanent Marine Disasters Fund of Newfoundland.

One of these stamps was mounted on a card printed *First Atlantic Air Post 1919* and signed by Hawker, Mackenzie-Grieve, Northcliffe and Thomas Sopwith as well as Captain John Alcock and Lieutenant Arthur Brown, who made it all the way across the Atlantic. The card, a gift from the aviators, was auctioned in aid of the same disaster fund and bought by a Colonel E. S. Halford, who presented it to the King for his collection. Also in the Collection is a letter with the 3 CENT overprint addressed to Lord Stamfordham with a manuscript note 'For His Majesty the King, C. A. H., St John's, 2 p.m. April 12th 1919'. There is also a letter from the Governor General Sir Charles Alex Harris, 'with details of the projected flight and issue of the stamps'.[16] Just to complete the picture, having successfully flown across the Atlantic on 14 June, Alcock and Brown were both knighted by the King at Windsor Castle on 21 June 1919, and the Collection has a card from Windsor Castle signed by them both. By way of a postscript, when Sopwith Aviation collapsed after the war, it was taken over and renamed H. G. Hawker Engineering Company. After Hawker was killed in a plane crash in 1921, Sopwith took over the company renaming it Hawker Aircraft Ltd. As Hawker Siddeley, the company produced the Hawker Hurricane, the mainstay of the Royal Air Force during the London Blitz of 1941 (and far beyond with the Harrier), as Sopwith's planes had been to the Royal Flying Corps in the First World War.

Although George V had 'an ingrained mistrust of flying, whether civil or military',[17] he had a particular liking for aerial postage stamps, which were very much a product of his reign.

Apart from his foreign collection, throughout his life the King parted with a negligible amount of philatelic material, preferring to keep all stamps, good, bad and indifferent, mounted together. But when a fellow collector sold an existing collection (quite often to the King's entire or partial benefit), its importance could be assessed both in quality and monetary terms. As the King so rarely sold, his collection could not be similarly assessed. However, like all very large collections, some areas are far stronger than others, and for George V, the Transvaal was of perpetual interest; over the years he built up one of the finest and most complete collections in existence.

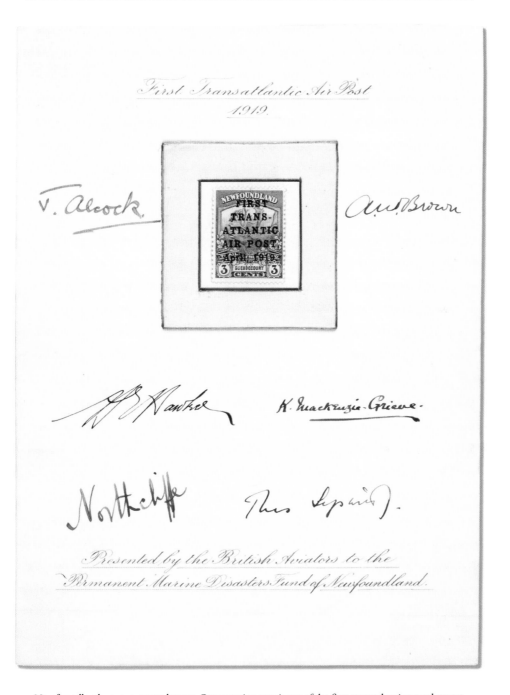

Newfoundland: 1919, 3 CENTS brown. Presentation specimen of the first transatlantic postal stamp, mounted on card with the signatures of the parties concerned – H. G. Hawker and K. Mackenzie-Grieve, pilot and navigator, Lord Northcliffe who put up the prize, Thomas Sopwith who made the 'plane, together with Alcock and Brown, the first men to successfully carry airmail across the Atlantic.

The Transvaal had resulted from the 'Great Trek' of Boers disaffected by the government of the Cape Colony, South Africa, who, between 1835 and 1845, moved north and settled in an area above the river Vaal. With their distaste for authority, they founded numerous independent republics that were eventually recognised by the British under the Sand River Convention of 1852. In time, these republics amalgamated into the Zuid Afrikaansche Republiek, but it was poorly funded and chaotic, with a dire system of communication. There were only twelve post offices linked by native runners to serve the whole republic, no prepaid postage, therefore no stamps. The Transvaal postal system was transformed by Frederick Jeppe, an *émigré* from Mecklenburg-Schwerin who was appointed Postmaster General in 1868. He reorganised the postal system by legislation, then ordered stamps from Adolf Otto through his brother Dr Julius Jeppe in Germany. The first stamps arrived in August 1860, with the plates, presses, matrix dies, rouletting wheel, paper and ink being delivered six months later, along with another batch of printed stamps.

However, the new republic could not come up with the £66 5s to pay for the stamps, so Jeppe sold the bulk of the issue to collectors and dealers; some, particularly the ONE SHILLING value, might have been sold as planned through the post office. There is an almost complete showing of this issue in the Royal Philatelic Collection. The plates made by Otto were used for seventeen years, but as they were made by electrotyping they were susceptible to wear, which at least made the plating of the later issues relatively easy. However, the early plates were pristine, and throw up only minor variations, including, most importantly, 'the inverted subjects which Otto incorporated into two of his plates'.[18]

From his earliest serious collecting days the King would have followed articles on the plating of the various issues, mostly by R. B. Yardley (from whom he bought the Griqualand collection). By the 1890s:

> The stamps of the Transvaal had achieved a remarkable popularity with collec-
> tors, possibly because they presented – and indeed still present – a particularly
> difficult challenge. There were many printings from the same plates to be identi-
> fied, many questions concerning these printings and the stamps themselves to
> be answered and a profusion of forgeries to confuse the unwary. But there was

also a very small number of particularly striking varieties to be competed for. A generation of philatelists deeply committed to plating studies could not have wished for a more fascinating country to espouse.[19]

George V was definitely of their ranks, particularly as Bacon was also an authority on the complexity of the Transvaal issues, and was fascinated by Yardley's first mention, in 1906, of the tête-bêche. The more he read, the more the King would have wanted examples of the error, and, as was so often the case, after a long period of wanting, he acquired several examples in a short space of time. He had bought an unidentified collection of Transvaal in 1915, but his real chance came with the sale of the Worthington Collection in 1919. George H. Worthington was the leading American collector before the war, and the King was able to select what he wanted from it before it was sold. He chose four tête-bêche items, including the unused block of four ONE SHILLING yellow green with a tête-bêche from the 26 April 1870 issue printed on thick, coarse paper. The remainder of the collection was sold to Mr Alfred Lichtenstein, another great American collector. Not long after, on 8 March 1920, Hugo Griebert, 'noted London dealer of German extraction'[20] sold the King

Transvaal: 1870 (1 May – 4 July) ZES (SIX) PENCE, pale ultramarine, imperforate, tête-bêche pair within a block of four from left of sheet, together with the 1870 (1 May) EEN (ONE) SHILLING, yellow green unused in block of four, another pair with a tête-bêche. George V was fortunate in being able to cherry-pick the Worthington Collection before it was sold.

three other tête-bêche in blocks of four, while the eighth Ferrari sale (see page 221) in 1923 produced some more pairs, like the ultramarine SIX PENCE unused vertical pair of 10 May 1870, one of six known. The H. J. Duveen sale also came up with a vertical pair of the 1876 printing of the bright blue SIX PENCE on stout, hard-surfaced paper.

The Collection holds the remarkable proof of a tête-bêche horizontal pair of the ONE SHILLING duty with a four ring target obliteration – the only other one being in the Tapling Collection. Then there is the unused block of four, in dull ultramarine, from the 4 April 1870 printing in Pretoria on thin paper, with one tête-bêche, one of three known examples. Thus, with a total of eight tête-bêche, the Royal Philatelic Collection has the greatest range of varieties of the SIX PENCE and the ONE SHILLING duties. There are also five tête-bêche, from the First British Occupation overprinted V. R. Transvaal, which make the Collection virtually complete in this most difficult of areas. A display of the First Republic and the two occupations was shown to the Royal Philatelic Society, London at their opening meeting of 1925.

George V reigned during one of the greatest upheavals in history. Whole countries were absorbed and new ones created: British military administrations of occupied territories gave way to colonial or national governments, and nowhere was this change so well charted than in the Royal Philatelic Collection.

In 1917–18, the Turks had been driven out of Palestine by the combined forces of the British, the Arab League and the Jewish Legion. A military administration ruled the country until 1920, when a civil government was set up. Britain's representative in Palestine, the High Commissioner of Jerusalem, was none other than the Rt. Hon. Sir Herbert Louis Samuel, who had been Postmaster General in Britain (with one short break) from 1910 to 1916 and had introduced the early stamps of George V's reign. With such vast expertise, it was only natural that he should take an interest in the design and production of the new stamps for Palestine. Nor did he forget the King with whom he had worked so closely in the past. On 12 September 1920, Samuel wrote to him:

A new series of Palestine stamps has just been issued [1 September], of a temporary character, pending the issue of the Mandate, and the definite settlement of the status of the country. I beg to enclose 4 copies of each value, together with copies of a set of rejected proofs containing errors in the Hebrew sur-charge. It has been difficult to find a suitable ink in which to sur-charge the one piastre value, and we have been compelled finally to use silver ink as the only one that would be visible – except gold, which was considered to be unsuitable.

Your Majesty may also be interested in an envelope showing all the various kinds of stamps that were obtainable at Salt at the time of my visit, with an explanation written by an inhabitant of Jerusalem who accompanied me and who is himself a philatelist. I enclose also some photographs that were taken of the sur-charging of the present issue of stamps at the printing office in Jerusalem.[21]

Through Samuel, the Collection holds the complete issue, including the essay of the overprint on the ONE PIASTRE in gold (which was rejected). These joined an already complete collection of Egyptian Expeditionary Forces (EEF) stamps, issued for the British military occupation of Palestine on 10 February 1918 – they were also valid in Lebanon, Syria, Trans-Jordan, parts of Cilicia and north-eastern Egypt. The first EEF stamps were printed by the Survey Department, Egypt, and the issue that Samuel sent to the King were EEF overprinted 'Palestine' in Hebrew, Arabic and English.

Palestine: 1920
FIVE MILLIEMES yellow-orange,
trial overprint in a block of four,
unused. George V received a
constant supply of each issue of
Palestine and Trans-Jordan from
the High Commissioner, Jerusalem,
the former Postmaster General,
Sir Herbert Samuel.

Further Palestine stamps followed in the King's favoured corner blocks of four, together with all the errors Samuel could find. He also saw that the King received the 'series being prepared for Trans-Jordania, with that word in Arabic only, sur-charged on the E.E.F. stamps'.[22] These were sent in October to Lord Stamfordham, with the observation 'I enclose for His Majesty's collection, specimens of the stamps we have issued for use in Trans-Jordania, with an Arabic inscription which is a translation of "East of the Jordan". Stocks do not yet allow the use of the other denominations, but they will be produced in due course'.[23] From then on, the King was supplied with every denomination and issue, right up to 1933.

The first issue for Iraq following the end of the war was produced by Bradbury Wilkinson, who had printed the Turkish pictorial issue of 1914. They used the original plates further surcharging them 'Iraq in British Occupation'. The Collection is remarkably complete, with every issue, mostly represented by corner blocks of four and many errors of the 'Baghdad in British Occupation' issue of 1917 presented to the King by Sir Percy Cox. However, when Iraq became a kingdom, though not fully independent, in 1921 a new issue was proposed. For this a Mrs Garbett, whose husband had served for a time in Iraq when it was still known as Mesopotamia as an assistant to the High Commissioner, was asked to design some of the stamps. The reduced watercolour designs of the 1½ ANNAS, the 2 ANNAS of a winged bull, the 3 ANNAS, and the 1 R – rupee – were largely inspired by the Assyrian and Babylonian sculptures in the British Museum, and were presented to the King. In the corner of each is a monogram MJM, standing for Mrs Garbett's maiden name, M. J. Maynard. The balance of the issue was reproduced from paintings by Miss Edith Cheesman, a local artist.

Queen Mary must have been profoundly grateful to Edward Bacon for she knew that any stamp or stamps that he suggested that she should buy – or more likely that should be bought on her behalf – would be something that the King *really* wanted. Sometimes they were bought and held in reserve for a Christmas or birthday present, like the Niger Coast Protectorate 20/- black surcharge on the ONE SHILLING green of Great Britain of the provisional issue of December 1893, overprinted 'British Protectorate' and 'Oil Rivers' on the bottom. It was thought that only one specimen had been made, but Bacon

Iraq: 1922 original watercolour sketches inspired by the Assyrian and Babylonian sculptures in the British Museum for the 1923–25, 1½ ANNAS, 2 ANNAS, 3 ANNAS and the 1 R[upee] painted by Miss M. J. Maynard.

Niger Coast Protectorate: 1893 (December) 20/- on ONE SHILLING green, black overprint BRITISH PROTECTORATE and OIL RIVERS. This was another instance of Edward Bacon finding a birthday present for Queen Mary to give to George V.

had spotted another in an auction in September 1920 and bought it secretly for the Queen. The stamp was well authenticated by letter. Writing from Old Calabar on 22 December 1893, the then Governor of the Protectorate, Sir Claude Macdonald sent the stamp with a selection of the current surcharged stamps. It was particularly welcome as the King already had the ONE SHILLING green of the same issue overprinted 20/- in black and violet.

The King was insatiable in his desire for stamps. At each appointment of governor or high commissioner, the new incumbent always had an audience with him before leaving for the post. Frequently, the new governor left with more than his good wishes and a handshake, for if he was going to a place where the King had a special interest, he was given a 'shopping list'. The same went for his family and their staff when on tours abroad. One such, Sir Godfrey Thomas B^t, Private Secretary to the Prince of Wales, wrote to his friend, Clive Wigram during a Royal Tour of Australia: 'Before I left London I was given a list of obsolete Queensland stamps which His Majesty desired.

I made friends with the PMG at Melbourne & gave him the list. I now enclose his reply together with an envelope containing those of the stamps which he has been able to supply.'[24] Although the Hon G. H. Wise, Postmaster General, did not have the earlier stamps on the list, 'the 1866 – 4d lilac, 5/- rose, 1875 4d pale yellow', he was able to send out everything the King wanted from the 1881 issue, the '2/- [TWO SHILLINGS] blue, 2/6 [TWO SHILLINGS & SIXPENCE] scarlet, 5/- [FIVE SHILLINGS] yellow brown 10/- [TEN SHILLINGS] reddish brown and 20/- [TWENTY SHILLINGS] rose'.[25] Each is in a block of eight overprinted SPECIMEN in large capitals and filled a gap in the Queensland section of the Collection. It appears that Sir Godfrey took his commission seriously as wherever he landed on the way out, westwards, in particular St Lucia, Samoa and Fiji, he went to the post office and bought the local stamps. One so fanatical about his collection, the King can only have been gratified by such loyalty.

In many ways, George V began collecting at exactly the right time, for not only was there still material to be had, it was available at affordable prices. By the 1920s his collection was such that the addition of another major collection in its entirety would produce so many duplicates that it would not be cost effective. Also at that time, the great collectors of the nineteenth century were disposing of their collections, either through their executors or extreme old age. One such was that of Baron Philip La Renotière Von Ferrari. He was reputed to have the largest accumulation of stamps in the world, even though the term 'Ferrarities' referred to the supposed number of fakes and forgeries within it. The Baron left his collection to the Berlin Postal Museum as he felt that this would most benefit philatelists. However, when he died (of a heart attack while trying to buy a Swiss stamp in 1917) the French government confiscated his collection and sold it piecemeal by auction between 1921 and 1925 for the benefit of the German War Reparations Account. The Royal Philatelic Collection has a good showing of Ferrari: the King minutely examined the catalogues against the 'lots that were most needed, and he missed very few of the stamps he most wanted'.[26] At the first sale he and Bacon settled on four lots, and dispatched his agent, Charles Nissen, to Paris to bid on his behalf. In the early days, both Tilleard and Bacon had used a variety of agents to bid on behalf of the King, but eventually Charles Nissen became their regular one, so much so that he received a royal warrant for his services. The system in the first Ferrari sale was unusual in that lots could only be paid for in cash, and the King had to buy a large amount of French francs. In the event Nissen only acquired one minor lot which seemed incredibly expensive after his fee and the loss in exchanging currency were added to the price. The 'experience displeased the King not a little'.[27] Nissen was more successful in later sales and the Collection is sprinkled with good 'ex-Ferrari' rarities. Some were acquired inexpensively, such as one of two recorded St Helena 1864–80 FOUR PENCE carmine-rose, the error FOUR PENCE surcharge omitted for a mere £42, and the unique imperforate and unused block of four, ONE PENNY carmine-rose, London Print of Queensland, November 1860. Ever with an eye for a bargain, the King was particularly pleased when he was able later to buy some coveted stamp for considerably less money than it had fetched in the Ferrari sale, like those carried off from an executor's sale of the American collector Arthur Hind in 1933. Charles Nissen was sent to bid at the mammoth

St Helena: 1864–80 FOUR PENCE on SIX PENCE carmine-rose, surcharge omitted. An inexpensive purchase from the Ferrari sale.

sale of Hind material; on the first occasion he secured twelve lots, and a dozen more in July 1934.

By 1923, it had become an established tradition that George V would send a display taken from a recently acquired collection to the opening meeting of the Royal Philatelic Society, London and that year he showed a selection of 'the Strait's Settlements stamps of Queen Victoria's reign',[28] with his latest acquisition, the major part of the W. A. Bicknell collection of Strait's Settlements and Native States, along with the unique block of sixty 10 CENTS on 30 CENTS claret of March 1880 that had come from the Ferrari sale. Also on view was another Ferrari gem, a block of forty-nine of the same 10 CENTS on 30 CENTS only these were from the April 1880 issue, a fine platform for Bacon's paper and talk at the meeting.

George V's diary entry for 17 May 1923 reads, perhaps endearingly:

> Arranged all the morning with Bacon my collection of stamps on long tables in picture gallery & at 3.0 I invited about 80 [nearer 100] members of the Royal Philatelic Society & Foreign Philatelists to come and see my collection, I think they were pleased with it.[29]

The visit was in aid of the Fiftieth Anniversary Fund so that a 'suitable home for the [Royal Philatelic] Society may be acquired'.[30] The King and Bacon spread the 150 carefully selected albums on tables in the Picture Gallery at Buckingham Palace, with its glass vaulted ceiling, for the benefit of the fellows, members and overseas visitors to the London Exhibition and Congress. He would have known in advance the guest list, and made his selection according to their particular interests and the specialities in his collection that might interest them. There is no hint in his diary that he *enjoyed* the visit, but he clearly did, for after he had been introduced to the guests he was reported 'most graciously remaining for over an hour conversing and personally pointing out special gems to his admiring guests'.[31] His remark 'I think they were pleased with it', when his philatelic peers were visibly enchanted by him and all they saw, shows a measure of self-doubt, even though he knew that what was on display was of the very best. His modest view of the occasion was in direct contrast to the report in the *London Philatelist*: 'After partaking of tea and light refreshments Members departed, feeling that they had taken part in an epoch-making occasion, which was at the same time one of the most enjoyable and instructive at which they had ever been present.'[32] The King should have been well pleased.

Henry J. Duveen had much in common with both Queen Mary and the King: he was not only an exceptional philatelist but also an antiques dealer of the highest calibre with a particular interest in Oriental porcelain. With his elder brother Sir Joseph, the Duveen brothers were the foremost dealers in London, New York and Paris, and it was this successful enterprise that supported a stamp collection second only to that of Thomas Tapling. What is more, Edward Bacon 'had assisted and advised Duveen in the formation of his splendid general collection of classic stamps'[33] and had mounted it for him. He knew exactly what was in the Duveen Collection, and consequently what would enhance the Royal Philatelic Collection. Shortly before Henry Duveen died on 16 January 1919, he had given his famous collection to his wife and their son, Commander Sir Geoffrey Duveen RNVR, and on Henry's death, it was given to C. J. Phillips to dispose of, the proceeds going towards the building of the Royal Ear Hospital in London.

Bacon knew Phillips as he had dealt with him over many years when he was managing director of Stanley Gibbons, and, volume after volume was sent to the Palace for inspection. Some of the collections, like Mauritius and Canada, were kept entire, and as the King's own holding was so good in those areas, there was little point in him buying them. However, as a special favour, he had first option on all of the others. The courtesy did not stop there: Mrs Duveen and her son allowed the King to buy stamps of great rarity and value at much-reduced prices.

The King must have been delighted: at a stroke, he had landed some of the world's most desirable stamps, which he must have despaired of ever owning, *and* at bargain prices. The list is indeed impressive, some of it unique like the pair of unused corner yellow green HALF PENNY of Barbados 1860, or just plain rare, such as the 1865 FIVE CENTS rose imperforate of Vancouver Island and the FOUR CENTS British Guiana of 1856, black on blue sugar paper on cover. Also chosen was the Ceylon 1857–59 FOUR PENCE dull rose, rare, expensive and beautiful. In the Collection from the same source is a block of four ONE PENNY red, Sydney Views of New South Wales from Plate 1. Imagine the

King's pleasure at being able to buy an unused block of four (9, 10, 14 and 15) of Plate 1 (thus no clouds) of this 1850 ONE PENNY red from Duveen, and to find that his existing position no. 13 was originally joined to this block. Then there was another Duveen gem, the 1856–57 no watermark dull emerald TWO PENCE unused of Tasmania, which had been on the King's wants list for the longest while, particularly as he had the other two denominations – the pale brick-red ONE PENNY and the blue (shades) FOUR PENCE.

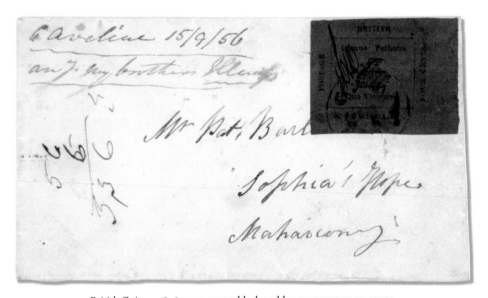

British Guiana: 1856 FOUR CENTS black on blue sugar paper, on cover.

Vancouver: 1865 FIVE CENTS rose unused.

New South Wales: ONE PENNY red.

Ceylon: 1857–59 FOUR PENCE dull rose.

Barbados: 1860 halfpenny yellow-green.

Examples of purchases of important stamps from the Duveen Collection.

With a collection of Western Australia as good as the King's it must have been galling for him to be wanting one of the great rarities of all time for so long, but with the pick of the Duveen Collection, he acquired the stamp that had eluded him: the so-called 'Inverted Swan', the FOUR PENCE blue of 1854–55. The King had several examples of the stamp in its correct form, including a sheet of 240 from the Crawford Collection, various creased transfer varieties, including one with the tops of the letters of AUSTRALIA cut off, this being one of two known examples.

In fact, it is not the swan that is inverted but the frame, which is upside down. This phenomenon is all the more extraordinary as unlike, say, the Indian FOUR ANNAS with the inverted blue head in a red surround (see page 196), this stamp is printed in just one colour, thus making it the fault of the lithographic artist, rather than the printer's error. By 1853, it had been decided

Western Australia: 1854–55 FOUR PENCE blue, error frame inverted, used.
Known as the 'inverted swan', this great rarity came from the Duveen Collection.

that Western Australia should have its own stamps, and a postage rate of one penny was fixed for letters under half an ounce. For these, Perkins, Bacon was commissioned to come up with a design that was to include *Chenopsis atratus*, the black swan indigenous to the area and a reference to Western Australia's origins as the Swan River Settlement. By late August the plate was ready and one million ONE PENNY stamps were printed and sent out to Perth with the plates, printing press, swan watermarked paper and ink. The stamps were neither perforated nor gummed and each post office was supplied with a pair of scissors, a pot of gum and a brush. Not long after their arrival, it was seen that higher denominations were also required, and it was decided to print locally a FOUR PENCE blue and a ONE SHILLING brown. As the manufacture of metal plates was beyond the fledgling Colony, the job was given to the government lithographer, a Mr Sampson in the surveyor-general's department. The process of building up the stone was well within his capability, but the process required skill and patience. For this, a transfer was taken from the ONE PENNY plate and two blocks of 60 (12 × 5), one each for the FOUR PENCE and ONE SHILLING values, laid down on a lithographic stone. The ONE PENNY frames were removed with an acid brush. A lithographic stone containing one frame design of each value was prepared, perhaps on transparent transfer paper, and placed around the central swan design one at a time to complete the intermediate stones. Four transfers were then taken of the intermediate stone of sixty and laid down, side by side, to produce the final printing stone of 240 impressions.

The transfers were so delicate that the printer could not even touch them with his fingers. The whole process was intricate and incredibly time-consuming. Consequently, it is not surprising that an error was made in one of the transfers on the FOUR PENCE stone: on the first stamp of the eighth row the frame was placed upside down. As the same transfer was used four times on the stone, four errors occurred on each sheet. When the error was spotted, some time after the stamps were issued around August 1854, the frame was replaced. It took some time, however, for collectors to notice it, the first mention appearing in the *Philatelist* on 1 April 1868: 'There is a 4d. octagonal blue known, with the swan upside-down.'[34]

There are just fourteen known examples of the 'Inverted Swan,' the

Collection holding an example, 'Cut square. Used. A very fine specimen'.[35] It was first recorded as being in the collection of a Reverend P. E. Raynor, who sold it to F. W. Ayer, the great American collector from Bangor, Maine, who in turn sold it to Henry Duveen.

The final set of stamps that passed from the Duveen Collection into the Royal Philatelic Collection was a selection of Cape of Good Hope – the incredibly famous error of ONE PENNY blue joined to a FOUR PENCE blue, se-tenant of February–April 1861 used on piece, and the ONE PENNY and the error FOUR PENCE red se-tenant on a cover together with a pair of Perkins, Bacon ONE PENNY. But to begin at the beginning.

Although a postal system had been mooted as early as 1846 in the Cape, no action was taken until 1852 when it was found that it would be 'a most desirable improvement which would be carried into effect at the earliest possible date'. The Board of Enquiry further found that:

> in order to obviate errors in sorting letters or stamping, we would suggest the adoption of a device and shape so different from those of the English postage stamps as to catch the eye at a glance, and we would propose that of a triangle with the figure of 'Hope' with the words 'postage', 'Four Pence', 'Cape of Good Hope' on the surrounding border, all on engine-turned field … We are disposed to recommend the triangle as most convenient, economical and distinctive. [36]

A sketch of the proposed stamp was made by the surveyor-general, Mr Charles Bell, and sent to Perkins, Bacon, with a request to print 50,000 ONE PENNY stamps for newspapers and 100,000 FOUR PENCE, the internal postage rate for letters under half an ounce. Perkins, Bacon then designed the stamp from Bell's drawing, adding the same engine-turned background that had been used on the PENNY BLACK and TWO PENCE blue of Great Britain, and the ONE PENNY value was engraved on to a mild-steel plate by William Humphreys. (The Collection holds a die proof of this in black on India paper.) This die (with its impressions) was hardened, and transferred on to two soft roller dies – the images are now standing proud. Humphreys took one, removed the ONE PENNY script, and hardened both roller dies. Taking the ONE PENNY roller die, he made two impressions on to a second flat die, positioning the bases of the triangles virtually parallel. The other die (the one with the value removed) was similarly transferred to a third flat die, and the FOUR PENCE value engraved in the blank space. Both pairs of dies were then hardened, and it was these that were used to make the ONE PENNY and FOUR PENCE plates. There was a minute difference in the dies, which when identified became known as Die A and Die B. These dies of two stamps were then transferred 120 times to make up sheets of 240 stamps. Again, the Collection holds plate proofs in black of both values.

The two values were printed, the ONE PENNY in shades of brick-red and brown-red, the FOUR PENCE in shades of deep blue to light blue. The paper was handmade wove and watermarked with a double row of anchors, the early issues being on blued paper. This bluing was caused by the chemical reaction of the prussiate of potash (potassium cyanide) added to the ink to prevent cleaning and the alum in the paper when wetted before both printing and gumming.

At last the stamps were ready and shipped to the Cape. They were distributed in good time to be issued on 1 September 1853. The Collection has a fine showing of both values, particularly the unused ONE PENNY brick-red on deeply blued paper and the FOUR PENCE deep blue on less blued paper.

Cape of Good Hope: 1853 FOUR PENCE deep blue, paper slightly blued, unused.

Sir John Wilson in his catalogue of the Royal Collection classified 'Wmk anchor Imperf 4d black'.[37] This is the triangular FOUR PENCE black, one of the most controversial stamps in existence. There are many different explanations of this variety. Some say that it was an issued stamp, and that the eleven surviving examples are all genuine, others would have it that it is an error of colour, or merely a deep-blue that has been heavily oxidised. It might even have been from a proof sheet and issued when stock ran short – the extant examples appear to have had an obliteration removed. Another explanation from a Mr Hirsch, a connection of the current Governor, was that the FOUR PENCE black was issued at the end of December 1861 as a form of mourning following the death of Prince Albert, consort to Queen Victoria. Hirsch maintained that:

> The Post Master General, at the instigation of the Governor of the Cape, had 300 stamps of the 4d. black to replace, for a few days, the blue stamps of the same value, solely with the object of having a token of mourning for the dead Prince. Eight days later these stamps were withdrawn from circulation and only the blue ones remained in currency.[38]

Of the 300 stamps, only eighty were reputedly sold, and it is thought that Hirsch's unused examples came from these. The remainder were supposedly destroyed. After the Collection acquired its copy in 1924, Bacon took a closer interest and pronounced that although Hirsch's story was flawed, there might be elements of truth in it. He thought it most likely that the Governor and the Postmaster General had discussed the possibility of such an issue, and dismissed it as impractical. The Postmaster General then found some proofs printed in black, and gave them to the Governor for his personal use, hence the source of Hirsch's stamp and story.

Cape of Good Hope: 1 September 1853, FOUR PENCE black, one of the most controversial stamps in existence.

The postal system worked well in the Cape of Good Hope, and stamps arrived at regular intervals from Perkins, Bacon. As the second issue, 1855–58, was still imperforate, the Standard Bank rouletted its own supply, usually the new denominations such as the rose-lilac SIX PENCE and ONE SHILLING yellow green. The roulettes were easily forged, and the Collection holds an example of the SIX PENCE genuine and the ONE SHILLING fake. In January 1860, the Postmaster General found that stocks were running low and immediately ordered another printing from Perkins, Bacon. These were duly dispatched, and although the stamps arrived in the Colony in mid-June 1860, the bill of lading did not, and the stamps lay with the Union Steamship Company for more than a year. By February 1861, the stock of the FOUR PENCE was exhausted and the ONE PENNY nearly so. After taking legal advice, the Postmaster General commissioned the Government printer, Saul Solomon, to produce the replacement stamps as quickly as possible.

Solomon had recently installed a new press for printing by the stereotype process. A die for each value had been produced on steel by a local engraver, C. J. Roberts, and a cast taken in plaster of Paris. After hardening, the mould was filled with molten metal. This 'stereo' or *cliché*, the philatelic term, was then replicated as many times as needed, each one mounted on sheets of strawboard, then glued to blocks of wood – hence the term 'woodblock', as opposed to a 'woodcut', which is entirely different.

For the first provisional issue, twenty-four FOUR PENCE *clichés* were put together and around a thousand sheets printed. At some time during the printing, one of the *clichés* was damaged on the bottom left hand corner, retouched *in situ*, leaving several irregular lines in the bottom right-hand corner. The Collection has two fine pale milky-blue used examples of this great rarity. These, and the first 150 sheets, were put on sale on 28 February 1861. In the meantime, a plate of sixty-four of the ONE PENNY *clichés* was put together and printed, 128 stamps (two panes of sixty-four) to a sheet. All was going so well that it was decided to step up production by making a new

Cape of Good Hope: 28 February 1861,
FOUR PENCE retouched *in situ*, hence the several
irregular lines in the bottom right hand corner.
As the *clichés* were stuck to strawboard,
they were known as 'woodblocks'.

230

plate with sixty-four of the FOUR PENCE *clichés*. Some of the original *clichés* were found to be serviceable and reused. Unfortunately (or fortunately for collectors), one of these FOUR PENCE *clichés* was included in the ONE PENNY plate, and a ONE PENNY *cliché* was included in the FOUR PENCE plate creating one error in each pane of sixty-four. So, on each sheet one stamp was printed in the wrong colour – the ONE PENNY in shades of blue and the FOUR PENCE in shades of vermilion, and it was these very stamps, on piece and cover, that the King was able to buy from Mrs Duveen and her son.

There are only four known examples of the error ONE PENNY blue and FOUR PENCE in se-tenant pair and the King's example was without doubt the finest. The first recorded owner was W. W. Blest, who sold the cover to Sir William Avery. His collection was bought by the London dealer W. H. Peckitt in 1909, who sold it to Henry Duveen. The other Duveen gem, one of five known, is the ONE PENNY and error FOUR PENCE vermilion on cover with the Perkins, Bacon pair of ONE PENNY. This is addressed to 'H. Crump Esqr.

Cape of Good Hope: 1861 FOUR PENCE vermilion error of colour in pair with ONE PENNY, used on entire.

Grahams Town' and is postmarked 'Bedford Ja[nuary] 12 1861' – interestingly dated a full six weeks before the issue of the first 'woodblocks'. The cover was bought by a Mr D. S. Bairstow, who passed it on to Stanley Gibbons, who in turn sold it to an Austrian collector, Herr Ludwig Schwartz. It was subsequently acquired by Duveen when the Schwartz collection was dispersed.

The February–April 1861 issue was reprinted in 1883 and in the Collection there are examples of the ONE PENNY red and the FOUR PENCE blue. By way of a postscript, in mid-1941 Mr A. A. Jurgens, a well-known collector, wrote to the secretary of the Governor General of Pretoria from Cape Town:

> On the 26th November 1940 I made reprints in colour from the original Woodblock plates in the possession of the South African Museum, Cape Town in order to illustrate the 1861 Woodblock issue in the collection of Cape Postal History, housed in the Museum, which I have donated in memory of my late daughter.
>
> After these prints had been made and owing to the very unsatisfactory way in which the plates had been defaced by the Colonial Treasury before being handed over to the Museum for safe custody in 1901, I received permission to have them properly defaced so they could not be made misuse of at any future date. It is now impossible to obtain a print without the white line showing through each of the stereos.
>
> The historical nature of these prints will reveal itself to His Excellency when I mention the fact that the only other time that prints therefrom in colour were made after the printing in 1861 by Saul Solomon was in 1883 when the official reprints were made.
>
> Permission was obtained by me to make an additional set with the object of presenting it for inclusion in His Majesty's Collection.[39]

Jurgens had first offered the reprints to Sir John Wilson, George VI's Keeper of the Royal Philatelic Collection, but was told to write again through the Governor General. All parties were delighted with the 'interesting historical addition' to the Collection.

After decades of serious collecting, it was almost like a reward to George V when he acquired the rarities that had eluded him for so many years. One such highly desirable stamp was the circular TWO CENTS rose of British Guiana, the

1850–51 issue commonly known as 'Cotton Reels' from their resemblance to the printed labels at the end of a cotton reel. On 5 November 1924 the King bought from Theodore Champion, a French dealer living in London, 'a vertical pair placed horizontally on entire letter, addressed to "Mr. Job Collier, Victoria Village, East Coast". Postmarked DEMERARA OC 24 1851'.[40]

The Royal Philatelic Collection of British Guiana stamps is remarkably complete, not least with 'Cotton Reels'. On 15 June 1850, the *Royal Gazette, Demerara and Essequibo* carried a notice that a mail service to carry letters from Georgetown 'upcountry' would begin on 1 July. The prepaid postage rates varied with the distance the letter was carried, FOUR CENTS the minimum distance, TWELVE CENTS the furthest, and EIGHT CENTS for anything in between. These, the simplest of all stamps, were produced by the *Royal Gazette* (after 10 May 1851 the *Official Gazette*) in Georgetown with the value followed by the word *'cents'* and 'BRITISH GUIANA' in roman serified capital

British Guiana: 1850–51 TWO CENTS rose. These early stamps are familiarly known as 'Cotton Reels' from their resemblance to the labels on the ends of cotton reels.

letters. The letters and numbers were inserted into a tube made up of brass printer's rules soldered together into a somewhat crude circle. The stamps were all printed in black, and to differentiate the three denominations, various coloured paper was used for each – shades of yellow to orange for the FOUR CENTS, green for the EIGHT CENTS, while the TWELVE CENTS varies between blue and indigo. As it was simplicity itself to forge these stamps, they were individually initialled by one of five members of the post-office staff. Fine examples of each colour variation, value and initials, amounting to twenty in all, are in the Collection.

But however fine and rare the three higher denominations of 'Cotton Reels' are, the finest of them all is the British Guiana TWO CENTS rose. Such was the success of the post to the interior that a simple house-to-house delivery service was set up for the few streets in Georgetown, and a TWO CENTS stamp, printed on rose paper, was issued on 1 March 1851, eight months after the others. The local delivery was not a success and soon withdrawn, so the stamp is extremely rare. There are only ten known examples, of which six are in pairs – the King bought a pair on cover, both initialled J. B. S(mith), the clerk of the Colonial Department of the Post Office. In fact, both stamps had been repaired. After delivery to Mr Job Collier in 1851, the envelope was found in 1888 and bought by a Mr E. C. Luard, a local philatelist operating in the right place at the right time – the first known pair. The cover was purchased in 1890, with the rest of Luard's collection, by the renowned dealers Pemberton, Wilson & Co. and sold to Baron Ferrari in the same year. When it was exhibited in May 1890 at the London Philatelic Exhibition there was a wedge-shaped bite out of the right hand stamp and a small nick to the left-hand side of the other. Ferrari would have arranged for it to be cleverly repaired by matching the wove paper and drawing in the missing lines and letters.

It was always said that George V would have liked to own the unique British Guiana ONE CENT magenta, reputedly the rarest stamp in the world – it is, of course, no rarer than any other unique stamp. But he always considered it an 'ugly thing' and of such poor quality that he did not bid for it when he had the chance in the third Ferrari sale in Paris. It was bought by Arthur Hind when it failed to reach its reserve in London on resale. However, a large proportion of the colossal figure of £7,343 Hind paid 'must be allotted to the pleasure of owning a highly publicised and unique item',[41] which was certainly not the King's form. It was, however, par for the course for Hind: he once wrote that his 'possession of the unique 1 Cent British Guiana … has changed me, philatelically, from an almost unknown modest collector to an almost best known prominent collector'.[42] However, in October 1938, an anonymous letter was received by the editor of the American *Stamp and Collectors Review* that outlined the amazing tale of how the writer owned a second specimen of the stamp. Having realised what a second ONE CENT magenta would do to the value of Hind's stamp, he went to see him at his home in Utica, New York State. Hind reputedly bought the stamp for cash, lit his cigar with a match, and then 'he held the stamp to the still burning match … It took not more than the bat of an eye to go up in smoke. "There's only one magenta One Cent Guiana," he said.'[43] There is a rather poor photograph of the 'One Cent Guiana' in the Collection, a present from Hind.

George V was always ready to include in his display at the opening meeting of the Royal Philatelic Society, London each year any particular rarity that the fellows and members would be unlikely to see elsewhere. For the Society's opening meeting of 1926, he chose Fiji for the second time. Out came the *Fiji Times* EXPRESS again (see pages 127–129), with the reconstructed sheets and the imitations. Out came the two issues, virtually complete, of King Cakobau's reign, with the 'almost complete reconstruction of the sheets of surcharged stamps overprinted "VR" and of those further overcharged 2d'.[44] However, for added interest, the King asked Bacon to include the 1878–99 TWO PENCE error of colour unused.

The first issue of the TWO PENCE Fiji inscribed 'VR' (Victoria Regina) was issued in September 1879 from the original dies with 'CR' (Cakobau Rex), and new plates made. It was printed in yellow-green at the Government printing office, Sydney, then sent to Fiji. For some unknown reason, all 50,000 of the next printing in 1881 were ultramarine. The consignment was condemned on arrival and a certificate exists for the destruction of

Fiji: 1878–99 TWO PENCE ultramarine, as opposed to yellow green. This example in the Royal Collection is one of three known – the fourth surviving stamp was burned in a forest fire in Australia.

49,940, leaving sixty stamps. Of the three now recorded, one is in the Royal Philatelic Collection, a fourth was burned in a forest fire in Victoria, Australia. Its owner, the late John Gartner, saved himself and his wife, but not the stamp.

Bacon made absolutely certain that every corner block of four of Great Britain and Colonial issue was sent to him at the Stamp Room for inclusion in the Collection. Although all of these formed an admirable basis for each collection, there were, of course, no errors, no surcharges, often no airmail stamps, all of which had to be purchased separately. Thus, on 19 May 1930, the King was extraordinarily fortunate to acquire, as he recorded in his diary, a 'collection of the Australian Commonwealth stamps ... which I have just bought from a Mr Purves in Australia ..., it is a very fine collection in 18 volumes.'[45] He was obviously delighted with it, and even went so far as to record in his diary the fact that he had shown his new acquisition to Bacon. It is impossible now to work out what came from the Purves collection and what the King had already, as Bacon had soon mounted them together. But what is in the Royal Philatelic Collection today is remarkably complete.

Although he was not related to the firm's owner, throughout his philatelic life Edward Bacon made a close study of Perkins, Bacon printings – at one time they sent him an invoice for £200, a lifetime's research fee. Consequently, he was close to them. When they found anything exciting, they told Bacon about it first and the King benefited. By 1932, the Royal Philatelic Collection of Great Britain and the Colonies was in a league of its own, so it was fitting in a way that George V was allowed to buy from Perkins, Bacon three of the most important items of colonial postal history: the last remaining drawings by Henry Corbould. The first was the Queen's Head first used in the stamps of Ceylon. It is a fine piece of work with the artist's signature in pencil in the left-hand corner, with the instructions to the engraver 'let the light fall on the drawing from the left'.[46] Then there was 'the miniature of the Chalon head made in May 1854 for the first stamps of Tasmania' and finally 'Corbould's original sketch from Levinge's crude idea for New South Wales 5s design'.[47] The King must have been delighted to own the drawings having seen them so often at exhibitions.

The famous Clutterbuck Collection of the West Indies was the last to make a serious impact on the Royal Philatelic Collection. By that time, 1933,

Ceylon: Queen's Head original drawings by Henry Corbould sold to George V by Perkins, Bacon.

there were, of course, still gaps in the Collection, but they could be filled satisfactorily through single purchases as and when the material became available. However, the Clutterbuck Collection was so good, and filled so many of his wants, that the King could not resist buying it through the dealer Thomas Allen in October after Clutterbuck died.

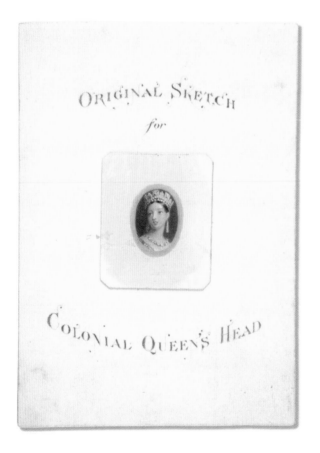

Tasmania: 1854 May, the original miniature sketch of the Chalon head by Henry Corbould.
It was originally prepared for the stamps of Tasmania (formerly Van Dieman's Land).
The image was subsequently used for the Bahamas, Grenada and Queensland. The Garter
in this watercolour was on the wrong shoulder and hence was omitted by the engraver.

The Crown Agents were, and indeed still are, great supporters of the Royal Philatelic Collection. Under the watchful eye of the Keeper, no issue was allowed to pass unrepresented in the Collection, generally a corner block of four with margins and the plate number. This source produced a rich harvest of rarities, often providing unique unused material, as in the case of the Kenya and Uganda with the two issues 1920–22 and 1925–27. Here the King received his usual blocks of four (often specimens from the Universal Postal Union through the Post Office), of every denomination from one cent to £100, as well as all the artwork from De La Rue – the prize being the very rare and valuable £25, £50, £75 and £100 corner blocks of four, again Plate 1.

Often when the Crown Agents awarded a printing contract they stipulated that the 'Proofs of the dies, and subsequent colour proofs in triplicate, were to be submitted before printing was commenced and, ultimately, the approved working designs were to be returned to the Crown Agents suitably mounted for presentation to His Majesty.'[48] One such example of their loyalty to their Sovereign was the commemorative issue they produced

Kenya and Uganda: 1922–27 ONE HUNDRED POUNDS, red and black, corner block of four, plate number 1. At this time, the Crown Agents were meticulous in sending corner blocks of all their issues to George V which made for a homogeneous collection.

for Sierra Leone in 1933 to mark the centenary of the death of William Wilberforce and the abolition of slavery.

Sierra Leone had been named by the Portuguese navigator Pedro de Cintra who had thought the thunder in the hills of the interior sounded like the roaring of a lion. In 1683 the country passed to the Royal Adventurers Company for the trading of slaves; who set up their headquarters first on Tasso Island in the Rockelle estuary, then on the nearby Bunce Island. In 1786, the settlement of Freetown was created for the repatriation of slaves mainly from Great Britain, the Bahamas and Newfoundland under the Sierra Leone Charter. By 1807 sovereignty of Sierra Leone had passed to the British Crown, and Freetown became the seat of government of West Africa, which included Gambia, the Gold Coast (Ghana) and Lagos.

The contract for the commemorative issue went to Bradbury Wilkinson, who produced thirteen designs from a HALFPENNY to ONE POUND. The original sketches from which the printers worked were drawn by a Father F. Welsh. Although the issue was supposed to honour one of the main abolitionists,

Sierra Leone: 1933 FIVE SHILLINGS, black and purple, corner block of 4. This issue, from a HALFPENNY to ONE POUND, commemorated the centenary of the abolition of slavery and the death of William Wilberforce.

Wilberforce does not appear on the stamp, but all the places and trappings of slavery are well represented. Freetown appears on the ONE POUND stamp, as does the slave market, with the vast cotton tree under which men, women and children were sold, on the TWO PENCE value, while the limestone fort of the old slaving headquarters on Bunce Island was depicted on the TWO SHILLINGS stamp.

Some time in early 1935, George V bought his last really important stamp: the *Onepenny* red on thick white paper dated 1853, from the 1848–61 series popularly known as the 'Bermuda Postmasters' after their creator William B. Perot, postmaster of Hamilton, Bermuda, between 1812 and 1862. By an Act of the Legislature of 1848, Perot was in the enviable, if not unusual, position of not only receiving a salary of £70 a year but also all of the postage revenue as well. Neither were his tasks particularly onerous, the population of Hamilton being small. A man of property, he operated from one of his own houses, now the Bermuda Natural History Museum.

With a secure income and time on his hands, Perot devoted his days to gardening. His friend and watchful neighbour, Mr J. B. Heyl, an American chemist, would summon him out of the garden when he was needed to receive the letters and collect the one penny postage dues. Letters were posted with the penny fee in a wooden box outside Perot's house at night, but in the morning Perot was considerably vexed as invariably there were more letters than pennies. Of course, there was no way of knowing who the

Bermuda: 1848–61
Onepenny black on bluish grey paper, of the known 'Perots' is dated 1848, one of the earliest.

Bermuda: 1848–61
Onepenny red on thick white paper dated 1853. This was the last important stamp bought by George V.

Bermuda: 1848–61
Onepenny red on bluish paper, of the 'Perots' it is dated 1854.

miscreants were, so Perot had to make up the shortfall. Heyl came up with the solution: adhesive labels as proof of payment, as supplied in his native America. Perot warmed to the idea, and proceeded to make his own stamps. For this, he took his postmark stamp and removed the date plugs, leaving just the year. Contained in a circle were the words 'Hamilton', at the top, and 'Bermuda', at the bottom, with two crosses between. These he struck on a sheet of paper and wrote, in his own hand, *Onepenny* above the year with his signature below. After gumming the back, he cut the paper to give strips of twelve impressions. The initial stamping was done with black ink, but around June 1849 it changed to red.

As Perot made the stamps, he did not see the need to further cancel them which meant that it was a long time before they were discovered, and even longer before they were recognised as genuine because no Act of the Legislature had confirmed the issue. Their authenticity was finally accepted after Edward Bacon had spent much time and energy researching them. Despite the number that must have been 'printed', there are only ten known examples, of which the Royal Philatelic Collection holds three.

In October 1922, the London dealer R. Roberts received a visit from a resident of Bermuda. He was astonished when the man produced from his pocketbook four 'Perot' labels that had been found among some business correspondence of a retired merchant from St George's. Roberts bought them all immediately and offered them to the King, who chose just two. The first was printed in black on bluish grey paper dated 1848. The stamp was clumsily cut round, so parts of all of the letters are missing, but nonetheless, it is from the first year of issue. The other is printed in red on bluish paper and dated 1854. It has been partially doubly struck as can be seen in the A, M, I, L, T, and O of HAMILTON. The King must have been thrilled when Arthur Hind, who bought one of the other two 'Perots' at the London International Philatelic Exhibition in 1923, came to see him in triumph: he was in the habit of exaggerating the numbers of rare stamps in his collection. At that time, the King had two to Hind's single 'Perot'.

★　★　★

There could be no more fitting tribute to George V than the Royal Silver Jubilee Stamp Exhibition in 1935 arranged by Sir John Wilson, President of the Royal Philatelic Society, London 'to express the Society's feelings of loyalty and esteem towards its Patron'.[49] Ninety fellows and members from all over the world contributed to the display of seven hundred sheets of British Empire stamps of the Victorian period. The entries were all anonymous, and the King was not asked to contribute.

The King recorded his visit, after the exhibition closed, in his diary:

> I went with Godfrey [-Faussett] to 41 Devonshire Place (R.P. Society) to see a wonderful exhibition of stamps. Bacon, Sir John Wilson (President) & Mr Bradbury [Honorary Treasurer] met me there. Some beautiful stamps, 8 Post Office Mauritius among them.[50]

The King was clearly flattered that the members of the 'Royal' had put together one of the greatest collections of rarities in his honour. He must have relished seeing so many good examples that he owned himself, but such pride must have been tinged with envy for those he did not have.

The Jubilee Year was a busy one for Edward Bacon: in reply to the honour shown to the King, fifty-five pages from the Collection were shown to the Royal Philatelic Society, London in October. In a way, this was a fitting finale for them both. Bacon had been a loyal, trusted servant and friend for twenty-two years. His salary and his travelling expenses were met out of the Stamp Fund, as was his Christmas present, which he bought himself – one year it was 'Teas Maid', an automatic electric kettle, from the Army and Navy Stores in Victoria costing £6. Both he and the King valued their friendship. Once at Balmoral, the conversation turned to Bacon and 'there was a certain amount of levity about the very deaf and slightly suburban philatelist with whom the King spent so much time'. The King entered the room while the conversation was in progress: 'Were you speaking about my friend Sir Edward?'[51] The company was deeply embarrassed. Bacon was created MVO (Member of the Victorian Order) in 1917, and CVO (Commander) in 1922. Finally he received his knighthood, KCVO, in 1932.

After the strain of the Silver Jubilee, the King and Bacon spent more and more time closeted in the Stamp Room. Christmas came, and the Royal Family repaired to Sandringham, while Bacon continued in London in his own quiet way. On 13 January, he paid the King's subscription of three guineas to the Royal Philatelic Society, London for 1936, but barely a week later, the King was dying. In the Royal Household dining room during the evening of 20 January, the royal physician, Lord Dawson, wrote on the back of a menu 'The King's life is moving peacefully towards its close.' Just after midnight, a bulletin was broadcast: 'Death came peacefully to the King at 11.55 p.m.'

The King was deeply mourned: he had served his country and the Empire to the very best of his ability. He was loved by some, but feared by many. He was a stickler for etiquette, and often appeared stiff and unbending, yet on the shooting field and in the Stamp Room, where he was an acknowledged expert, he was a different man: kind, courteous, generous and knowledge-able. Shortly after he died, John Betjeman penned a few lines, 'On the Death of King George V':

> Spirits of well-shot woodcock, partridge, snipe
> Flutter and bear him up the Norfolk sky:
> In that red house in a red mahogany bookcase
> The stamp collection waits with mounts long dry.

CHAPTER NINE

✿❖✿

To Sir Edward Bacon, the Stamp Room at Buckingham Palace was a gloomy place after George V had died. He missed his friend of so many years, and was lost without his leadership. Added to that, the future of the Royal Philatelic Collection which they had put together so assiduously was in serious doubt: it had always been rumoured that the first thing that the Prince of Wales would do on becoming King was to dispose of it. Bacon knew that the Collection was regarded as an heirloom and therefore would not be sold. But it might be abandoned.

As long ago as 1905, the then Prince of Wales feared for his beloved collection, and had sought advice from Tilleard, who was also a respected City solicitor. In July he wrote to him from York Cottage, Sandringham thanking him for an outline of possible wording to make the Collection an heirloom. It would appear that at that time he had no other motive than to ensure that it was kept intact as a collection after his death rather than keeping it out of the hands of his eldest son and heir, Prince Edward of Wales (later Edward VIII, then Duke of Windsor). Although often irritated by the eleven-year-old boy, he certainly did not then despair of him – as he came to in later years, once remarking to Stanley Baldwin, his last Prime Minister: 'After I am dead, the boy will ruin himself in twelve-months'. Further, the then Prince was a keen stamp collector himself. At the 1906 International Philatelic Exhibition (see page 93) in London, he had exhibited 'A book containing a great collection of unused stamps of France and the Colonies'[1] in a class 'For Collectors under 16 years of Age with over 2,000 stamps'. Clearly Prince Edward was a keen collector in his own right. He wrote home from the Royal Naval College,

245

Osborne requesting some stamps of the Virgin Islands 'Contributions will be welcome.'[2] Philately was also a useful point of contact between father and son: 'Showed David [as Prince Edward was always known] & Hansell [his tutor] my stamps after tea.'[3] Later, as Prince of Wales, he was often to be seen scouring the stamp shops of the Strand, although he never exhibited again.

The facts do not bear out the persistent rumour that Edward VIII wanted to sell the Collection at the time of his Accession. Barely a week into his reign, the Private Secretary to the Governor General of South Africa, Colonel the Hon. Malise Hore-Ruthven, (formerly ADC to George V), received a letter from H. J. Lenton, the Postmaster General:

> My Department have, in accordance with the usual arrangement, sent me a corner block of Voortrekker stamps for presentation to His Majesty The King through the Governor-General.
>
> I am a little doubtful about sending these on as I saw a reference recently to the disposal of King George's collection. Perhaps you would be kind enough to find out and let me know whether I should still continue to send them.[4]

The reply was swift, well considered and to the point. Alan Lascelles, Assistant Private Secretary to Edward VIII, wrote on 6 February 1936: 'I am to inform you that the stamp-collection made by His late Majesty will be maintained by the present King'.[5] The Secretaries of the Governors General of the Dominions, Australia, Canada and a little later, India and New Zealand, received a similar letter: 'I am to inform you that the stamp-collection made by his late Majesty will be maintained by the present King.

It is requested, therefore, that the existing arrangements for forwarding new issues of stamps to The King may be continued exactly as heretofore.'[6]

All the replies came back in the affirmative often accompanied with a new or part issue – a corner block of four with margins – as before. But even more important for the Collection, Lascelles wrote a similar letter to E. B. Boyd, Private Secretary to the Colonial Secretary, requesting that 'the existing arrangements for forwarding new issues of stamps from the Colonies to The King is [to be] continued exactly as before'.[7] Boyd obliged.

Not long after, on 24 March 1936, Edward VIII, an honorary President of the Royal Philatelic Society, London since 1919, agreed to become its patron – hardly the action of a man hell-bent on selling his father's most treasured possession. At that time, the King's mind was very much on stamps as the 'Accession Issue' was being planned. He had already requested 'a selection of the best of the newer foreign stamps'[8] to be sent to him for ideas, and received some specimens of a Bavarian issue of 1914, which he thought 'particularly attractive'. Less appealing were the essays of the suggested mourning stamp for George V – the current 1½d stamp with the words IN MEMORY substituting the value THREE HALFPENCE. The new King dismissed them outright, nor are they in the Royal Philatelic Collection.

There is further evidence that Edward VIII was content that the Collection should go on as before – so long as it was self-financing. Bacon must have made the suggestion in the first place that duplicates could be sold to finance new purchases, for Major the Hon. Alexander Hardinge, the King's Private Secretary, wrote to him: 'I have spoken to The King and His Majesty approves of your dividing the block of four of the K. E. [King Edward VII] Straits Settlements 500 dollar issue and disposing of the top pair to the gentleman who is prepared to give £1,000 for these two stamps. This will give you a nice sum in hand which you are authorised to use, at your discretion, in filling up any gaps there may be among the earlier issues in the Royal Collection.'[9] Bacon must have been amazed when Edward VIII called on him in the Stamp Room to discuss the Collection, and personally confirmed the arrangement

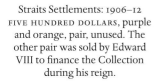

Straits Settlements: 1906–12
FIVE HUNDRED DOLLARS, purple
and orange, pair, unused. The
other pair was sold by Edward
VIII to finance the Collection
during his reign.

to split the block of four, purple and orange $500 Straits Settlements (Malaysia) stamps of the 1906–12 issue (given by the Crown Agents). Bacon saw the purchaser, the dealer Tommy Allen, and the cheque was handed over for the pair, Bacon making it a condition of sale that Allen would not 'divulge where he had got the specimens'.[10] A special account was opened with Coutts Bank on which he was empowered 'to draw for any purchases' to be made in the future. The purchases were few, but important, including some Oxford and Cambridge college stamps and a fine example of a Great Britain unused TEN SHILLINGS 1883–84 cobalt blue. Bacon had not lost his touch, just his heart.

Great Britain:
1883–84
TEN SHILLINGS
cobalt blue unused.
One of the last stamps
bought by Bacon for
the Collection.

With the photogravure process for printing adopted by the Post Office in 1934, stamps could be produced direct from a photograph. A comparatively short time after his accession, the first stamps of Edward VIII's reign appeared in August and September 1936, and examples of the printings were sent to the Stamp Room and were mounted by Bacon. The close confidant of George V, Bacon would have been less enthusiastic about the new King and the stamps of his reign, but his concern was short lived for on 10 December 1936 Edward VIII abdicated. His brother, the Duke of York, became King George VI. The ex-King Edward VIII sailed into exile to join Mrs Wallis Simpson, not as first planned in the Admiralty Yacht *Enchantress*, but more appropriately aboard the destroyer HMS *Fury*.

Although the now Duke of Windsor had amassed a great fortune as Prince of Wales, mostly through the Duchy of Cornwall revenues, he was unhappy about his financial settlement, and it was at this time that he may have looked into the possibility of selling the Royal Philatelic Collection. The rumours began all over again, as the news of the supposed sale leaked out. A report appeared in the *Sunday Express* that prompted G. & A. Cosens, a firm of City solicitors, to write to the Private Secretary's office, stating that they had a client who wished to purchase the whole Collection but was prepared to donate a representation of it to the nation. They received a curt reply:

Edward VIII (when Prince of Wales) in the uniform of the Cameron Highlanders.
The King particularly liked this portrait and wanted to use the head for the new stamps of his reign.
[Photo: Bertram Park, Camera Press, London]

'there is no truth in the report that the collection of Stamps made by His late Majesty King George V is likely to be sold.'[11]

The upheavals within Buckingham Palace took their toll on Sir Edward Bacon. With the stamps of two reigns from Great Britain, the Dominions and the Colonies piling up, he felt that he could not cope on his own. As he was not mounting the new material, he lost track of what he had and what was missing. No longer the friend and trusted confidant of the King, he was not consulted on the stamps of the new reign. George VI, like his father, made it known that he wanted to be informed on every stage of his new issues, particularly as Queen Mary had made suggestions over the colour in the past.

In April 1938 Bacon wrote to Sir Ulick Alexander, sending 'a short Report on the Royal Collection of Stamps' which he thought that the King might be interested in seeing. He went on,

> If it meets with the King's approval I should like to retire from the post I now hold on Sept. 30th. I shall be 78 in August & I do not feel I can face the difficulties of getting to & fro Town during another winter. I hope by the end of September I may be able to get all the stamps with the head of King George V arranged in the albums. Some of those stamps continue to appear even now, but by the date named I expect that they will have been superseded by new issues. I think that this change in the postage stamps of the British Empire forms, perhaps, a suitable time for the appointment of a new curator of the Collection.
>
> Whoever my successor may be I shall be pleased to give him all the assistance I can & explain to him the lines on which the Collection has been built up. [12]

He knew who should succeed him; Sir John Wilson, the President of the Royal Philatelic Society, London. Edward VIII and later George VI had continued their father's practice of allowing members of the Expert Committee of 'the Royal' to consult the Collection. Wilson was one of their number, and thus was fully acquainted with all aspects of it. At one such visit, Bacon called him aside and suggested to him that he should take over as his successor, but first that he should act as his assistant or understudy.

Wilson considered the informal proposal and wrote to Bacon:

You asked me when I called whether I would consider taking on the position as understudy to you in connection with the Royal Collection with a view to looking after the Collection in the event of your retirement, and I am writing to let you know that I am willing to help as far as I possibly can.

The Royal Philatelic Society, London have so much to thank King George for in the past, and so much also to thank King Edward for in placing his marvellous collection at the disposal of interested parties and particularly the Expert Committee of our Society that I feel I owe the benefit of any knowledge I may have to the King, and I should be very proud to follow in your footsteps though I know very well I have not got your qualifications.

I hope however you will regard this letter rather as a promise for the future as I cannot think that anybody could easily follow in your path on the lines which you have recently undertaken. Without a deep knowledge of the collection over a long period of years it would be impossible to decide what surplus material should first be exchanged to fill any gaps, and I hope that you may long be spared to use your exceptional knowledge at Buckingham Palace.

I should like you to know however that I am available as a very second string.[13]

All parties were delighted with Sir John's reply. The King was 'very glad'[14], Sir Godfrey Thomas hoped to 'have the pleasure of making your [Wilson's] acquaintance before long' while Bacon knew the worth of his successor. The only reservation came from Sir John himself. In May 1938 he went to see Sir Ulick Alexander, where he learned that he 'did not think the King would be prepared to spend any money on the purchase of new stamps other than money he might be able to obtain though the sale of duplicates in the existing Collection'.[15] Wilson was concerned, and said 'that the sale of duplicates could not go on for ever without spoiling the Collection, and that it would be difficult to keep this Collection up to its present standard unless His Majesty from time to time was prepared to spend a little money on the purchase of new stamps, other than the moneys he might be able to obtain through the sale of duplicates in the existing Collection'.[16] Alexander thought this unlikely, but hoped that 'this would not prevent him from allowing his name to be considered as a successor to Bacon. Wilson told me that he would much like his name considered for this post'.[17] So, Sir John Wilson continued to visit the Stamp Room very much as before, and talk to his friend of many years.

As was his habit, Bacon took a few days holiday in May 1938 in Worcester-shire, and finally returned to the Stamp Room having suffered a severe attack of influenza. Then in early June, Sir Ulick Alexander received a letter from Bacon's daughter, Constance:

> I am very grieved to have to tell you that my Father Sir Edward Bacon passed away early this morning. His heart was very bad all day yesterday and he had a temperature so the Doctor advised me to have a Nurse for him and he died peacefully in his sleep at about 6.30 this morning.[18]

So he had died in harness after all. Alexander replied to Miss Bacon's letter by return of post offering his and the King's sincerest condolences, commenting 'I know that the King is much grieved to hear of your sad news and he well realises the fine work carried out by your father as Keeper of the Royal Phila-telic Collection.'[19] As a postscript to the same letter to Miss Bacon, Alexander added, 'Do you think you could kindly send me the keys to the cupboards in which the Stamp Collection is kept.' He also wrote to Lord Wigram: 'It is most unfortunate that Bacon should have died before he was able to hand over to his successor, Sir John Wilson. I expect, however, that everything in connection with the Collection is in good order, and Wilson should find no difficulty in taking on the work. I am going into this matter now.'[20]

On 20 June 1938, Sir John Wilson Bt was appointed Keeper of the Royal Philatelic Collection, the third man to hold the post, with a salary of £250 per annum. He was not quite forty.

Bacon had certainly chosen the right man for the job. Although Wilson undoubtedly looked up to Bacon for his vast philatelic knowledge and they were great friends, the two men could not have been more different. Sir John was the second baronet (his father was given the title for services to Scottish agriculture) and had a large house and estate just north of Glasgow. Where Bacon was comparatively tall and thin, his successor was short and stocky, but his patrician nose and bearing gave him a certain presence. In his youth, Sir John had been an accomplished games player, sweeping the board in all sports at school. At Harrow he was a 'triple school blood', being in the first cricket, rugby and Harrow Football teams. Commissioned into the

Coldstream Guards towards the end of the First World War, he ended up in hospital in Stirling, not far from his home. There, his father's 'stuck-down' collection of stamps was produced as something that might amuse him, and from that moment, Wilson became a dedicated philatelist. After the war, he practiced as a barrister, but retired from the Bar in the early 1930s to concentrate on his estate and collections.

Sir John Wilson always chose to concentrate on comparatively small areas – the German Levant, second issue Romanian, Russian and Norwegian locals – but once it was as complete as the material or his pocket allowed, he lost interest and sold it. Much of his expertise came from a phenomenal memory: when his son, the present Baronet, Sir David Wilson, produced a stamp for him to look at in the late 1950s, Wilson declared it a forgery. He went to a bookcase, thought for a moment, then pulled out a volume of the *London Philatelist* and turned up an article on the stamp, which he had not seen since he first read it thirty years before. A world class bridge player, he was invited to play for England, but declined on the grounds that he would play only for Scotland, who did not have a team at that time.

Sir Edward Bacon had always called himself 'Curator of the King's Stamp Collection', but Sir John was the 'Keeper of the Royal Philatelic Collection', as the post is described today. Although George VI was interested in the Collection, he had neither the time nor the inclination to play an active part in it. Consequently, the Stamp Room was relegated from its smart position on the ground floor to the second floor on the other side of Buckingham Palace. After the furniture and albums had been moved to their new quarters, the first action of the new Keeper was to apply for a telephone to be installed; it had not been needed before as his predecessor was so deaf. He then set about looking at the post-George V material, and found that 'Sir Edward Bacon had not mounted any stamps with designs of the present reign, and this material is all in envelopes.'[21] Like Bacon, Wilson had no assistance and all his letters are in manuscript. He identified what was missing, such as the 'issue of Great Britain with head of King Edward VIII ... The ... "coronation" issue which was used in nearly all the Empire... [and] the new permanent issue of Great Britain with head of H. M. the King'.[22] In fact, the Edward VIII stamps had been received and mounted by Bacon. The Private Secretary's

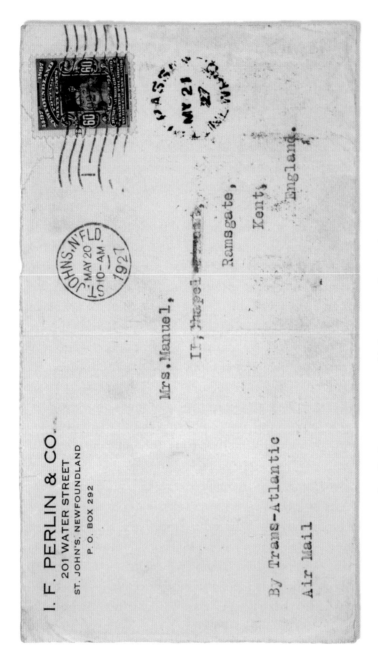

Newfoundland: 1927 SIXTY CENTS black, overprinted Air Mail DE PINEDO 1927.
This airmail stamp celebrated the first flight from Newfoundland to Italy by the Marchese de Pinedo.

Office and the Privy Purse had been there before – the age-old system was revived and Wilson received his missing proofs and essays.

It was not until mid-December that Sir John Wilson had his audience with George VI, a full half-hour when the King saw him in the Stamp Room. The next day, 17 December 1938, Wilson wrote to Sir Ulick with the solution to his problem of keeping the Collection alive:

> The King has decided to start a fresh collection of stamps commencing with the designs of his own reign. This collection is to be mounted in blue albums instead of red, and I shall refer in this letter to the … [George V] … collection as the Red collection and to the new George VIth collection as the Blue.[23]

An early purchase by Wilson, and one that certainly appealed to the King with his early experience in the Royal Air Force, was a 'Pinedo' stamp on cover. To commemorate the first flight from Newfoundland to Italy made by the Marchese de Pinedo in 1927, 300 of the SIXTY CENTS black stamps were overprinted with the words 'Air Mail, DE PINEDO, 1927'. The cover came up at an auction held in aid of the Red Cross in 1940 and it was bought for the Collection for £410. It was said at the time that the King was lucky to secure the lot, as competition was hot against two other keen philatelists, President Roosevelt of the USA and King Carol of Romania. In fact the Collection already had a de Pinedo on cover, as it had been mounted by Bacon. The cover bought by Wilson is not now in the Collection.

From here on, Sir John Wilson set the tenor of the Royal Philatelic Collection that has lasted to the present day. There was another good, practical reason to separate the two collections. By the time Bacon died, he had virtually completed arranging all of the stamps of George V's reign, and this collection is therefore homogeneous. Had the George VI issues been added to these pages, with another's style of mounting and annotating, they would have looked out of place in the album. Also, with extra material, the volumes would have had to be renumbered. As it was, the wants list for the Red Collection was minimal, and when a particular specimen on it was found, it usually found a home on a page annotated by Bacon.

As now, the bulk of the new material for the Blue Collection came from the Post Office and the Crown Agents, but also from the Universal Postal Union,

Berne, and from the Governors General of the Dominions. The King set out the guidelines, in that he wanted all proofs and colour trials supplied by the Crown Agents for the Colonies as well. As in his father's day, artists' drawings for many Colonial issues were submitted to him for his approval, and were mounted in the Blue Collection, along with the proofs and colour trials and, of course, the issued stamps.

Wilson mounted the first printings for the George VI stamps for Great Britain and the Colonies, but after that he merely filed the new submissions. Also, as the purchases for both collections were few, the demands on the Keeper were not especially taxing. Once the design and format of the blue albums had been approved by the King in December 1938, Wilson set about mounting the George VI material. But he suffered from phlebitis in the leg, a serious ailment that kept him in bed sometimes for months at a time – in March 1939 the King was so concerned for his health that he sent his own physician to attend him.

The Royal Philatelic Collection was not all that was taking up Wilson's time: he was the prime mover behind the exhibition to celebrate the centenary of 'The First Day of Postage, 6 May 1840' scheduled for the same day in 1940. The King agreed to become patron and to lend extensive material from the Collection. The celebrations caused a great deal of excitement among philatelists on both sides of the Atlantic – there was even a suggestion from the United States that Great Britain should issue a stamp with the joint images of President Roosevelt and George VI. The King was less than enthusiastic about the idea. However, the exhibition could not go ahead, at least in its proposed form, because war with Germany was declared on 3 September 1939. A few days later, Wilson wrote to Alexander: 'The outbreak of war has forced me to give up any hope of organising the Stamp Centenary Exhibition for 1940 for reasons which are self-evident, but none the less as His Majesty was graciously pleased to grant the Exhibition his patronage, I feel I should notify you of my intention and get your permission to cancel.'[24] In fact, under his chairmanship and the King's patronage, a token exhibition was held at Lancaster House in aid of the Duke of Gloucester's Red Cross and St John Fund. The King had lent some Great Britain stamps from both Collections for the exhibition, and he visited it with the Queen.

Great Britain: 1940 ½ᴰ green, 1ᴰ scarlet, 1½ᴰ red-brown, 2ᴰ orange,
2½ᴰ ultramarine and the 3ᴰ violet commemorative issue to celebrate the centenary
of the first adhesive postage stamp.

Towards the beginning of August 1939, Wilson ordered eight large wooden
crates and began to pack the Royal Philatelic Collection. He had arranged for
it to be stored in the bomb-proof safe in the Cox and King's branch of Lloyds
Bank in Pall Mall, but delayed sending it over in the hope that, as he wrote to
Alexander:

> the King could possibly find time before he goes away to Sandringham to have
> a look at the Collection. The reason is this; that I am keen to know his wishes
> about the annotation of the pages of new material which I am mounting and
> have delayed writing them up in order to get instructions.
>
> Every collection has its own methods and I cannot copy the script style
> adopted by Sir Edward Bacon. I am a little frightened that my additions will look
> patchy in consequence.[25]

The Collection remained safely in the bank for the duration of the war, and
no charge was made for the service. However, although the Luftwaffe bombs
fell on that side of the Palace in the daylight raid of 13 September 1940, demol-
ishing the chapel, they would not have damaged the Collection. There was
always the risk, but as it was lodged less than a mile from Buckingham Palace,

it was readily available for Wilson to remove material when it was needed for displays such as the Royal Philatelic Society, London's opening meetings throughout the war.

Sir John Wilson was deeply committed to the Royal Philatelic Collection. On his appointment as Keeper, he disposed of a large part of his 'private collection, including all my British and British Colonials, and most of the foreign, except three or four largish specialised collections'.[26] He did not, however, sell three items, two from India and one from Western Australia that were important and missing from the Red Collection. They must have been very special: he wrote to Sir Ulick Alexander that he was prepared to sell them for £200 as that way he felt he 'would not altogether be parting from them and that makes a very great difference'.[27] Predictably, the Keeper of the Privy Purse said that any purchase had to come from sales of duplicates in the Red Collection. Wilson replied that 'Mr Mann and I were going to make a survey of the Red Collection, but the War has stopped us and the Collection is in the Bank vault in packing cases so that nothing can be done on these lines until happier times.'[28] Although nothing could be done with the Red Collection for the duration of the War, Wilson made good progress with mounting the Blue, – pointing out to Alexander that he would soon need some more albums. As the war dragged on, postage stamps were needed more than ever. There were the Great Britain stamps: there were new issues for the Colonies, mostly from the Crown Agents and the Dominions.

Sir John might have been a renowned philatelist, but his record as a correspondent was dire: when he died, 'every drawer in the house was filled with unanswered correspondence'.[29] Mr L. A. Beadle of the Crown Agents for the Colonies wrote to the King's Private Secretary's Office:

We have addressed several letters to Sir John Wilson, Bart., Buckingham Palace s w 1 regarding specimens of British Colonial Stamps for His Majesty's Philatelic Collection but have received no replies.

Would you be good enough to confirm that the letters in question ... were duly delivered to Sir John and that we are in order in sending the correspondence to the Palace.[30]

Cartoon of Sir John Wilson, drawn by Ledoux, a fellow member and habitué of the Arts Club, London.

The Private Secretary's Office sprang into action. Memoranda flowed as if in a whirlpool: one writer 'was under the impression that all correspondence about stamps for The King's Collection should be with the Private Secretary & <u>not</u> with Sir John Wilson',[31] and it was 'a strict rule in his predecessor's time, & when broken it always caused trouble'. They were baying for Sir John Wilson to give them answers. Sir Eric Mieville had 'been trying to see him about the attached for the last few days, but he has not been in … It is <u>not</u> a very good show ignoring letters!'[32] Sir John was finally tracked down and carpeted. He was 'exceedingly sorry about the official receipts'[33] and promised to resolve the matter. Secretly, Wilson was delighted: Lascelles, in command of secretaries, each with a typewriter, and filing clerks, said that his office would acknowledge all correspondence in future.

Throughout long periods of the Second World War the Royal Philatelic Collection lay dormant – either nothing was happening, or the Keeper was laid up in bed with phlebitis. During these occasions, Lady Wilson acted as courier, liaising for her husband with the Private Secretary's Office. When he managed to go into the Stamp Room, Lady Wilson would pick him up and take him to lunch at the Arts Club in Dover Street. On one occasion, she was late and arrived at the Palace as the guard was changing. She saw a gap between the Colour and the Colour Guard, and drove her Morris Minor between them. Later that day, Sir John received a visit from the colonel of the Grenadier Guards who spelt out what had happened. 'Pray ask Lady Wilson not to do it again, the last time the Colour and the Colour Guard were separated was at Waterloo!'[34]

There were, of course, philatelic events throughout the war. There were exhibitions and displays, meetings and stamp auctions, although the market was not as buoyant as it had been during the First World War. At one such important auction, the Yardley sale at the end of October 1944, Wilson was delighted to find a British Guiana FOUR CENTS lemon-yellow 1850–51 'Cotton Reel'. He had intended to buy the stamp for Alfred Lichtenstein, a fitting present for the great philatelist who had looked after and paid for the education of

British Guiana: 1850–51 FOUR CENTS lemon-yellow 'Cotton Reel' bought for the Collection at auction by Sir John Wilson B[t].

Wilson's three sons in the United States for over three years of the War. He had already bought another specimen of the same stamp for the Red Collection 'at the beginning of the war when stamps were rather under a cloud, a very nice clean one cut round came up at auction'. The black impressions on lemon-yellow paper, were cut round and initialled 'H. A. K. [illikelly] (Clerk Post Office, Georgetown)'.

With his phenomenal memory, Wilson had remembered his conversation of many years before with Bacon about the FOUR CENTS lemon-yellow. Bacon had expounded on the one in the Tapling Collection in the British Museum, and thought it the only perfect example of the *square-cut* FOUR CENTS and had never seen another, except in the Duveen collection with one corner repaired. Bacon 'thought [it] too dear at several hundred pounds'. Although the famous Ferrari Collection had five of the TWO CENTS rose, including two of the pairs, as well as many FOUR CENTS orange and pale yellow, there was 'no decent lemon stamp'. Wilson was surprised to see the first Duveen specimen offered in the Yardley sale and 'anticipated that it would fetch a biggish figure'. He had heard, however that 'various people thought it had been entirely re-backed and that others were frightened of it as it lacked the postal clerk's signature in ink which was sometimes, but seldom, omitted and it was supposed to provide a guard against forgery'.

As he had already bought one example of the stamp for the Red Collection, he did not think that George VI would care for another, particularly in wartime, so he did not ask the Privy Purse for funds to buy it. So Wilson put in a bid of £115 and, to his utter amazement, 'It was knocked down at £65' plus the 5 per cent for the commission agent who bid for him – Wilson never bid himself: as he always said, 'The price is liable to rise if the room knows that I consider an item worth having and it therefore is far cheaper to pay a small commission.' In this case, the agent was Mr E. O. Holmes; Charles Nissen had recently died.

After an 'extension to permit full examination', Wilson 'spent some hours removing nine old stamp hinges from the back' and found, as he suspected, 'that it was not rebacked and that only one corner was repaired. His colleagues on the Expert Committee of the Royal Philatelic Society, London all pronounced the stamp genuine, so it was paid for and offered to His

Majesty. Members of the Royal Family are invariably shrewd enough to spot a bargain when offered, and the King thanked Wilson himself as they were photographed together in the Stamp Room by the American magazine *Picture Post* The two stamps bought separately by Wilson were truly remarkable as they were used on the same day, 10 November 1851, but the date was wrongly stamped as 'NO 01', when it should have been 'NO[vember] 10'. It was subsequently sold.

At last the War was over. On 8 May 1945, VE Day was celebrated, and VJ Day three months later on 15 August. Life returned to a semblance of normality, particularly in the Stamp Room. Wilson received the 'eight wooden boxes and one brown paper parcel' that contained the Red Collection. It returned in remarkably good condition having been kept dry and

George VI examines the spine of one of his blue-bound albums with his Keeper of the
Royal Philatelic Collection, Sir John Wilson in the Stamp Room in Buckingham Palace.
The photograph appeared in the *Picture Post*, December 1944.
[Photo: Hulton Getty]

at a constant temperature. Sir John Wilson had his work cut out: he had not only to check the condition, but feed into the Red Collection the stamps he had bought throughout the war.

Although George VI took an interest in the Collection he was never a hands-on philatelist like his father. At one point, he looked at stamps as an investment, but never took it up other than buying for the Collection. The Royal Philatelic Collection still enjoyed a great reputation and, as his father had, George VI received unsolicited gifts. In June 1945, James Kitto, former head of the Postal Department of New South Wales, Australia wrote indirectly to the King, through Captain Bracegirdle, secretary to the Governor General, to tell him that he had in his possession a sheet of forged scarlet 2d stamps, depicting the Sydney Harbour Bridge of 14 March 1932 issue, which he thought would make a useful addition to his 'choice collection'[35]. Wilson was consulted and declared that it would indeed make a useful addition to the Collection, but since 'forgeries were in circulation before they were discovered. I wonder whether there is a used example as well available for the collection?'[36] There were none, and a complete sheet of twenty forgeries is now in the Red Collection.

Of all the victory stamps to appear after the Second World War, none are more emotive than those unique to Hong Kong. Miss E. K. Baker of the Colonial Office wrote to Sir Alan Lascelles:

I enclose, to be laid before the King, a drawing for a stamp to commemorate the 'Resurrection' of Hong Kong.

The drawing is the work of the Postmaster General of Hong Kong, Mr Wynne Jones, who says that he conceived the idea while in the Stanley Internment Camp for Civilians, and that he was assisted in its execution by Mr W. E. Jones, Chief Draftsman of the Hong Kong Public Works Department.

The date 1944 will, of course need to be altered to read 1945, and the Chinese characters will require to be amended as shown in the separate leaflet which has been prepared by a Chinese expert at the School of Oriental and African Studies.

The literal translation of the Chinese inscription on the left hand side is "China and Britain perpetually at Peace", while that on the right-hand side reads "The Phoenix revives in Prosperity."

264

It is proposed that this commemorative set should comprise only the two denominations of 30 cents (not 25 cents) and 1 dollar, which represent the postage rates for ordinary and air-mail letters respectively. The 30 cents stamp would be printed in blue and red, as in the enclosed drawing, and the 1 dollar stamp in brown and red, both on white paper.

In order to ensure accurate registration in printing it would probably be necessary to have a surface printing process rather than the intaglio process. The medallion portrait would, of course, be copied from the approved 'Dorothy Wilding' photograph.

Will you be so good as to ascertain whether these proposals meet with His Majesty's approval.[37]

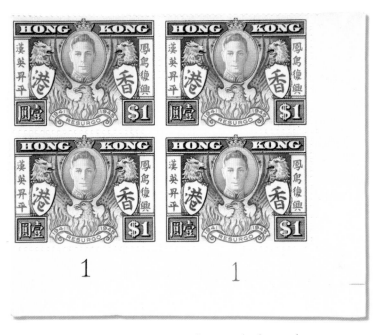

Hong Kong: 1946 Victory $1 brown and red, unused.

Opposite: Hong Kong: 1946 artwork by W. E. Jones for the 25c (later changed to 30c) 'Victory' issue. It was conceived by Mr Wynne Jones in Stanley Internment Camp for Civilians.

Michael Adeane, Assistant Private Secretary to the King, wrote back to say how pleased the King was with 'the design and colour'.[38] Later, Wilson received the original 'sketches from Hong Kong and before writing to acknowledge them' he thought that 'they should be shown to His Majesty with the interesting accompanying letter'.[39] The Collection holds both of Mr Jones's drawings on what appears to be brown rice paper, one in pencil, the other coloured. There is also a card from the printers, De La Rue, with their artist's trial drawings of some of the detail of the original. Unfortunately, there is no record of Wynne Jones's original letter.

Victory stamps in the design used for Colonies (other than Hong Kong) were proposed and printed for Singapore and the Federation of Malaya, but for some reason the Governor of Malaya decided that the stamp was inappropriate. As one could not be issued without the other, the entire two issues were incinerated. However, an enterprising local raked through the ashes and recovered a few examples. The Collection has a corner block of four of each of the two values of both countries.

Despite Wilson's periods of enforced absence from the Stamp Room through ill-health, he was coping well with managing the Collection. However to him, as an expert philatelist, the work involved in arranging material that had merely come direct from 'the GPO, the Crown Agents or the Dominions', however colourful, must soon have palled. Just occasionally there was something different to interest him. As a rule he did 'not bother with minor non-recurring flaws as it would make the Collection tedious' but concentrated on genuine 'misprints, errors & varieties' when they became available. In December 1947, Wilson had gathered together 'a little group of items' for the King's consideration, bearing in mind that 'the collection of stamps of the present reign is very popular as it does not require a long training in philately. There is consequently a very strong demand for items such as these.' The rarities he came up with were:

Item 1. [Great Britain] Block of four used ½d imperf... This I should certainly advise purchasing. It came from a booklet & therefore there were only six copies ever. After posting these four somebody told the owner the other two were very rare & he took them off letters which he had prepared for the post. They are therefore singles and the gum has gone. The stamps are the old shade no longer used.

Item 2. [Great Britain] 2½ᵈ two blocks mint one all imperf the other perfᵈ at bottom only. One sheet passed the checkers with the top three rows imperf.

Item 3. [Great Britain] 7ᵈ block 4 with top row imperf.

Item 4. Channel Islands proofs printed in Paris during the war... I cannot find out how many more there are but I am always suspicious of French printing establishments.

Item 5. South West Africa 1ᵈ. bilingual pair overprint inverted. ... There are two other values existing with inverted overprints but I think the owners are asking too much for them and I am laying off at the moment.

There is also floating around a few blocks from a 4ᵈ G.B. sheet similar to the 2½ᵈ. with the three top rows imperf. At present the blocks are very firmly held, and I have not had a reasonable offer.[40]

The King, trusting Wilson's judgement implicitly, 'decided he would like to buy all the stamps'.[41]

Wilson's memorandum ended with: 'I would like to discuss with you the best way to deal with preliminary enquiries from Australia 1950 & Canada 1951' – a reference to the centenary exhibitions planned to mark their first issues. George VI was only too delighted to lend material from both collections, firmly believing in the 'value of philately in the creation of international goodwill, and [he] realised how much pleasure he could give by permitting portions of the Collection to be seen'.[42] He sent his collection of Nevis to Switzerland in 1946, a tribute to his father whose only foreign loan had been to an exhibition in Berne. The next year, a collection of the Treasury Essays of 1839 and other 1839–41 material went to New York for their centenary exhibition; in 1949 the collection of Trinidad went to Paris. In the Dominions, Melbourne, Australia, was loaned the first Ham printings of the ONE PENNY, TWO PENCE and THREE PENCE of Victoria and the first printings of the lower values of the Sydney Views. The same courtesy was extended to Canada for their centenary exhibition: the Royal Philatelic Collection came up with examples of the earliest stamps of the Province of Canada, British Columbia and Vancouver Island, New Brunswick, Newfoundland, Nova Scotia and Prince Edward Island.

Commemorative stamps for both Great Britain, the Dominions and the Colonies had long found their way into the Collection, their design and production being treated like any definitive issue; a commemorative issue is linked to a particular event or anniversary and is sold for a short time, while a definitive issue is only replaced by a subsequent issue. Two stamps, 2½ᵈ blue and 3ᵈ violet had been issued as peace stamps after the war, and were followed in 1948 by a fine commemorative issue celebrating the King and Queen's Silver Wedding anniversary, the 2½ᵈ ultramarine and the £1 deep blue. This showed a fine double portrait in silhouette of the King and Queen bearing the legend '1923–1948'. St Vincent and most other Colonies used the same design for their Silver Wedding issues. The original St Vincent £1 denomination was

Great Britain: 1946 2½ᴰ blue and the 3ᴰ violet 'Peace and Reconstruction' stamps issued to mark the end of the Second World War.

Great Britain: 1948 2½ᴰ ultramarine and the £1 blue issue to mark the Silver Wedding of George VI and Queen Elizabeth.

printed in black, but the whole issue was stolen before it reached the island and its replacement was printed in bright purple. There are a few archive examples in black, of which there are blocks of four from Plates 1 and 1a in the Collection.

It was indeed a just honour for Sir John Wilson to be elected President of the Royal Philatelic Society, London in 1950 for the second time to coincide with the exhibition to commemorate the centenary of 'The First Day of Postage, 6 May 1840', delayed from 1940. The Royal Philatelic Collection lent twenty pages of Great Britain, and the great rarities of the early issues of the Empire, being 'one page of classic stamps from each of the forty-eight British Possessions to issue their own adhesive Postage Stamps arranged in chronological order. The selection made from the collection formed by the late King George V.'[43] (see Appendix VII, page 320). The King visited the

St Vincent: 1948 £1 black, block of four, unused. The whole of this Silver Wedding commemorative issue was stolen. The replacement was printed in purple.

exhibition after hours at Grosvenor House with his younger daughter, Princess Margaret, who was interested in stamps but not a serious philatelist.

At the end of January 1952, George VI stood on the windswept tarmac of Heathrow Airport waving as his daughter, Princess Elizabeth, and the Duke of Edinburgh left for their tour of East Africa, Australia and New Zealand. But the King was far from well. As Winston Churchill, the prime minister wrote: 'During these last months the King walked with death, as if death was a companion, an acquaintance, whom he recognised but did not fear. In the end, death came as a friend.'[44] George VI died peacefully in his sleep during the night of 6 February 1952.

In comparison with his father, he had been no philatelist, but he had kept alive George V's Collection, and saw to it that his own modern collection lacked nothing, in particular the essays for all of the stamps that bore his image. It is for his loans to exhibitions, particularly abroad, that philatelists around the world chiefly remembered the King. As was remarked at the 1950 exhibition, no one forgets a display from the Royal Philatelic Collection.

CHAPTER TEN

⚜️⚜️⚜️

The Postmaster General waited upon Her Majesty Queen Elizabeth II's pleasure at Balmoral in August 1952 as she considered the essays of the first stamps of her reign. Ernest Marples had not held his post for long in Winston Churchill's cabinet, and certainly had no experience in the issue of postage stamps. But fortunately the Stamp Advisory Committee, under the chairmanship of Sir Kenneth Clark, had been through the process many times before. The competition for designs of the stamps for the new reign opened in early March 1952, and as the artwork came into the Postmaster General's office, it was considered by the Committee. The panel was made up of specialists, with representatives from the Council of Industrial Design, the Fine Arts Commission and the Arts Council of Great Britain. The Royal College of Arms sent an expert on heraldry, but the guiding force was Sir John Wilson, the Keeper of the Royal Philatelic Collection.

In all, seventy-four designs from twenty-eight artists were considered. At least there was no argument over the choice of photograph: for the Queen had selected it herself from a series of existing portraits by the Dorothy Wilding Studios, Court Photographer and holder of the Royal Warrant. Wilding's 'formidable technical abilities and eccentric charm combined to make her one of the foremost society portraitists of the day'.[1] The Queen selected a three-quarter-face portrait, much in the manner of the 'Downey Head' photograph of her grandfather, George V. Since then, the photogravure method of printing had been perfected, and it translated well to the stamp.

The Stamp Advisory Committee concentrated on the frames and their suitability to surround the portrait. A short list of essays was finally drawn up by August and submitted to the Queen for her final choice and approval. In the end, five basic designs made up what became known as the 'Wilding Definitives', with a variety of artists responsible for them. Miss Enid Marx, better known as a book illustrator, designed the frame of the 1½ᵈ value: she surrounded the portrait with a 'circlet of the national emblems, rose, thistle, shamrock and daffodil'.[2] For the 2½ᵈ value, M. C. Farrar-Bell, whose speciality was painting signs for public houses and designing stained-glass windows, produced an ornamental oval with the entwined national emblems in the lower left hand corner. The higher denominations were entrusted to three artists with experience of designing stamps, G. Knipe, the resident artist-designer at Harrison and Son, Miss Adshead, and Edmund Dulac, who had designed the Coronation stamp of George VI.

Princess Elizabeth examining an album of stamps at Buckingham Palace.
This is not one from the Royal Philatelic Collection. [Photo: Hulton Getty]

272

With the new issue came a new watermarked paper. Obsessed with security, the stylised version of the Sovereign's monogram had long been used by the Post Office. For this new issue, what became known as the 'Tudor Crown Watermark', with the Imperial Crown and 'E2R' staggered over the sheet, was adopted. Like her father and grandfather before her, the Queen monitored the progress of each stamp, right up to the day of issue, 5 December 1952, of the 1½ᵈ green and the 2½ᵈ red – produced in time for Christmas.

Having mounted all of the early original material from the inaugural stamps of George VI, Sir John Wilson was in a prime position to make sure that the essays, proofs and colour trials of the present reign came to the Royal Philatelic Collection. But he apparently believed that the stamps of a reign could only be properly mounted when it ended, and until then they should remain in storage. Thus, he committed the material for Queen Elizabeth II to a series of folders for another era and continued, or (predominantly) not, with mounting the George VI material.

The Coronation of Queen Elizabeth II on 2 June 1953 was celebrated with great enthusiasm throughout her realm, the Colonies and by the countries

Great Britain: 1953 artwork for commemorative Coronation stamp.
It was used with modifications for the 1/3 value.

that made up (or would become) the British Commonwealth; it was a welcome respite from the grim period after the Second World War, with rationing and the rebuilding of the nation. The day was marked in dozens of ways, not least with a Coronation Commemorative issue. As Coronation Day was a public holiday, the four values – 2½ᴰ carmine, 4d ultramarine, 1/3[D] deep yellow-green and 1/6[D] deep grey-blue – were issued on 3 June. Again, the Wilding portrait was used except for the 1/3[D] that was designed by Dulac, 'startling in its novelty and dignified approach, showing a full-face half-length portrait of the crowned Queen in her coronation robes and holding the orb and sceptre'.[3] The Queen was said to have been unhappy with this stamp, but it is thought that she was reconciled to it because its higher value meant the image would not be seen as often had it been used for the 2½ᴰ as first planned.

The origin of special, or commemorative, postage stamps (rather than the definitive issues) lies in the adhesive paper medallion that marked the Crafts and Trades Exhibition in Vienna of 1845, and the commemorative envelope for the centenary of the Declaration of Independence in 1876. In Great Britain, a brick-red adhesive label with a crown and suitable inscription having a stamp-like appearance was issued for the Great Exhibition of 1851. In 1890 Great Britain marked the fiftieth anniversary of the Uniform Penny Postage with a fine postal stationery envelope and a postcard. However, although the rest of the world issued commemorative stamps by the score, Britain remained aloof. But that was before the British Empire Exhibition of 1924 held at Wembley Stadium. For this first proper commemorative, six artists were invited to submit designs, the winner being Harold Nelson who came up with a sturdy lion to portray Britain's greatness. The same stamp was put on sale the next year with 1924 changed to 1925. Again, the Collection holds bromides of not only Nelson's essays, but those of three of the losers as well. Once the Post Office had broken its own rule, they felt empowered to mark the Ninth Congress of the Universal Postal Union held in London in 1929. The designs of two artists, Linzell and Farleigh, were chosen for the lower values, while one of Nelson's unaccepted designs for the British Empire Exhibition, known as the St George and Dragon, was used for the £1. Later, Farleigh wrote in his autobiography, 'Stamp collectors – a race as difficult to please as farmers – referred to the lack of England's

Great Britain:
1953 Coronation
2½ᴰ carmine,
designed by
E. G. Fuller.

Great Britain:
1953 Coronation
4d ultramarine,
designed by
Michael Goaman.

Great Britain:
1953 Coronation
1/3 deep yellow-green,
designed by Edmund
Dulac. The Queen
preferred the
Wilding portrait
in the other values
to this stamp.

Great Britain:
1953 Coronation
1/6 deep grey-blue,
designed by
M. Farrar-Bell.

Great Britain:
1924 rejected designs
by Eric Gill for
British Empire
Exhibition issue.

Great Britain: 1924 British Empire Exhibition
ONE PENNY and THREE HALFPENCE.

Great Britain: 1929 £1 black, colour trials of the 'St George and Dragon'.

beauty spots in the new designs, while one more imaginative critic discovered a resemblance to a beer bottle label in one of mine.'[4]

George V's Silver Jubilee commemorative stamps followed, the last issue of his reign. The King took the greatest pleasure in them and followed their progress from the well-known artist Bertram Freedman's sketch to the final issued stamps – the HALFPENNY green, ONE PENNY scarlet, THREE HALF PENCE red-brown and the TWOPENCE HALFPENNY ultramarine. However, legend has it that a resident of north London, who was also a stamp collector, sent his secretary to buy some of the TWOPENCE HALFPENNY stamps. He noticed that they were 'in that deep shade, with a greenish tinge, known as Prussian blue'.[5] The collector rushed round to the Post Office and bought up the remaining stamps. A few of the error were sold locally, while the rest were offered to a major firm of stamp dealers, who eventually bought them when no more came to light elsewhere. The error, as Wilson pointed out beside an example of the Prussian blue in the Red Collection, was thought to have been caused by four sheets of the colour trials being accidentally perforated. This has now been disproved, for although there is a trial of that colour, the stamp is of a different size from the issued stamp.

The Crown Agents were responsible for producing definitive postage and commemorative stamps for the Colonies. Throughout the reigns of George V and George VI, and up to 1960 of the present reign, the recess printed pictorial stamps produced by the Crown Agents are considered to be among the finest of the Colonial issues. They used a well-tried format, with representative views or local scenes to give a romantic impression of the country and its people, combined with the Sovereign's head. In the main, they were all beautifully produced, with attractive colour combinations and, being engraved, they were well printed. One such typical issue is the 1938–52 Jamaica with values from $\frac{1}{2}^d$ to £1. Through these stamps, the world was acquainted with the beauty of the island, its industry, and crops – citrus (4^d brown and green), bananas (3^d ultramarine and green) and sugar cane (1/- green and purple-brown). By August 1949, the Crown Agents gauged that the time was right to introduce the £1 value, and instructed the printers Waterlow and Sons to produce 48,000 stamps depicting tobacco growing and cigar manufacture in chocolate and violet with the head of George VI.

Great Britain: 1935, cover with all George V's Silver Jubilee commemorative stamps,
from the HALFPENNY to the TWOPENCE HALFPENNY used.

Great Britain: 1935 Silver Jubilee TWOPENCE HALFPENNY Prussian blue, an interesting error of colour.

Jamaica: 1938 artwork George VI.

When the King died in 1952, the Crown Agents instructed Waterlow to reprint the same £1 value, but with the Queen's head. The stamps were shipped out to Jamaica in 1954, where there was still a stock of the £1 with the late King's head. It was then decided to issue a completely new set of Jamaican Queen Elizabeth II definitives, with all values from ½d to £1, which eventually appeared between 1956–1958. This caused a dilemma as it was deemed unfair to philatelists to produce one £1 stamp with the Queen's head, only to replace it a year or so later with another completely different stamp in a new set. The solution was to reissue the George VI £1 stamp and destroy the Elizabeth II version. The whole batch was incinerated. Just seven examples escaped the flames, and the Royal Philatelic Collection holds an unused block of four, with the plate number in the margin below.

But these definitive and commemorative issues remained in their envelopes as Sir John Wilson had concentrated, in part, on mounting the initial stamps of the reign of George VI and working on his epic *The Royal Philatelic Collection* which was finally published, to great acclaim, in 1952. It is a masterly

Jamaica: 1956–58 £1 chocolate and violet. This unissued block of four (of the seven known examples) are all that remained after the whole batch of the Elizabeth II £1 value was destroyed and George VI £1 reissued as a concession to philatelists.

study in which he has described and catalogued the whole of the Red Collection, including the purchases made after the death of its founder, George V. At this time, few purchases were made for either the Red or the Blue collection (and none of the present reign), but the material flooded in as usual from the Post Office, the Crown Agents and Dominions. As regards the Universal Postal Union specimens, those germane to the Collection – Great Britain and the Commonwealth – were kept, and the rest were sent on to the Royal Philatelic Society, London, as is the practice today. At the time of writing, a backlog of U.P.U. specimens is caught up in the Postal Heritage Trust.

Sir John Wilson continued to present displays from the Collection at the opening meeting of the Royal Philatelic Society, London where

on these occasions he gave attractive talks on the Colony being shown. He took great care in the preparation of these addresses, consulting all that had been previously written on the particular stamps, and then speaking for about 30–45 minutes without any notes to assist him. His legal training was of great assistance in doing this as he was able to read the earlier writings as he would have read a brief and then proceed to include all the necessary information in his speech. As a speaker he was in the first rank ... [where] he was never once seen to have recourse to notes as the exhibits were passed round the table.[6]

At the end of September 1955, for example, he spoke about the display from the Collection of the New Zealand first type. Prime among the exhibits was not one of the rare 1855 (18 July) ONE PENNY dull carmine, unused, but *three*, with another two used.

New Zealand: 1855 ONE PENNY, dull carmine, unused, one of three in the Collection. The first was a birthday present from Queen Mary to George V in 1920.

The first body of immigrants had arrived in New Zealand on 22 January 1840, and eight days later Captain Hobson RN hoisted the Union Flag and read the commission under the Great Seal of Great Britain that extended the boundaries of New South Wales to include the whole of New Zealand. Shortly after, at the treaty of Waitangi, the native chiefs ceded all powers to Great Britain while retaining their territorial rights. By 3 May 1841, New Zealand was proclaimed a separate Colony in its own right. Initial efforts to establish a post office failed due to the high postal charges, but by 1851 the system had shaken down and notice of the prepayment of letters was published in the *New Zealand Gazette*.

New Zealand. Proof of an engraving taken from the Chalon portrait of Queen Victoria.

As was so often the case in emergent Colonies, the postal system was willing but the stamps were missing. On 18 July 1855, the *Gazette* announced that the new stamps had arrived from London, and were for sale and use.

These stamps are truly wonderful. The image was taken from the A. E. Chalon portrait of Queen Victoria in her state robes for the ONE PENNY, TWO PENCE and ONE SHILLING values. The engraver William Humphreys prepared the master die, which was used to make the subsidiary dies on which the values were inserted. These in turn were used to make the steel plates. Humphreys was the leading stamp engraver of his day working on the early designs of Ceylon, St Helena, South Australia, the triangular Cape of Good Hope, and the famous George Washington portrait for the early issues of the United States of America. The first issue was printed by Perkins, Bacon, London – hence the term 'London printing' to distinguish them from the local 1862 printing, also on a six-ray star watermark paper that was sent to the Colony with the plates, inks, and press.

The first unused example of this ONE PENNY carmine in the Collection was a birthday present from Queen Mary to George V in 1920, so marginally predates the other fine copy bought from the Duveen Collection. The other unused specimen came from Perkins, Bacon, and was a truly remarkable find. On one of Sir Edward Bacon's frequent visits to the printer, a director told him that he remembered finding some early Colonial stamps, which he had put into a manila envelope and subsequently lost. He promised to let him know if he found them. In 1928, W. D. Heath turned up at the Stamp Room at Buckingham Palace and, to Bacon's amazement, he produced the envelope with the most perfect set of the early Colonials, as bright and brilliant as when they were first printed. Out of it came the third of the Collection's London Printed 1855 New Zealand ONE PENNY, along with TWO PENCE blue, and a ONE SHILLING yellow-green, all of the same 18 July 1855 issue. Out slid another set, the 1855–58 issues ONE PENNY, TWO PENCE, FOUR PENCE, SIX PENCE and ONE SHILLING of Tasmania, also with the Chalon Head, and finally two stamps of Victoria, the ONE PENNY green of October 1856 and an imperforate example of the SIX PENCE bright blue of November 1858, and they are mounted beside other examples in the Collection.

However, in the Collection (and often on the same page) there are some examples of equally brilliant stamps, known as the 'Cancelled by Perkins, Bacon'. These stamps were prepared at the instigation of, and as a favour to, Ormond Hill, nephew of Rowland Hill. In 1861, Hill wrote to Joshua Bacon, the head of Perkins, Bacon, asking if he would pass on any specimens of new or uncommon Colonial stamps for six of his collector friends and family. Bacon obliged, starting with some examples of Queensland, quickly followed by other Colonies like St Vincent. More than likely these were

New Zealand: 1855 (July) ONE PENNY carmine, the TWO PENCE blue,
and ONE SHILLING yellow-green, unused.

Victoria: 1856 Queen on Throne ONE PENNY green, and 1858 SIX PENCE bright blue imperforate.

Tasmania: 1855 ONE PENNY carmine, TWO PENCE deep green,
FOUR PENCE blue, 1858 SIX PENCE dull lilac, and 1863–71 ONE SHILLING vermilion.

These were all the contents of an envelope of 'forgotten' stamps in pristine condition
found in a drawer at Perkins, Bacon and sold to George V.

Newfoundland: 1860 (August)
ONE SHILLING orange-vermilion,
CANCELLED by Perkins, Bacon.

Bahamas: 1860 (October)
ONE PENNY, lake,
CANCELLED by Perkins, Bacon.

Around 450 stamps from about twenty Colonies were illegally distributed by Perkins, Bacon to collector friends. The practice led to Perkins, Bacon losing their contract with the Crown Agents.

printed clandestinely from the plates entrusted to them by their respective governments, rather than leftover specimens at proof stage. When Penrose Julyan, Agent General of the Crown Colonies, learnt of the practice, he used it as an excuse to terminate their contract with Perkins, Bacon to print Colonial stamps. But that was after around 450 stamps from about twenty countries (mostly Colonies) had been produced. George V, encouraged by Tilleard and Bacon, was particularly interested in these stamps and was fortunate to be able to cherry-pick a collection that came on the market in December 1934. Consequently, the Collection has a virtually complete set – those from Chile being outside the scope of the Collection – along with some from Newfoundland.

Throughout the whole of the 1950s and 1960s, Wilson worked alone on the Collection, although while he was writing his book, the Palace allowed him a secretary. Besides putting together the displays for the Royal Philatelic Society, London each year, which required a great deal of planning and research, and his work on the Expert Committee of the Society, he had a full programme of exhibiting selected parts of the Collection abroad. In 1950 he had been to Melbourne with the first Ham printings (see page 63) of Victoria, and the Sydney Views, and was in Toronto the following year with all the important Canadian material. He travelled to Cape Town, Lisbon and New Delhi. Sometimes, as in 1955, he went to several venues, Stockholm, Oslo and New Zealand (with the famous 'first type'). 1960 was particularly busy: Wilson took parts of the Collection to Barcelona, Johannesburg, Poland and contributed to the London International Stamp Exhibition at the Festival Hall with 'a display of stamps in use 100 years ago including *Great Britain, Private Telegraph Companies, Queensland, South Australia, Western Australia, Malta, India, Mauritius, British Guiana, Natal, Jamaica, Barbados,* and *Trinidad*'.[7] His work on the Stamp Advisory Committee became particularly eventful after the Labour Party's election victory in 1964 and the appointment of the radical Anthony Wedgwood Benn as Postmaster General.

Long before his appointment as Postmaster General, Benn had campaigned for the improvement of British stamps and, on the same agenda, the removal of the Queen's head from them. In his diary, he wrote:

> One of the other preoccupations of my first months as Postmaster General was stamp policy. The GPO had a narrow and limited view about commemorative stamp issues which were primarily connected with State and Commonwealth occasions and one or two international events. Above all, they were determined that British stamps should not become 'cheap and flashy' which was the way they interpreted the mass of modern design that was emerging all over the world. Indeed it was impossible to do a good design when about a third of all commemorative stamps were occupied by a large portrait of the Queen which, in effect, involved attaching a regular stamp to the side of every commemorative stamp, thus destroying any integration of design or free-flowing picture across the whole. I therefore urged a more imaginative policy, which was greatly resented, and invited designers to put their own designs for public display. The Stamp Advisory Committee under Sir Kenneth Clark argued that the Queen herself did not wish to appear with faces of other people, however famous, who were dead. The ordinary, or definitive, postage stamp had always carried the Monarch's portrait and because Britain was the originator of postage stamps, it was and is the only country whose stamps do not bear the country's name.
>
> Historically, sovereigns in this country have always been intensely interested in the design of coinage, stamps and all medals issued.[8]

Great Britain: 1964 1/6 deep slate purple – the
Shakespeare Festival was the first commemorative
issue where, against the Queen's wishes,
her head appeared with another.

The issue became focused when the Queen's head appeared jointly with a portrait of Shakespeare on a stamp, ostensibly to mark the four-hundredth anniversary of his birth, and the proposed Burns stamp to mark the two-hundredth anniversary of *his* birth made 'the issue a live one at the Queen's request'.[9] The Postmaster General had his way. On 15 December 1964 he announced that the criteria for commemoratives had been too restrictive in the past, and that besides celebrating events of national and international importance, and anniversaries, stamps in future would reflect 'the British contribution to world affairs, including the arts and science; and to extend public patronage to the arts by encouraging the development of minuscule art'.[10] Having opened the 'floodgate' to new 'commemorative' issues, Benn then set about removing the Queen's head altogether from the stamp. For this he had an ally in the husband-and-wife artist team David Gentleman and Rosalind Dease 'one of the best – if not the best – stamp designers in the country'[11] who had been commissioned to design the stamp to honour Sir Winston Churchill. They stressed that it was impossible make a decent stamp 'until the Queen's head was removed'. They tried 'a tiny Queen's head on Churchill's massive shoulder, and asked if they could have the stamp printed without the Queen's head to see what it looked like'. Benn agreed and said that he would put it to the Stamp Advisory Committee. The civil servants in his office had other ideas, and the essay without the Queen's head was not submitted.

In March 1965, Benn was granted an audience by the Queen at Buckingham Palace. He was met by Sir Michael Adeane, her Private Secretary, and taken to her private apartments. After he had bowed and shaken hands, the Queen beckoned him to sit down, whereupon he started on his carefully prepared speech. He said that he was grateful for the audience, as he 'knew the keen interest that she took in postage stamps'[12] and that he wanted to talk about stamp design policy in general. He told the Queen that 'the new Government saw stamps in an entirely new context as part of the arts and not just as adhesive money labels for postage purposes'; he thought that there were many things about Britain that should be projected abroad, 'perhaps through postage stamps'. The Queen 'smiled graciously' when Benn suggested that the government 'would like to have new definitives which would have a more beautiful picture' of her on them, and outlined how he wanted to widen the scope of the postage stamp with pictorial images of a wide range of subjects.

'However,' he continued, 'this raised the whole question of the use of the head on the stamp,' at which the 'Queen frowned and smiled'. Undaunted, Benn continued pointing out the difficulty of the Burns stamp under the present arrangement, along with other planned issues. He battled on, saying that it was understood that it had been Her Majesty's personal command that stamps 'that did not embody the [Queen's] head could not even be submitted [to her] for consideration', but as he did not know if this *was* the case, he thought he should ask her in person if it had been a 'personal command' or not. 'The Queen was clearly embarrassed and indicated that she had no personal feeling about it at all.' Clearly, she did not want to be an 'obstacle to new design', but Benn had manoeuvred her into a difficult position. He knew that the removal of her head from the stamp would cause an outcry unless it was done with the Queen's blessing. What Benn then proposed was that designers could submit their designs for new stamps, with or without her head, which would then be forwarded to the Queen for her approval. That way, in answering a question in the House of Commons, he could truthfully say that 'The Queen had approved a procedure under which all stamps of all kinds were submitted to her for her consideration.'

Great Britain: 1966 1/3 black, slate-blue and orange.
This Burns commemorative issue was almost the last
to have a photographic portrait of the Queen.

The Queen replied that she knew that various Commonwealth countries had removed her head from their stamps, but replaced it with a crown. Benn thought that a good alternative, adding that her head might well be right for some stamps, or that it might be embossed in white or in silhouette. All he wanted was the right to submit stamps of all kinds to her. When the Queen told him that she had never seen any of these headless designs, Benn said that by chance he had some by David Gentleman with him, and asked if she would like to see them? As both of them knelt on the floor, he then spread out the twelve large design models of the Battle of Britain stamps with the words GREAT BRITAIN and without the royal head. The audience over, Sir Michael Adeane escorted Benn to his car, said goodbye, and added 'But I think the monarch's head has to be on the stamps, doesn't it?'

After his meeting with the Queen, Benn was elated. He proposed to commission Gentleman for an entirely new series, and present it to the Stamp Advisory Committee. 'There will no doubt be some trouble from them but it is not a discussable issue any more since it has already been settled with the monarch.'[13] He was surprised that the Committee warmed to the proposals of the new policy, but the Chairman, Sir Kenneth Clark, told him that George V had made him promise as a junior member 'never [to] let the sovereign's head come off the stamps',[14] then added that so long as the Queen's head remained on the definitive stamps, his pledge would be honoured. But the *entente cordiale* between the Postmaster General and his Stamp Advisory Committee did not last. When they saw the designs for the Burns stamp, some without the head of the Queen, it was too much. Sir Kenneth Clark resigned as chairman, ostensibly as he had been on the committee for thirty years and felt it was time for a change. Sir John Wilson wanted to resign too but, with Clark gone, he felt it 'incumbent to stay on'.[15] The artist James Fitton RA took over as Chairman.

By December 1965, the Committee had become thoroughly irritated with Benn, who had not always accepted their recommendations. Benn noted in his diary that 'Sir John Wilson, Keeper of the Queen's Philatelic Collection, had told them that The Queen would never accept stamps without her head on them',[16] but when he reminded them of his meeting with the Queen in March, Paul Reilly said, with some feeling, that 'There certainly have been second thoughts since then.' Benn admitted (albeit privately) that realistically it was unlikely that he would ever 'get the Queen's head off the stamp'. A set of four pictorial landscapes was issued on 2 May 1966, for the first time bearing a white silhouette of the Queen's head adapted by David Gentleman from the coinage. The following day, Benn attended the Stamp Advisory Committee and presented the next issues. He thought the British Technology issue was disappointing, but that the stamps to commemorate the Battle of Hastings 'were very good carrying a small cameo of the Queen's profile in gold'.[17] 'Sir John Wilson,' he continued, 'just muttered all the time about the size of the Queen's head and said with a thick Scottish accent [which he did not have] "People seem to forget that it is the symbol of the country, that it must be significant, that it must be big, that it must be important and we can't accept anything less than that."'[18]

In the end, both factions were appeased. By dogged persistence, Benn changed the face of Great Britain stamps, but men like Sir John Wilson fought and won the battle to keep the Queen's head upon them. The Queen monitored the situation throughout, and directed her Private Secretary Sir Michael Adeane to write to Benn:

> Her Majesty ... hopes that the wide public interest in British stamp design which you have aroused in this country and is now being re-echoed in the United States of America, will continue to have fruitful results. You can rest assured that this is far from being a subject which Her Majesty regards in any way as 'routine'; she looks forward to the design which you should submit, because she realised, better than most people perhaps, that the postage stamp, which we invented, remains one of the best ways of reminding the world of what we are and what we are doing.[19]

Benn was promoted to the Cabinet in July 1966 on his appointment as Minister for Technology, and was succeeded by Edward Short as Postmaster General. It is ironic that one who was so keen to remove the Queen's head from the Great Britain postage stamp should have been indirectly responsible for one of the best designs of all time. When Sir Kenneth Clark, Chairman of the Stamp Advisory Committee, proposed a new profile portrait stamp

Great Britain: 1977–87 £2 colour essays, design after the plaster cast by Arnold Machin.
The light emerald and purple-brown was chosen and the stamp was issued on 2 February 1977.

the year before, it was Lord Reilly who suggested using the Earl of Snowdon's portraits of the Queen, his sister-in-law (the Queen famously dislikes having her photograph taken) for the new issue. In fact, Snowdon's portraits of the Queen were used in the first instance by Arnold Machin, who had been selected to design the new coinage in 1964. For the stamps, five artists – Arnold Machin, John Ward, David Gentleman, Reginald Brill and Stuart Devlin – were each asked to produce by January 1966 a 'rendering' of a profile portrait of the Queen, based on the Snowdon photographs. Machin produced a drawing of the Queen's head, and in consultation with Brill and Gentleman, advanced his work into a first plaster cast, still largely based on the coinage head, although it faced the opposite direction. By the spring of 1966, essays were produced from this plaster cast, and these were subsequently simplified over the summer.

Although the Stamp Advisory Committee greatly admired Machin's work, they also wanted a photographic alternative before finally committing themselves. For this, they commissioned John Hedgecoe to take new photographs of the Queen on 22 June 1966, and it was these photographs that were subsequently used by David Gentleman to create various photographic designs and essays. The Committee then compared these with the simplified Machin essays. After much deliberation, it was decided that the diadem in the Hedgecoe photographs was better than the tiara proposed by Machin. Consequently, the next plaster cast produced by Machin in October 1966 was based on his earlier work, but with certain features, like the diadem, taken from the Hedgecoe photographs. The Queen had the final say, and asked for a corsage, rather than being cut off at the neck (she could well have been reminded of the controversy over the Edward VIII stamps). Mindful of the Queen's wishes, Machin then produced the final plaster cast.

When the issue was launched on 5 June 1967, Short declared it 'a classic of stamp history, one of the greatest stamps of all time'.[20] It had 'captured the delicate lines of the moulding', and at the end, it was generally agreed that nothing served so well as just the profile head of the Queen and the value of the stamp. Queen Victoria kept the same youthful profile of herself aged fifteen for the whole of her long reign, and the classic simplicity of the Machin Head, the hallmark of a great stamp, could well do the same for Elizabeth II.

In 1969, Sir John Wilson decided to retire as Keeper of the Royal Philatelic Collection. He had not been well for some time and was over seventy. He had served Elizabeth II and George VI loyally for over twenty-eight years, a service for which he was made a KCVO (Knight Commander of the Victorian Order) in 1957. His contribution had been great, he had single-handedly kept the Collection going, but the time had come to hand over to a younger man. He recommended as his successor John Marriott, whom he knew well as they had served together on the Expert Committee.

John Marriott inherited an enormous backlog of material stuffed into envelopes and boxes, and a mountain of unanswered letters – the only advice he received from Sir John Wilson was 'to do what I do with all correspondence!'.[21] It was said by some wit that the greatest philatelic rarity was a signed letter from Sir John Wilson. Marriott, then aged forty-seven, was a mathematics master at Charterhouse, the English public school founded in 1611 on the site of a Carthusian monastery in London but now situated near Godalming, thirty-five miles south west of London. He had been housemaster of Girdlestoneites (named after the first housemaster, a Mr Girdlestone) for nine years, and when the offer came to take over the Royal Philatelic Collection, both his mathematics classes and his house were running so smoothly that arrangements were made by the headmaster whereby he could accept. The timetable was revised to allow him to be in London by midday, having taught at least two classes in the morning. His wife, Mary, covered for him during his absence from his house. The salary he received as Keeper of the Royal Philatelic Collection exactly matched what the headmaster docked from his salary for his reduced teaching hours.

A mild, unassuming man, Marriott excelled in many areas. He had gone up to St John's College, Cambridge, with a major scholarship in 1941. In just two years, he read for Part II of the Mathematics Tripos, graduating with a first. He was appointed to Bletchley Park, the code-breaking centre, where he worked with the legendary Max Newman (also a St John's Fellow) on the Colossus, an electronic machine designed specifically to decipher the German Lorenz code. This eventually led to the breaking of the 'Enigma Code'. With that monumental breakthrough, the Axis Powers' initiatives and movements could be decoded, undetected by the enemy. Such invaluable intelligence helped to shorten the Second World War. He played cricket and rugby for Cambridge, but he dismissed this with the words 'they were only wartime blues'. He was a fine batsman though, and he went on to play for Hertfordshire. After the war, Marriott was 'demobbed' early to teach mathematics at Charterhouse. He remained there for thirty-seven years.

Another of John Marriott's fortes was philately. He had started as a twelve-year-old schoolboy who spent his pocket money on stamps (rather than cigarettes like his contemporaries). His interest widened when an aunt sent him the first airmail letter from South Africa, and family legend tells of regular letters arriving with exotic stamps from Samoa sent by his missionary grandfather. This interest developed after the war into serious philatelic research and collecting. His first love was Trinidad (his collection of Tobago was sold to furnish his first house when he married in 1952), which was virtually complete when it was sold shortly after his death in 2001; it was

Sir John Marriott, KCVO. A housemaster at Charterhouse School, he divided his time between teaching and as Keeper of the Royal Philatelic Collection. *[Photo: RPSL]*

awarded gold medals at international exhibitions in London, South Africa and Amsterdam, and the Tilleard Medal in 1968. In fact, Marriott's collection of and publications on Trinidad were so famous that his wife was known in philatelic circles as 'Lady McLeod' (see page 49).

So John Marriott worked quietly in the Stamp Room at Buckingham Palace, initially twice a week 'after break' during term time, and more often during the school holidays. He began by reorganising what Sir John Wilson had left unfinished – when Wilson died, his son found stamps from the Royal Philatelic Collection among his father's papers and returned them to Buckingham Palace.

The material of Elizabeth II's reign had accumulated to an enormous volume, and Wilson had made no provision for mounting it. Marriott asked the Queen what colour she would like to distinguish her albums and produced some swatches of morocco leather. After careful consideration, the Queen chose dark green, and cut off a snippet. When the new sample album was produced for her approval, she declared it was the wrong colour, and produced the snippet to prove it. The album was soon replaced in the correct colour. Such attention to detail is typical of the Queen's commitment to the Collection although, like her father George VI, her interest in it is from afar.

Marriott enjoyed mounting and writing up, often working in pencil first, then inking in his annotations. The Great Britain and the Commonwealth issues were still sent automatically to the Stamp Room, but he kept up to date with all notable errors, particularly Great Britain. These had to be bought or, on rare occasions, were donated.

One of the few notable errors that Marriott bought at this time was the 1964 50th Anniversary of the Battle of the Falkland Islands commemorative SIX PENCE black and light blue, error of centre. The battle was fought on 8 December 1914 at the beginning of the First World War. On 1 November, Vice-Admiral Maximilian Graf von Spee, the commander of the German East Asiatic Fleet, engaged a British squadron under Rear-Admiral Sir Christopher Cradock at the battle of Coronel, off the south coast of Chile. Cradock's flagship, the armoured cruiser HMS *Good Hope*, and another HMS *Monmouth* were sunk. Fresh from his success, von Spee sped towards Port Stanley, Falkland Islands, to attack the British radio station and coaling depot.

Falkland Islands: 1964 commemorative issue to celebrate the 50th Anniversary of the Battle of the Falkland Islands. The 2½ᴰ (black and red) has HMS *Glasgow* in the centre, the 6ᴰ (black and light blue) has HMS *Kent*, while the 1/- value (black and carmine red) shows HMS *Invincible*, while the 2/- value (black and blue) depicts the War Memorial.

Falkland Islands: 1964 Battle of the Falkland Islands 6ᴰ black and light blue, error of centre. A whole sheet of 60 was printed with HMS *Glasgow* instead of HMS *Kent*.

Unbeknown to him, a British squadron under the command of Vice-Admiral Sir Frederick Sturdee had been sent by First Sea Lord Admiral of the Fleet Lord Fisher to avenge the British defeat at Coronel. His flagship, the modern, fast battle-cruiser HMS *Inflexible* along with HMS *Invincible,* the armoured cruisers HMS *Carnarvon, Cornwall* and *Kent*, and two light cruisers, the *Bristol* and the *Glasgow,* had put into Port Stanley to recoal when von Spee arrived. The German Admiral began his attack on 8 December 1914. Too late he realised his danger and, having missed the golden opportunity to shell Sturdee's squadron while in port, he dashed for the open sea, pursued by the

British. He knew he could not hope to outrun *Invincible* and *Inflexible*, so decided to bring about an engagement. Four German cruisers, including von Spee's flagship *Scharnhorst*, were sunk, and the Royal Navy carried the day. It was hailed as a great and morally uplifting victory.

To mark the fiftieth anniversary of the battle, a set of four Falkland Islands stamps was issued, three showing British cruisers: 2½ᴰ HMS *Glasgow* in black and red, 6ᴰ HMS *Kent* in black and light blue, 1/- HMS *Invincible* while the 2/- value showed the war memorial commemorating the ten British sailors killed in the battle. The stamps were engraved and recessed-printed by De La Rue in the two colours, the centre being in black. A little later, a Canadian collector bought the set from a New York dealer, and noticed that the 2½ᴰ and the 6ᴰ both had HMS *Glasgow*. At first he did not identify the error, but then read a report of the issue and realised what he owned. It is thought that as it was a two-colour operation, a single sheet of sixty stamps was first printed with the 2½ᴰ vignette, HMS *Glasgow*, and then mysteriously found its way into the pile of HMS *Kent* sheets waiting for their second printing of a frame in blue. Hence the error: HMS *Glasgow* with a 6ᴰ value with a blue border. It is suggested that there are no more than seventeen known examples out of a possible sixty.

Marriott bought a variety of Great Britain errors for the Collection, one of the rarest being the 'missing value' in 13p stamp of the 'roses' June 1976 issue to commemorate the Centenary of the National Rose Society. The error occurred when a minute sheet of copper was placed over the cylinder during some temporary repairs, and left in place when the printing resumed. When the error was discovered, the faulty stamps were removed and destroyed, but three known examples slipped through the net. The Royal Philatelic Collection has two, one unused, the other used on cover.

Other contemporary errors that Marriott bought include examples where one or more of the colours were omitted from reel-fed printings. Here the pressure

Great Britain: 1976 13p rose-pink, lake brown, yellow-green, pale greenish-yellow, grey-black and gold, commemorative issue Centenary of the National Rose Society, unused. With the value omitted, it is known as the 'roses error'.

on the drum is relaxed to realign the colour register, but just long enough to skip three or four rows. One of the first of the famous errors occurred when the blue was omitted from the National Productivity Year 3d. commemorative stamp. As this shade of blue had been used to print the portrait of the Queen, it meant that her head was completely missing – hence the sobriquet 'The Headless Queen'. Similarly, the 3d. value of the 1965 issue to commemorate the opening of the Post Office Tower where the shadowy tower is missing.

A very small fund was allocated annually by the Privy Purse to the Collection, which was topped up by the sales of duplicates and fees from articles and works by the Keeper. Decisions about where and what to buy were for him to take, and he made purchases for a purpose, rather than for personal choice as George V principally had with the Red Collection. Thus, Marriott believed that the Collection would benefit from the purchase of the Lovegrove Collection of 'free franks', a fine collection put together by

Great Britain: 1764–1840 Free Franking. Letter from the Duke of Clarence.

Sir John Marriott, a much sought-after judge for philatelic exhibitions the world over.

J. W. Lovegrove, an authority on the subject. Before the introduction of the universal 1d postage and the postage stamp in 1840, members of the House of Commons and the House of Lords, were allowed to send their letters free of charge. This privilege had been widely abused since introduction by the Council of State in 1652, when a wax seal, rather than a signature, identified the MPs' free post. The Collection holds a very large number of envelopes, all with the signatures. The other big Marriott purchase was a collection of Canadian airmails.

In 1975 John Marriott retired as housemaster and in 1982 from teaching. He planned to devote more time to his own pursuits, in particular philately, but retirement can create a vacuum and the demands on his time were just as great, but from other quarters. He was elected President of the Royal Philatelic Society, London, in 1983 which added to his already heavy philatelic workload: where Sir John Wilson approached the opening meetings of the Royal Philatelic Society as a barrister does a brief, John Marriott had spent weeks putting together his display (when he was teaching it took all the summer holidays). It was always accompanied by a learned paper, which was published in the *London Philatelist*. Although his particular expertise was the stamps of the West Indies, he did not favour them in his displays at the expense of other countries. Over his twenty-six years as Keeper, there was something for everyone. And the showing of the Royal Philatelic Collection at home and abroad, which Wilson had begun, escalated with Marriott.

Every year there was an international philatelic conference or exhibition somewhere in the world, and John Marriott, invariably accompanied by his wife, took to each one a display from the Royal Philatelic Collection. Mrs Marriott was an important member of the team; not only was she essential as a hostess but also, being small, 'The case with all the valuable stamps could be put safely on the floor in front of me like a footstool, so it was quite safe.'[22] The early exhibitions during Marriott's tenure took place in Europe – Posnan, in Poland, Madrid, Copenhagen, Amsterdam; later ones were held further afield in Auckland, Bangkok, Tokyo, Hong Kong – even, in 1994, Seoul. Each display was chosen with great care: Marriott believed that there was little point in taking the country's own stamps unless, of course there was something unique in the Collection.

For his great contribution to philately, John Marriott was honoured throughout the world: in 1982 he received the Lichtenstein Award from the Collectors' Club in New York and the Lindenburg Medal from Germany among many others. He had 'signed the Roll of Distinguished Philatelists' (RDP), in 1972. There was, however, one event in connection with the Stamp Room that was not of Marriott's making: Michael Fagan's break-in to Buckingham Palace. Some years previously, Marriott had moved the Stamp Room from the first floor (the room was needed as another bedroom) to the ground floor, overlooking what is now the Queen's Gallery beside the Ambassadors' Entrance. The vault was at the back of this room on one side, and on the other, a door led into a small room with a bathroom where dignitaries could change. On the afternoon of 9 July 1982, a housemaid had cleaned the set of rooms, but had left the window of the side room ajar. That night, Fagan climbed over the Buckingham Palace wall and walked along the west side of the Palace. There he saw the open window and entered the Stamp Room, triggering the burglar alarm. As the door was securely locked, Fagan retraced his steps and climbed out of the window, triggering the alarm again. The police turned it off, twice, without investigating. Fagan entered the Palace through another open window on the first floor on the south side and made his way to the Queen's bedroom. The footman, who had replaced the armed policeman at six o'clock in the morning, was out walking the corgis. Fagan received a prison sentence.

Eventually, the strain of looking after the Collection and his other duties took their toll on John Marriott. In 1993, he asked that his friend Charles Goodwyn (who was elected fellow RDP in 1995) be brought in to help. Goodwyn was summoned to a meeting at Buckingham Palace by the Keeper of the Privy Purse, Major Sir Shane Blewitt, to discuss his proposed role as assistant to Marriott. Blewitt asked him to give an account of himself, which Goodwyn did and easily passed muster. But before his position was confirmed, Sir Shane told him that he would have to have a reference from the President of the Royal Philatelic Society, London. 'That is not difficult', Goodwyn replied, 'I can give it to you right now'.[23] Charles Goodwyn, a former honorary secretary to the Society, was then nearing the end of his two-year term as President.

Soon Marriott realised that the time had come for him to retire, and he asked Goodwyn to draw up a list of suitable candidates to take over, which he duly did. Without looking at it, Marriott screwed it up, tossed it into the waste-paper basket and put forward Goodwyn's name. Eventually, he was named as Marriott's successor and he took over as Keeper of the Royal Philatelic Collection in September 1995.

On his own appointment, Marriott had had an audience with the Queen. She told him about her collection of first-day covers of Great Britain and the Commonwealth, which she had begun in 1952. She asked him what he thought of them in general. Marriott was deeply embarrassed, and put it as politely as a serious philatelist could. He thought that first day covers were a somewhat sub-standard form of collecting. The Queen roared with laughter, and said, 'Sir John [Wilson] did not think much of them either!'[24] At the end

Charles Goodwyn, LVO, LLB, RDP, FRPSL.

of his tenure, the Queen made Marriott a Knight Commander of the Royal Victorian Order. He died in 2001.

Like most serious philatelists, Goodwyn's interest was sparked in boyhood. 'My father had a collection, and when I was at Wellington [College] I heard a Colonel Latham talking about his Chinese collection. I started with an all-world general collection, then started collecting Hong Kong, and went naturally into China.'[25] The fine collection of Hong Kong was largely sold, and his present collection is very specific: Wei Hei Wei, an erstwhile leased territory in the north-east corner of China.

Wei Hei Wei was a strategic port founded in 1898 when Britain took a lease from the Chinese government of the tiny island of Liu-Kung-Tau, with a strip of the mainland about ten miles deep around the bay. At first, the settlement was somewhat primitive, with a postal system that relied on passing ships to carry the mail to and from the nearest Chinese post office at Chefoo, some fifty-six miles away. This was thought unsatisfactory, so some of the residents put together their own system of a courier post and received permission from the commissioner in December 1898 to issue 2 and 5 cents stamps to cover their expenses. These stamps were ordered from Shanghai, but were needed long before they arrived. In the meantime, a number of stamps were printed locally by a Captain Harrison of the Royal Engineers. For these, a piece of 'dark room paper' – a fine Chinese red wove paper – was stamped with the company symbol of Cornabé and Co., who were in the habit of marking every genuine dollar bill with their mark or, as it was widely

Wei Hei Wei: 1899 2 cents red-brown and 5 cents pale olive green.
This lithographed issue replaced the locally printed 'dollar chop' stamps.

known, the 'dollar chop'. The 'chop' was made up of the letters C & C and W.H.W. (Wei Hei Wei) between two concentric lines with the company name in Chinese characters (Ho Kee) in the centre. The value, either 2 or 5 cents was written in manuscript on the top, with the letters c and p, standing for courier post, on the bottom. Before it was cut up into little pieces one inch square, the sheet was signed several times by G. L. Fergusson, Cornabé and Co.'s local representative, so that each 'stamp' would be authenticated with a fragment of his signature. These red labels had a life of about a month, after which they were replaced by a proper printed issue, in the same values, on white wove paper in Shanghai. While Charles Goodwyn's collection is considerable, the British Post Offices in China section of the Royal Philatelic Collection contains a token representation with several fine examples of the 'dollar chop' issue and the replacement lithographed series of January 1899.

The tradition that the Keeper of the Royal Philatelic Collection served for decades was sadly broken when Charles Goodwyn resigned his post after a little over seven years. But during that short time, he left an impression that has set the scene for the twenty-first century. Where the Red Collection had been the personal property of George V, and was thus rarely seen outside the Stamp Room and the Royal Philatelic Society London, Goodwyn's brief was to make the entire Collection, Red, Blue and Green, available to the widest possible audience, both at home and abroad. He continued where Marriott left off, collating material, mounting, and exhibiting. Again, he worked single-handedly and, most of his correspondence, like his predecessors', was hand-written. His great contribution, however, was to encourage research. Until he took over, the only outsiders to use the Collection had been, almost exclusively, members of the Expert Committee of the Royal Philatelic Society London. Goodwyn encouraged those with a valid research project to study the Collection. He continued to take the displays to international exhibitions around the world, travelling to such places as Canada in 1996, Hong Kong in 1997, and Australia in 1999. But what Charles Goodwyn will also be remembered for is his purchase of the Kirkcudbright Cover for the Collection.

There are around seventy known covers with the Penny Black dated 6 May 1840, the first day on which it was valid for postage. These are mostly single stamps, very occasionally pairs. Some are better than others: they were imperforate so much depended on the scissor work of the Post Office counter clerk or the sender as they cut the stamps out of a sheet. But one of the excitements of philately is that just when it is thought that there could not possibly be anything new to discover, something rare and exceptional comes on to the market. In 1968, the Kirkcudbright Cover suddenly appeared for sale. It was unique – a block of ten Penny Blacks used on the first day of postage. The cover, in fact a wrapper, had been sent from a London solicitor to a James Burnie Esqre in Kirkcudbright, a pretty harbour and centre of the Stewartry of Kirkcudbright in the southwest corner of Scotland. The letter weighed between four and five ounces, which was why it was so expensive to post, was known to contain a will and a collection of legal documents as the list of them has also survived. It was a find of the century, for it is the largest block of Penny Blacks used on the first day. The vendor was 'an elderly resident of Kirkcudbright' who had been given it by a descendant of Mr Burnie. As she had no knowledge of stamps, she took it to a local philatelist, a Mr W. G. Morris, who naturally recognised what it was, and advised her to sell it at auction. It was sold by H. R. Harmer in London on 27 May 1968 for £4,800 and was taken out of the country.

Great excitement surrounded the auction when it came up for sale again through Stanley Gibbons on 24 June 1998, estimated at £250,000–300,000. It failed to reach its reserve and was bought in by the auctioneers for £220,000. It was then offered to all likely purchasers, private individuals and museums – the British Library considered it for their collection, but even if they had wanted it, the price was far out of their reach. Eventually, it was offered to the Royal Philatelic Collection at £250,000, the lower end of the auction estimate. The discussion on whether it should be bought or not lasted for several weeks. There was certainly not the money in the bank to buy it, and the question was raised, 'what would it do for the Collection?'[26] Eventually, after lengthy discussions with the Keeper of the Privy Purse, it was decided that with the strength of the early material, the Treasury essays and the existing Penny Blacks from every Plate, it would enhance the Collection. The next

Opposite: Great Britain: 1840 ONE PENNY black Plate 1a, a block of ten (5×2) used on wrapper on the first day of the postage stamp, 6th May, 1840. It is known as the 'Kirkcudbright Cover'.

James Burnie Esq

Kirkcudbright

hurdle was to raise the money. Clearly the Privy Purse was not going to fund the purchase.

With Sir John Wilson's stricture in mind that the Red Collection should fund new purchases, Charles Goodwyn went through the albums again marking off 'certain duplicates and surplus items'.[27] Spink, the London-based dealers specialising in stamps and medals, were nominated to sell the items to 'fund the purchase and to establish a reserve for the future enhancement of the Collection'. The stamps of Egypt and the Suez Canal, were included in the sale as they were outside the scope of the present Collection. The auction took place on 17 May 2001 and raised £645,000, against an estimate of £320,000. There was now more than enough to buy the Kirkcudbright Cover, and to ensure that the Collection continued to live.

The other great contribution that Charles Goodwyn made to the Royal Philatelic Collection was in recognising that he needed others to assist him in his ever-escalating task. His first assistant was Surésh Dhargalkar, who joined in April 1996. It was a fortuitous appointment on all sides. Dhargalkar had been the superintending architect to the Royal Household for over twenty years – one of his first projects, in 1975, had been to create the first purpose-designed Stamp Room in Buckingham Palace. He has had an eventful time throughout, not least in overseeing the initial part of the restoration after the devastating fire at Windsor Castle in November 1992, and the underpinning of the Round Tower. Charles Goodwyn first met him when he sought him out to guide him back to the Stamp Room by a circuitous route to avoid doors that were being alarmed during the overhaul of the Palace security and fire alarm systems. Dhargalkar was invested as a Lieutenant of the Royal Victorian Order for his architectural services in 1994. With his background as an architect in conservation practices, he suggested that on his retirement he might join Charles Goodwyn as a conservator, and his position was confirmed by the Keeper of the Privy Purse. Dhargalkar has proved invaluable: together with Charles Goodwyn he made substantial inroads into mounting the vast backlog of George VI stamps and, although he is not a philatelist, has masterminded the first ever travelling exhibition in the United Kingdom of the Collection during the Queen's Golden Jubilee celebrations of 2002. He was made a Fellow of the Royal Philatelic Society

London, in recognition of his services to philately, and appointed Deputy Keeper of the Royal Philatelic Collection from January 2003.

Surésh Dhargalkar also helps to prepare for the various exhibitions, and on occasion accompanies the displays to their destination. In November 2002 he took one to Tortola, which included the famous black and rose-carmine ONE SHILLING 1867 'Missing Virgin of the Virgin Islands'. This remarkable stamp is one of the most dramatic errors, and has intrigued philatelists since it was discovered in the late 1880s; it is still not absolutely clear as to how and why it came about.

The higher values of the Virgin Island stamps were printed in two colours, and therefore two separate processes, by the English firm of Nissen and Parker. In fact they subcontracted the making of the master die to Waterlow. This die was only used to prepare the outer part of the stamp, or the 'glory'. So, from that die, twenty single impressions were made and transferred to a lithographic stone in four rows of five stamps. This was used for the first stage to print the outer part of the stamp in carmine on white wove paper. The Collection holds a proof copy in black. The second stage was done by typography. Twenty images of the Virgin Mary were transferred to a copper plate (the unwanted parts were cut away so she is raised) to align exactly in the centre of each of the lithographed frames. These were then printed in black.

In all, there were four separate printings, yet in the thousands of ONE SHILLING carmine that were produced, only half a sheet of the 'missing Virgins', where the centre of the carmine 'glory' is blank, is thought to have been made. Thus, of the ten possible copies, eight are known. All are unused. It would appear that the error occurred during the second stage of the printing – that is, adding the Virgin Mary – when a sheet was partially

Virgin Islands: 1867 ONE SHILLING black and rose carmine, error figure of Virgin omitted, unused together with an example of the correct form. Known as the 'Missing Virgin', it was the centrepiece of the loan exhibition from the Collection to Tortola in 2002. It is one of eight known examples.

damaged. Rather than let it run all the way through the press, the sheet was removed so leaving the top half (all ten stamps) without the image of the Virgin. It is also likely that the stamps were never delivered to Tortola (the parent island), but found their way into the philatelic market direct from the printers. When Surésh Dhargalkar took the 'Missing Virgin' from the Royal Philatelic Collection to the British Virgin Islands, it is more than likely that it was its first visit there.

Around the time of Surésh Dhargalkar's arrival in the Stamp Room, Charles Goodwyn saw an opportunity to advance the scope of the Collection further. He had known Michael Sefi as a member of the Council of the Royal Philatelic Society London. Goodwyn also knew that he might be available to assist him, as Sefi had taken early retirement and was not certain that he wanted to join another firm of chartered accountants. Sefi took up Goodwyn's offer and was appointed Deputy Keeper of the Royal Philatelic Collection in 1996.

Philately partially runs in Michael Sefi's veins. He is a distant cousin of Alexander Joseph Sefi, who was once editor of the *Philatelic Journal of Great Britain*, a position he combined with that of stamp-dealer, in partnership with Percy L. Pemberton, and as author of many learned works on philately. Shortly before he died in 1934, he was elected to the RDP. Michael Sefi's grandfather, also a collector, gave him 'thirds, not even seconds to start off his collection'.[28] However, he had also been given a page of photogravure George V Great Britain stamps of all the different values, sizes and shades. His schoolboy collection remained dormant for just over twenty years until his children were given a 'starter pack' of stamps and an album for Christmas. This reminded Sefi of his own collection in the attic. When he dug it out, his interest was rekindled and, in a short period of time, he had specialised in the early Great Britain stamps of the reign of George V.

When he joined the existing team of two in the Stamp Room, there were the exhibitions to prepare and researchers to be supervised. The routine was working well until Goodwyn took a display to Hong Kong from which he returned unwell. His trip to Australia in 1999 took a further toll on his health. Sadly, he never fully recovered. There was further strain when the Stamp Room transferred from Buckingham Palace to St James's Palace, half–way up

Michael Sefi, FCA, FRPSL, the present Keeper of the Royal Philatelic Collection at the first meeting of the year of the Royal Philatelic Society London. Traditionally, the Keeper mounts a display from the Collection. He is only the sixth Keeper in over 110 years.

the Mall, where there is more room and a larger strong room. But even with three people working, albeit part-time, the work kept piling up. There was a major international philatelic exhibition at Earls Court in 2000 with material from the Collection, the largest and most important that the Collection had ever mounted, then the travelling exhibition for the Golden Jubilee in 2002, which went to the Palace of Holyroodhouse, Edinburgh, for eight days, Sandringham, the Queen's private estate in Norfolk, for another eight days, and ended up at Hampton Court Palace just outside London. It was a wonderful display with all the 'favourites' and great pieces from the Collection:

the treasury essays, the Kirkcudbright cover, Mauritius items [including the TWO PENCE and ONE PENNY Post Office] the biggest block of 2d blue extant from plate I, Cottonreels from Bermuda, the Tyrian Plum and three frames of Seahorses. There was also the Silver Jubilee artwork from 1935 from De La Rue, Bradbury Wilkinson and Waterlow, and items from the Canadian decorative album presentation to the then Duke of York.[29]

The displays were accompanied by five frames of items from the Crown Agents Stamp Bureau, which included, for the first time, the letters commissioning them to produce the first stamps for Trinidad and Mauritius, alongside frames from the British Forces Post Office with covers from the original Army Postal Corps. Shortly afterwards, there was a request by the Smithsonian Institution National Postal Museum for a major exhibition to be loaned entirely from the Royal Philatelic Collection to be displayed in Washington in 2004.

When the excitement of the Queen's Golden Jubilee had died down, Charles Goodwyn decided that he should step down for reasons of ill health. Just before Christmas 2002, he was invested a Lieutenant of the Royal Victorian Order at a private audience with the Queen. He had long since been elected a signatory of the RDP, and was a Chevalier de St Charles, an order given by Prince Rainier of Monaco. In the United States, he had received the Smithsonian Medal for Philatelic Achievement.

The choice of Michael Sefi to replace Goodwyn as Keeper of the Royal Philatelic Collection was by no means automatic. The position was advertised in the *London Philatelist* and a short list of four, which included Sefi, was drawn up. After interview, he was finally chosen to succeed by the Keeper of the Privy Purse. When he took up his position in January 2003, he was only the sixth Keeper of the Royal Philatelic Collection in 110 years.

★   ★   ★

The stirring music of the 1st Battalion of the Grenadier Guards fades as they swing into the Mall from St James's Palace, then the whir of the CD-ROM in the computer in the Stamp Room can be heard. Michael Sefi views

Surésh Dhargalkar LVO, FRPSL, Deputy Keeper of the Royal Philatelic Collection (right), with
Rod Vousden FRPSL, formerly curator at the British Library. Dhargalkar, a former superintending
architect to the Royal Household, created the first purpose-designed Stamp Room in Buckingham
Palace. In 2002, he masterminded the travelling exhibition of the Collection during the
Queen's Golden Jubilee celebrations.

the catalogue of a forthcoming stamp sale on the screen, and marks down
a few items to consider buying that were even on George V's wants list for the
Red Collection. At another table by the window, Rod Vousden, formerly a
curator at the British Library and expert in the stamps of George VI's reign,
is mounting part of the huge backlog into the Blue Collection. It is a busy
day. Surésh Dhargalkar, the Deputy Keeper, goes to and from the strong
room with volumes from the Red Collection for Patrick Pearson, chairman
of the Expert Committee of the Royal Philatelic Society London, to compare
with the 'patients' (the stamps under review) he has brought along. In the
afternoon, a Ph.D. student from Sydney, Australia, has an appointment
with the Keeper to discuss her thesis on the Post Office Mauritius. This is

the way forward for the living Royal Philatelic Collection, a far cry from the days of even the last Keeper, Charles Goodwyn, who wrote his letters in manuscript with no help from any quarter.

The form set by Goodwyn continues under the present Keeper. With Dhargalkar and Vousden, the mounting of the Blue Collection of George VI is nearing completion, while Sefi continues with his work on the Great Britain part of the Collection. The future is exciting. In parallel with the mounting is the conservation of the Collection, to preserve it for many generations to come – to be seen and enjoyed by countless philatelists around the world.

The Royal Philatelic Collection was founded through the scholarship, dedication and passion of George V, who made it his life's work to have the best collection of Great Britain and what was then the Empire. This he largely achieved, and although his heirs have not followed him as philatelists, they have at least shared his commitment to the Collection. Thus it is only fitting that the Sovereign of the country that gave the world the postage stamp should have the most important collection in private hands, respected and known as The Royal Philatelic Collection.

✿✿✿

APPENDICES

⚛⚛⚛

APPENDIX I

Gift from the Sydney Philatelic Club to the Prince of Wales.

Views: 1d., Plate II., pair and single on blue wove paper; 2d., Plate II., on yellowish wove; 3d., on blue wove.

Laureates: 1d., on blue wove, unused; 2d., Stars; 2d., Plate II., no wmk; 2d., Plate II., wmk. 2, reconstructed plate of fifty types, and a pair; 6d., coarse background; deep orange.

Large Square: 5d., wmk. 5, unused; 5d., sage-green, imperf., pair, unused; 1s., rose perf., unused.

Diadems: 3d., pair, imperf., wmk 3; 3d., wmk. 10, block of four unused; 3d., wmk. NSW and Crown, pair, imperf., unused, and a block of four, imperf. vertically, both unused.

De La Rue Series: 9d., double surcharge, unused, and an unused pair without any surcharge (10d., red-brown).

Centennial: 1s., pair, imperf., unused; 5s., wmk. 5/- (old paper) unused.

There were also blocks of the Record Reign series, of the first dies, unused, the Hospital stamps, 6d., green, block of four, unused; the first postcard, both types of 'To', unused, several official and private envelopes on coloured paper, all unused and entire.

APPENDIX II

Extract from the *London Philatelist*, vol. XV, 1906, pp. 111, 112 with details of the Prince of Wales's Mauritius entry at the 1906 International Philatelic Exhibition at the Horticultural Hall, Vincent Square, London.

Apart from the two POST OFFICES and the PENOE error, the Prince of Wales showed

> 'the other native-printed stamp specimens … used and unused from the earliest to the latest states of the plates, especially noticeable being the three superb unused 2d. … The used stamps include a large number, in every state of the plate,

of the issues of 1848. The provisional FOURPENCE on the green stamp of April, 1858, was shown unused and used [*sic*]. The rare 1862 1s. dark [*sic* – deep] green, perforated [12 to 16] is also included unused. The later issues were practically complete both used and unused, and included in the collection are no-water-mark stamps, imperf., cut from the *imprimatur* sheets registered at Somerset House. His Royal Highness is to be congratulated upon the possession of such a superb lot of these interesting old issues.'

APPENDIX III

A. S. Tompson BARBADOS

International Philatelic Exhibition, London 23 May – 1 June 1906, official catalogue (pp 50, 51):

A most complete collection comprising a great range of shades unused in pairs and blocks of the imperf. amongst others a block of 4 6d. unused and various bisected stamps. A fine lot of pin-perf. 14 and 12 ½ *unused*. Three copies of the 1d. blue, clean-cut, unused. The rough perfs., no wmk., are particularly strong, especially the 4d. and 6d., which are shown in great range of shade, also in pairs and blocks.

A pair of 1s. imperf. between the 1s. blue, error and various other varieties imperforate.

The large and small stars, both clean-cut and rough perfs., are particularly strong, especially 4d. and 6d.; amongst others, a pair of 4d large star.

A particularly strong exhibit of the CC 12½ 6d. bright and dull yellow, and the CC perf. 14 are well represented by a fine range of shades and blocks of each value. Also the 4d. compound perforation.

The Provisional stamps consist of ten used pairs of the 1d. on 5s., showing all types: surcharged to the right and to the left, with slanting serif, and with straight serif, and straight and slanting *se tenant*; and in addition a strip of three used as 3d., and also three singles and a pair unused.

Amongst the latter issues, which are well represented, will be found the ½ d. 'Half-Penny' double surcharge in red and black, two blocks of four, and a vertical pair showing varieties without hyphen; and also one used on entire.

APPENDIX IV

Frances Teresa Stewart (1646–1702) was the daughter of the Hon. Walter Stewart, physician to Queen Henrietta Maria (widow of Charles I) in exile in France. After the Restoration of Charles II, Frances Stewart was appointed Maid of Honour, at the age of fourteen, to his wife, Catherine of Braganza. From the start, she captivated the Court, and was universally known as 'La Belle Stewart'. Pepys described her as the 'finest site to me … that ever I did see in all my life. Miss Stewart … is the greatest beauty I ever saw, I think, in all my life,' while Henrietta Maria thought her the prettiest girl in the world.

Charles II was struck from their first meeting, but she managed to resist his importunities, though her behaviour was far from modest and 'she had no aversion to scandal'. In 1667, the King commissioned John Roettier to strike a silver medal with her on the obverse, which Pepys noted in his diary: 'At my goldsmith's did observe the King's new medal, where, in little, there is Mrs [*sic*] Stewart's face as well done as ever I saw anything in my whole life, I think: and a pretty thing it is, that he should choose her face to represent Britannia by.'

Frances Stewart had numerous suitors, including the Duke of Buckingham and 'Francis Digby, son of the Earl of Bristol, whose unrequited love for her was celebrated by Dryden'. In March 1667 she eloped with the Duke of Richmond and married him secretly. She died in 1702.

APPENDIX V

Extract from the *London Philatelist*, vol. XX, 1911 p. 140.

The two sets of Nevis colour trials consisted of: 'thin wove paper, 1d lake and 1d red; 4d grey-lilac; 4d deep blue; 4d yellow; 4d deep blue SP [specimen]; 6d grey; 6d violet; 6d violet SP; 1s deep green; 1s deep green SP.

Proof impressions on white card of the plate of 12 types. 1d blue-green and green; 4d two shades of violet; 6d two shades of orange; 1s two shades of deep rose; 1s lake.

APPENDIX VI

Tyrian purple was first produced in Tyre, hence its name. The ancient dyestuff was first mentioned in texts in 1600 BC and was produced from the mucus of the hypobronchial gland of various species of marine molluscs, notably the *Murex*. It was widely used throughout the Roman Empire, but its use declined, and finally ceased with the fall of Constantinople in AD 1453. Although produced in massive quantities, it was always very expensive. It was replaced by other cheaper dyes, like lichen purple and madder. Pliny the Elder left a detailed description of how the mucus was extracted and turned into dye.

APPENDIX VII

The Court of Honour
His Majesty the King

The Exhibit comprises one page of classic stamps from each of the first forty-eight British Possessions to issue their own adhesive Postage Stamps arranged in chronological order. The selection is made from the collection formed by the late King George V.

Frame 911

1847 TRINIDAD: "Lady McLeod" 5c. blue, privately issued by David Bryce, owner of the Steam Ship bearing that name, which were sold at five cents each for the prepayment of the carriage of letters by this vessel between Port of Spain and San Fernando; an uncancelled example on a folded letter which is dated Port of Spain, June 2nd 1847. The first known date is April 16th.

1847 MAURITIUS: Inscribed "Post Office," locally engraved on copper by J. Barnard; 1d. red on envelope dated Sept. 21st, 1847, which originally contained an invitation to the Governor's Ball. Also 2d. blue unused. This stamp is normally on a page by itself but has been mounted below the cover for this Exhibition.

Frame 912

1830 VICTORIA: Ham's first printing 1d. vermillion and 3d. blue used together on a folded letter dated Jan. 10th, 1830; the first recorded date of use.

1850 BRITISH GUIANA: The circular type-set stamps, set up and printed at the office of the "Royal Gazette" at Georgetown and initialled by the Postmaster or Post Office clerk before issue; examples of the 4c. on orange, 4c. on primrose (two) and 4c. on pale yellow pelure paper. Of the 4c. on primrose there is only one other recorded cut-square example (in the Tapling Collection).

1851 CANADA: Engraved and printed by Messrs. Rawdon, Wright, Hatch and Edson, New York (later known as the American Bank Note Co.); 6d. on laid paper, two singles and a pair used on folded letters, part of a series of twelve such letters in the Collection.

1851 NEW BRUNSWICK: Engraved by Perkins, Bacon & Co., 1/- reddish-mauve, two examples on folded letters to New York dated June 24th and July 30th, 1853.

1851 NOVA SCOTIA: Engraved by Perkins, Bacon & Co.; 1d. red-brown, a single and a bisect used with 6d. deep green on an envelope to Antigua dated Annapolis Jan 26th, 1860. The only recorded cover bearing a split 1d.

1852 BARBADOS: Engraved by Perkins, Bacon & Co.; 1860 no watermark, pin-perforated 12½ ½d. yellow-green, two singles and a marginal pair unused, three used, and 1d. blue, two used.

1852 INDIA: Scinde District Dawk embossed stamps issued under the authority of the Commissioner, Sir Bartle Frere, printed by De La Rue & Co.; the page includes three examples of the ½d. red.

Frame 913

1853 CAPE OF GOOD HOPE: Stereotyped provisionals of 1861, 1d. blue error of colour caused by insertion of one 1d. cliché in the plate of the 4d.; a single, another single used on a large piece of the finest known pair of 1d. and 4d. *se-tenant*.

1853 TASMANIA: Locally engraved and printed at the office of the "Courier" newspaper, 1d. blue unused, an unused block of four with original gum, and two unused.

1864 WESTERN AUSTRALIA: Locally lithographed by M. Sanson, Government Printer, 4d. blue error frame inverted and 4d. with "AUSTRALIA" in squeezed letters (creased transfer), of which only one other example is said to exist.

1855 SOUTH AUSTRALIA: Engraved by Perkins, Bacon & Co., London Printing, the un-issued 1/- violet unused and another with "CANCELLED" obliteration in barred oval.

1855 NEW ZEALAND: Engraved by Humphreys and printed by Perkins, Bacon & Co., London, 1/- green, two unused, one with "CANCELLED" obliteration in barred oval, three used, and a bisect used on cover dated Dec. 9th, 1857.

1856 ST HELENA: Engraved by Perkins, Bacon & Co., essays of overprints on the 6d.; blue imperforate "ONE PENNY" (two) and "FOUR PENCE" (five), made to effect economy by use of only one engraved plate for all values. Also 1863 Crown CC imperforate 6d. lake, error surcharge omitted.

1857 NEWFOUNDLAND: Engraved by Perkins, Bacon & Co., 2d. scarlet vermillion, two unused examples, one used and a used pair.

Frame 914

1857 CEYLON: Engraved by Perkins, Bacon & Co., imperforate 4d. dull rose unused with original gum, three used and a pair (one of three recorded pairs).

1857 NATAL: Embossed on coloured paper, 3d. rose unused (from the Natal Government Archives), used pairs, a tête-bêche pair, and another pair with one stamp doubly embossed, one impression inverted.

1859 IONIAN ISLANDS: Engraved by Perkins, Bacon & Co., ½d. orange and 1d. blue used together on front dated Sept. 10th (1859), and the same two stamps used on a folded letter dated Oct. 15th, 1859.

1859 BAHAMAS: Engraved by Perkins, Bacon & Co., a die proof and plate proofs of the 6d; 1861 rough perforation 6d. grey-lilac two unused, one used, and 6d. dull lilac, two unused singles and an unused block of four with original gum, a little close but unique.

1860 QUEENSLAND: Engraved by Humphrys and printed by Perkins, Bacon & Co., imper-forate 1d. carmine-rose, two unused singles and an unused block of four with original gum, a little close but unique.

1860 JAMAICA: Typographed by De La Rue & Co., watermark Pine 6d, the range of shades including an unused pair, two unused blocks of four, and the deep purple shade unused.

Frame 915

1860 MALTA: Typographed by De La Rue & Co., blued paper ½d. buff, three unused singles, an unused block of four, and one overprinted "SPECIMEN."

1860 ST LUCIA: Engraved by Perkins, Bacon & Co., watermark Star 6d. green, two unused singles, an unused block of six, an unused pair imperforate between, and one with "CAN-CELLED" obliteration in barred oval.

1860 SIERRA LEONE: Typographed by De La Rue & Co., 6d. original die proofs in black and in colour. Also the issued 6d. dull purple on blued paper, unused singles and a block showing plate number.

1861 PRINCE EDWARD ISLAND: Electrotyped by Charles Whiting, Beaufort House, London, perforated 9 2d. rose, five unused, one used, and another used on envelope.

1861 NEVIS: Engraved by Nissen & Parker, London, greyish paper, perforated 13, 4d. rose, a complete unused uncut sheet of twelve with margins. The 1d. and the 2d. of this issue are the rarest of Nevis in uncut sheets.

1861 ST. VINCENT: Six drawings made by Perkins, Bacon & Co. for the St. Vincent stamps. The heads are pulled from a die and stuck down on backgrounds of different design.

Frame 916

1861 GRENADA: Engraved by Perkins, Bacon & Co., no watermark, rough perforation 1d. bluish-green, two unused, another with "CANCELLED" obliteration in barred oval, and 1d. green unused.

1862 ANTIGUA: Engraved by Perkins, Bacon & Co., no watermark, rough perforation 6d. blue-green, three unused singles and an unused pair; perforated 11 to 12 6d. unused and compound perforation 6d., two unused.

1862 HONG KONG: Typographed by De La Rue & Co., Crown CC 8 issue of 1863, 18c lilac, two unused singles, an unused block of four, an imperforate example and one overprinted "CANCELLED."

1865 BRITISH COLUMBIA AND VANCOUVER ISLAND: Typographed by De La Rue & Co., the 2½d. stamp for the two Colonies, a progress die proof, a finished die proof and two pairs from the imprimatur sheet, one with plate number.

1866 BRITISH HONDURAS: Three drawings Perkins, Bacon & Co. for stamps to be produced by the engraved process.

1866 VIRGIN ISLANDS: Lithographed by Waterlow & Sons and supplied by Nissen & Parker, perf. 15 1/- block and crimson with coloured margins, two unused examples on bluish paper with wide border and one without the figure of the Virgin.

Frame 917

1867 HELIGOLAND: Engraved by Herr Schilling, embossed and printed at the Government Printing Works, Berlin; 1873 perforated 13½ × 14½ ¼sch. Rose and green, a postally used block of nine.

1867 TURKS ISLANDS: Engraved by Perkins, Bacon & Co.; the 1881 2½d. or 1/- slate-blue provisional, the main varieties and the complete setting in an uncut block of fifteen.

1867 STRAITS SETTLEMENTS: Indian stamps surcharged, a page of the 12c on 42 green, including an unused block of four.

1869 GAMBIA: Typographed and embossed by De La Rue & Co.; 1886 watermarked Crown and CA 1d. maroon used. The stamp is the same colour as the 1d. of the previous Crown CC issue; normal stamps are provided for comparison.

St. Christopher 1888 "ONE PENNY" on 2½d., both types including the rare small surcharge

1870 ST. CHRISTOPHER: Typographed by De La Rue & Co.; the 1888 "ONE PENNY" on 2 ½d. ultramarine provisional with small surcharge, one unused and another used on piece, together with one with large surcharge.

1870 FIJI: The first adhesives were the locally type-set "Fiji Times Express" stamps. The Islands were ceded to Great Britain on Oct. 10th, 1874 when the 1871 stamps bearing the cipher of King Cakobau were overprinted "V.R.". The page of these overprints on the 12c. rose includes the cross pattée included in a block of four, inverted "A" for "V" unused and used, three with inverted overprints, and other varieties.

Frame 918

1874 DOMINICA: Typographed by De La Rue & Co; 1886 provisionals include the "One Penny" on 6d. green used and the "One Penny" on 1/- magenta with double surcharge.

1874 LAGOS: Typographed by De La Rue & Co.; the 1884–86 10/- purple-brown unused, an unused marginal block of four, one overprinted "SPECIMEN" and another imperforate.

1875 GOLD COAST: Typographed by De La Rue & Co., a page of split provisionals used on pieces, including quarter, half and three-quarter stamps, and the "POSTAGE" label only of the 6d.

1876 MONTSERRAT: Printed and overprinted by De La Rue & Co., 6d. green a page including the inverted "S" variety included in a block of four, and 6d. blue-green, a single and pair.

1878 FALKLAND ISLANDS: Engraved by Bradbury, Wilkinson & Co., no watermark 1d. claret, an unused block of four and 4d. grey-black, an unused block of nine.

1879 LABUAN: Engraved by De La Rue & Co.; the 1881 "Eight Cents" on 12c. carmine provisional, the "Eight" error in a vertical pair with normal, the sheet showing the corrected setting, and the invert in a vertical pair with normal.

NEW ZEALAND: The lovely Chalon Heads provide classic rarities in the 1d. and 1/- values of 1855 London and local printings, and in the bisected 1/- values provisionally used as 6d. stamps (see frame 380). Primitive perforations on the 1856 and 1862 issue are of considerable interest and rarity, and the 1862 printings on pelure paper include the exceedingly rare 3d. Rarities continue amongst the later Chalon Heads and increasing interest is taken in the later Victorian issues, with their rare perforations, and in a variety of rare cancellations.

GLOSSARY

⚜⚜⚜

ADHESIVE – a stamp with a gummed back: one intended to be stuck on an envelope, instead of a stamp to be printed on a post-card or wrapper.

BISECTS – a stamp cut in half, usually with scissors or perforated, to denote half the original face value.

BLOCK OF STAMPS – a number of undetached stamps in the form of a rectangle. A block implies that there are a minimum of four stamps in two vertical rows.

CHECK LETTERS – letters printed in the corners of certain stamps, as the early issues of Great Britain, to denote the position of the stamps on a full sheet. Really used against fraudulent imitations.

COMMEMORATIVE STAMPS – stamps issued to commemorate some worthy event; often used to denote stamps issued more with a view to selling to collectors than for general use.

CONTROLS – letters and numbers printed on the margins of sheets of stamps to distinguish one printing from another. The controls were followed by the last two figures of the year.

CUT-OUT – a stamp that is cut out of an embossed envelope or printed post-card as opposed to an adhesive.

DOUBLY-FUGITIVE – term applied to such lilac or green inks as a protection against the removal of pen and postal cancellations.

DUTY-PLATE – where a stamp is printed in two operations, the plate that prints the value is known as the duty-plate.

ELECTROTYPING – where the design is stamped in a sheet of wax or gutta-percha which is dusted with plumbago and placed in an acid bath which was then electroplated in copper, backed in type metal and mounted on a block of wood.

ERROR – a stamp bearing some fault in one or more of its particulars but generally in the spelling of some words.

ESSAY – a trial stamp for a design.

FACSIMILE – another word for a forgery but sometimes applied to an official imitation.

FISCAL – a stamp serving some revenue purpose.

FUGITIVE – a term applied to inks that are designed to fade or wash out as proof against the removal of postmarks.

IMPERFORATE – stamps that require cutting with scissors.

IMPRIMATUR – literally, 'let it be printed', usually imprimatur sheet, that indicates the first impression from a plate endorsed with an official certificate to that effect, and a direction that the plate be used for printing stamps.

JUBILEE LINE – a raised line run round the margin of a plate of stamps to protect the outside edges of the stamps. Introduced in 1887, hence the name.

KEY-PLATE – the plate that prints the sovereign's head or vignette in a two printing operation.

MINT – a stamp or entire in perfect condition as when issued; in the case of an adhesive, including the original gum.

MOUNT – the hinge used for fixing a stamp to the album.

OBLITERATION – any mark that cancels a stamp.

OBSOLETE – term denoting that a stamp has been withdrawn from postal service.

ON PIECE – the remaining part of an envelope or wrapper with used stamp or stamps affixed, usually with the postmark.

OVERPRINT – something printed over a stamp to give it a different use than originally intended.

PANE – a number of undetached stamps often with blank margin paper running round part or all of it.

PERFORATED – stamps with edging of small holes so arranged that they may be easily separated without the aid of scissors.

PLATE NUMBERS – numbers engraved on stamps or the margins of sheets to enable the authorities to recognise from which plate any particular stamp was printed.

PROVISIONAL – a stamp pressed into service temporarily.

REMAINDER – a stamp that remained in the government's hands after its withdrawal from postal use and subsequently came onto the market.

REPRINT – a stamp printed from a plate after it has become withdrawn.

RETOUCHING – when a plate is corrected after manufacture by hand. It is relatively easy to retouch a lithographic plate, but often crudely executed. A steel plate is more difficult as has to be softened, retouched, and hardened again.

SE-TENANT – a French term translating as 'joined together' for two adjoining stamps that differ in either design or value.

SILK-THREADS – these were worked into the paper manufactured by Dickinson amongst others to serve as a check against fraud. It was thought that stamps printed on this paper could not be imitated as the absence of the silk threads clearly indicated their origin.

SPECIMEN – a term used to describe stamps overprinted 'specimen' or 'cancelled' for official distribution.

SURCHARGE – an overprint placed on the face of a stamp to alter the postal value.

TÊTE-BÊCHE – when two stamps are joined and so printed that one is inverted in relation to the other.

BIBLIOGRAPHY

❖∘❖∘❖

Albert Victor, Prince, and George, Prince, *The Cruise of the Bacchante,* London 1886

Anglesey, The Marquess of, *A History of the British Cavalry 1816–1919*, London, 1986

Barker Nicholas, *Bibliothecia Lindesiana*, London, 1977

Bailey, Edmond, *The Stamps of Barbados*, London, 1989

Beale, P. O., *The Postal Service Sierra Leone, Its History, Stamps and Stationary until 1961*, London, 1988

Beaumont, K. M. and Stanton, H. C. V., *The Postage Stamps of Great Britain, Part Four, The Issues of King George V*, London, 1957

Benn, Tony, *Out of the Wilderness, Diaries 1963–67*, London, 1987

Bennett, Russell, and Watson, James, *Philatelic Terms Illustrated*, London, 1972

Boggs, Winthrop S, in collaboration with Strange, Arnold, *The Foundations of Philately*, London, 1955

Chambers's Encyclopedia, London, 1959 edition

Collins, R. J. G., *A Philatelic Handbook*, Christchurch, New Zealand, 1967

Drysdale, Dr Alan R. and Criddle, Major Harold, *The Tête-Bêche Varieties of Transvaal*, Bournemouth, 1993

Easton, John, *The De La Rue History of British and Foreign Postage Stamps 1855 to 1901*, London, 1958

Evans, Major R. B., *The Mulready Envelope*, London, 1891

Farleigh, John, *Graven Images*, London, 1940

Friedman, Dennis, *Darling Georgie, The Enigma of King George V*, London, 1998

—— *Inheritance, a psychological history of the Royal Family*, London, 1993

Goodwyn, Charles, *Postal Reform, Bristol, 1999*

Gore, John, *King George V, A Personal Memoir*, London 1941

Graffey-Smith, Laurence, *Bright Levant*, London, 1970

Hobson-Jobson, *The Anglo-Indian Dictionary*, Bombay, 1886

Houseman, Lorna, *The House that Thomas Built*, London, 1968

Ibbotson, Peter, *The Postal History and Stamps of Mauritius*, London, 1991

Jefferies, Hugh, *The Queen's Stamps*, London, 2000

Johnston, Stanley, *The Stamp Collector*, London, 1920

Kirk, A. J., *King Edward VIII, a study of the stamps in the reign of King Edward VIII*, London, 1974

Lawrence, M. R., *The Home Letters of T. E. Lawrence and his Brothers*, Oxford, 1954

Mills, Anthony R., *Two Victorian Ladies*, London 1969

Nicolson, Harold, *Comments, 1944-1948*, London, 1948

—— *Diaries and Letters about King George V*, London, 1949

—— *George V, His Life and Reign*, London, 1952

Ponsonby, Sir Frederick, *Recollections of Three Reigns*, London, 1951

Potter, David, *British Elizabethan Stamps*, London, 1971

Rogers-Tillstone, Captain Benjamin (ed.), *The Royal Philatelic Society 1869–1969*, Glasgow, 1969

Rose, Kenneth, *King George V*, London, 1983

—— *Kings, Queens & Courtiers*, London, 1985

Staff, Frank, *The Penny Post, 1680-1918*, London, 1964

Stanley Gibbons, *Great Britain Volume 2, King Edward VII to King George VI*, London, 1996

St Aubyn, Giles, *Edward VII Prince and King*, London, 1979

Storrs, Sir R., Orienetations, London, 1937

van der Kiste, John and Jordan, Bee, *Dearest Affie … Alfred Duke of Edinburgh*, Gloucester, 1984

Walker, J. Reg, *New Zealand, the Great Barrier Island 1898-99 Pigeon Post Stamps*, New York, 1968

Wallace, Sir Donald Mackenzie, *The Web of Empire: a diary of the Imperial Tour of their Royal Highnesses the Duke and Duchess of Cornwall and York in 1901*, London, 1902

Wilson, Sir John, Bt, *The Royal Philatelic Collection*, London 1952

Williams, L. M. & M., *Stamps of Fame*, London, 1949

—— *Commemorative Postage Stamps of Great Britain, 1890–1966*, London, 1967

—— *Encyclopaedia*, Geneva, 1993

—— *Biographies*, Geneva, 1997

ARTICLES AND PAMPHLETS

Cole, Henry, *Queen Victoria and the Uniform Penny Postage – A Scene at Windsor Castle*, pamphlet bound in with Part XIII of *Nicholas Nickleby*, April 1839

Moorshead, Sir Owen, 'King George, a Broadcast to Children', *Listener*, 30 January 1936

Negus, Ron, *The Earl of Crawford K.T., A Short Biographical Sketch*, supplement in the *London Philatelist*, December 2002

Spink, *Stamps and Covers from the Royal Philatelic Collection*, catalogue, Thursday 17 May 2001

NOTES

⁂

Abbreviation: RA = Royal Archives.

PREFACE

1 Personal comment to the author.

INTRODUCTION

1 Cole, Henry, *Queen Victoria and the Uniform Penny Postage – A Scene at Windsor Castle*, pamphlet bound in with Part XIII of *Nicholas Nickleby*, April 1839.
2 Hansard, xxxviii, pp. 1462, 1464.
3 Staff, Frank, *The Penny Post, 1680–1918*, London, 1964, p. 77.
4 *The Ninth Report of the Commissioners Appointed to Inquire into the Management of the Post Office Department*, 1837.
5 *The Times*, 6 September 1839.
6 *Inventor's Advocate and Journal of Industry*, 4 January 1840.
7 Hill, Rowland, evidence given at 9th Duncannon Commission, 7 July 1837.
8 Hill, Rowland, journal entry, 30 January 1840.
9 *Ibid.*, 31 May 1840.
10 Goodwyn, Charles, *Postal Reform,* Bristol, 1999, p. 37.
11 Evans, Major R. B., *The Mulready Envelope*, London, 1891, p. 4.
12 Hill, journal entry, 12 May 1840.
13 *Ibid.*

14 Cole, Henry, letter to Mr Turner enclosing impression of embossed paper.
15 Hill, journal entry, 10 April 1839.
16 Melville, F., *Chats on Postage Stamps*, London, 1911, p. 115.
17 *Punch*, July–December 1842, p. 201.
18 Melville, *Chats*, p. 116.
19 *Ibid.* p. 122.

CHAPTER I

1 RA VIC / EVIID / 1856: 15 May.
2 *Ibid*: 3 January.
3 *Ibid*: 8 April 1856.
4 Wilson, Sir John, Bt, *The Royal Philatelic Collection*, London, 1952, Great Britain p. 18.
5 Marriott, Sir John, *The Philatelist*, vol. 80, p. 189.
6 *Ibid*: p. 191.
7 Coburg MMS Prince Albert to Alexandrine 6 December 1857.
8 Mills, A.R., *Two Victorian Ladies*, London, 1969, p. 117.
9 Rogers-Tillstone, Captain Benjamin (ed.), *The Royal Philatelic Society 1869–1969*, Glasgow, 1969, p. 111.
10 Melville, F., *Chats on Postage Stamps*, London 1911, p. 306.
11 George V to Tilleard, letter book, Royal Philatelic Collection, 14 January 1894.
12 Rose, Kenneth, *King George V*, London, 1983, p. 7.
13 RA GV / GVD / 1881: 3 November.

14 RA GV/AA6/383 and 382: 26 and 18 May 1889.
15 RA GV/GVD/1882: 9 May.
16 Albert Edward, Prince, and George, Prince, *The Cruise of the Bacchante,* vol. 1, London, 1886. p. 576.
17 RA GV/GVD/1887: 19 March.
18 *Ibid*: 29 January.
19 *Ibid*: 19 April.
20 *Ibid*: 2 March.
21 RA GV/AA6/366: 3 February 1887.
22 Houseman, Lorna, *The House that Thomas Built,* London, 1968, p. 125.
23 *Ibid.*
24 RA GV/AA 68/119: 21 July 1889.
25 Wilson, *Royal Philatelic Collection,* p. 6.
26 Spink, Sir John Marriott Collection sale catalogue, 18 September 2001, lot 538, p. 111.
27 RA GV/AA6/ 398: 9 March 1891.
28 RA GV/GVD/1891: 20 April 1891.
29 *Ibid*: 4 April 1891.
30 *Ibid*: 24 July 1891.

CHAPTER 2

1 Wilson, Sir John, Bt, *The Royal Philatelic Collection,* London, 1952, p. 6.
2 *Ibid.,* p. 3.
3 RA GV/GVD 1893: 28 February.
4 Castle, M.P., in *London Philatelist,* vol. XXII, September 1913, p. 227.
5 *Ibid.*
6 RA GV/GVD 1895: 15 December.
7 Nicolson, Harold, *George V, His Life and Reign,* London, 1952, p. 61.
8 Rogers-Tillstone, Captain Benjamin (ed.), *The Royal Philatelic Society 1869–1969,* Glasgow, 1969 p. 35.
9 *London Philatelist,* vol. 2, July 1893, p. 129.
10 *Ibid.,* p. 131s.
11 *Ibid.*
12 *Ibid.,* pp. 183, 184.
13 *Ibid.*
14 *Ibid.*
15 *London Philatelist,* vol. XXXVII, 1928, p. 104.
16 Williams, L. M. & M., *Encylopedia,* Geneva, 1993, p. 286.
17 RA GV/GVD 1894: 15 March.
18 Houseman, Lorna, *The House that Thomas Built,* London, 1968, p. 127.

19 RA GV/GVD 1894: 10 May.
20 *London Philatelist,* vol. III, 1893, p. 111.
21 *Ibid.,* vol. V, 1896, p. 2.
22 *Ibid.,* Vol.VI, 1897, p. 188.
23 *Ibid.,* Vol.VII, 1898, p. 308.
24 *Ibid.,* Vol.VI, 1897, p. 188.
25 Wilson, *Royal Philatelic Collection,* p. 34.
26 GV/GVD/1910: 22 January.

CHAPTER 3

1 Quoted in Wilson, Sir John, Bt, *The Royal Philatelic Collection,* London 1952, p. 11.
2 Duke of York to Tilleard, letter book, Royal Philatelic Collection: 11 January 1894.
3 Wallace, Sir Donald Mackenzie, *The Web of Empire: a diary of the imperial tour of their Royal Highnesses the Duke and Duchess of Cornwall and York in 1901,* London, 1902, p. 88.
4 RA GV/GVD 1901: 17 April 1901.
5 Wilson, Sir John, Bt, *The Royal Philatelic Collection,* Victoria, British Australia, p. 62.
6 *Ibid.,* p. 64.
7 *London Philatelist,* vol. X, 1901, p. 171.
8 *Ibid.,* p. 172.
9 RA GV/GVD/1901: 31 May.
10 *Ibid.,* 17 June 1901.
11 Walker, J. Reg, *New Zealand, the Great Barrier Island 1898–99: Pigeon Post Stamps,* New York, 1968, p. 15.
12 RA GV/GVD/1901: 5 July.
13 *Ibid*: 25 October.
14 *Ibid*: 3 November 1901.
15 *Ibid*: 17 January 1902.
16 Barker, Nicholas, *Bibliothecia Lindesiana,* London, 1977, p. 274.
17 Negus, Ron, *The Earl of Crawford K.T., A Short Biographical Sketch,* supplement in the *London Philatelist,* December 2002, p. 4.
18 *London Philatelist,* vol. XXII, 1913, p. 26.
19 Quoted, Negus, *The Earl of Crawford,* p. 7.
20 *Ibid.,* p. 10.
21 *London Philatelist,* vol. XXII, 1913, p. 26.
22 Rogers-Tillstone, Captain Benjamin (ed.), *The Royal Philatelic Society 1869–1969,* Glasgow, 1969, pp. 14, 15.
23 Prince of Wales to Tilleard, letter book, Royal Philatelic Collection: 6 January 1902.

24 RA GV/GVD/1904: 4 March.
25 *London Philatelist*, vol. XIII, 1904 p. 58.
26 Johnson, Stanley, *The Stamp Collector*, London, 1920, p. 101.
27 *The London Philatelist*, Vol. XIII, 1904, p. 61.
28 Wilson, Sir John, Bt, *The Royal Philatelic Collection*, p. 13.
29 Mauritius line 'shall pass free of postage' Mauritius Government Ordinance No. 13, 1846 (Enacted 1 January 1947).
30 Bonar to Tilleard, letter book Royal Philatelic Collection: 24 December 1903.
31 RA GV/GVD/1904: 14 January.
32 Ponsonby, Sir Frederick, *Recollections of Three Reigns*, 1951, p. 281.
33 Wilson, *Royal Philatelic Collection*, p. 41.
34 Rose, Kenneth, *King George V*, London, 1983, p. 227.
35 Williams, L. M. & M., *Encyclopedia,* Geneva, 1993, p. 196.
36 Prince of Wales to Tilleard, letter book, Royal Philatelic Collection: 14 January 1904.
37 *Ibid*: 29 September 1909.
38 Ibbotson, Peter, *The Postal History and Stamps of Mauritius*, London, 1991, p. 134.
39 Wilson, *Royal Philatelic Collection*, p. 23.
40 Brownrigg to Colonial Secretary, 2 May 1848, quoted in Williams, *Encyclopedia*, p. 171.
41 Williams, *Encyclopedia*, p. 176.
42 *Ibid.*, p. 177.
43 RA PS/GV/PS 19931/01/STAMP: 26 May 1911.
44 RA GV/DVD/1906: 23 May.
45 Williams, *Encylopedia*, p. 143.
46 *London Philatelist*, vol. XV, 1906, p. 121.
47 RA GV/DVD/1905: 5 October.
48 Wilson, *Royal Philatelic Collection*, p. 14.
49 *London Philatelist,* vol. XV, 1906, p. 121.
50 *Ibid.*, p. 15.
51 *Ibid.*

CHAPTER 4

1 *London Philatelist*, vol. XV, 1906, p. 118.
2 RA GV/GVD/1908: 5 March.
3 *London Philatelist*, vol. XVII, p. 83.
4 Bayley, Edmond, *The Stamps of Barbados*, London, 1989, p. 27.
5 *London Philatelist*, vol. XVII, 1908, p. 85.

6 Wilson, Sir John, Bt, *The Royal Philatelic Collection*, London 1952, p. 8, Plate II.
7 Colonial Office to George Baillie, joint colonial agent in London, letter book: 4 October 1848.
8 Perkins Bacon & Co. to W. P. Clarke 31 August 1863: Bayley, *Stamps of Barbados*, p. 42.
9 *London Philatelist*, vol. XVII, 1908, p. 87.
10 *Ibid.*, p. 92.
11 RA GV/GVD/1908: 13 March.
12 Prince of Wales to Tilleard, letter book, Royal Philatelic Collection: 3 September 1906.
13 *Ibid*: 24 August 1906.
14 Prince of Wales to Tilleard, letter book, Royal Philatelic Collection: 5 March 1905.
15 Wilson, *Royal Philatelic Collection*, London 1952, British Australia, p. 53.
16 Prince of Wales to Tilleard, letter book, Royal Philatelic Collection: 16 April 1904
17 *Ibid*: 17 January 1908.
18 *London Philatelist*, vol. II, 1893, p. 184.
19 RA GV/GVD/1910: 5 February.
20 Prince of Wales to Tilleard, letter book Royal Philatelic Collection: 4 February 1910.
21 *London Philatelist*, vol. XX, 1911, p. 140.
22 Wilson, *Royal Philatelic Collection*, British America, p. 31.
23 *Ibid.*, p. 15.
24 *Ibid.*, p. 16.
25 Personal comment to author.
26 *Chambers's Encyclopaedia*, vol. VII, p. 4.
27 *London Philatelist*, vol. XXVIII, 1919, p. 259.
28 Wilson, p. 13
29 *Ibid*
30 St Aubyn, Giles, *Edward VII, Prince and King*, London, 1979, p. 473.

CHAPTER 5

1 RA GV/GVD/1910: 28 September.
2 RA PS/GV/PS 4130/43: 30 June 1910.
3 Stanley Gibbons, *Great Britain volume 2, King Edward VII to King George VI*, London, 1996, p. 126.
4 *Ibid.*
5 Houseman, Lorna, *The House that Thomas Built*, London, 1968, p. 146.

6 Johnston, Stanley, *The Stamp Collector*, London, 1920, p. 113.

7 RA PS/GV/PS 2090/1/STAMP: 28 June 1911.

8 *London Philatelist*, vol. CVI, 1997, p. 111.

9 *Ibid.*

10 *Ibid.*, p. 113.

11 *Ibid.*

12 Prince of Wales to Tilleard, letter book Royal Philatelic Collection: 4 May 1910.

13 *Stamps of Fame*, London, 1949, p. 181.

14 Williams, L. M. & M, *Encyclopaedia*, Geneva, 1993, p. 219.

15 *London Philatelist*, vol. XXXII, 1923, p. 206.

16 *Ibid.*, vol. XXII, 1913, p. 98.

17 Williams, *Encyclopaedia*, p. 59.

18 *Fiji Times*, 24 September 1870.

19 Wilson, Sir John, Bt, *The Royal Philatelic Collection*, London, 1952, British Australia, p. 20.

20 Williams, *Encyclopaedia*, p. 61.

21 *London Philatelist*, vol. XXII, 1913, p. 98.

22 George V to Tilleard, letter book, Royal Philatelic Collection, 1 March 1912.

23 *London Philatelist*, vol. XXI, 1912, p. 71 and Wilson, *Royal Philatelic Collection*, British Africa, p. 41.

24 Wilson, *Royal Philatelic Collection*, p. 22.

25 RA PS/GV/PS 31402/19/STAMP: 2 February 1932.

26 RA PS/GV/PS 55686/1/STAMP: 3 February 1935.

27 *Ibid*: 23 April 1935.

28 RA PS/GV/PS 06193/2/STAMP: 18 May 1912.

29 *Ibid.*

30 *Ibid*: 29 May 1912.

31 Wilson, *Royal Philatelic Collection*, p. 53.

32 *Ibid.*

CHAPTER 6

1 Friedman, Dennis, *Darling Georgie, The Enigma of King George V*, London, 1998, p. 101.

2 *Ibid.*

3 Moorshead, Sir Owen, 'King George, a Broadcast to Children', *Listener*, 30 January 1936, p. 56.

4 Wilson, Sir John, Bt, *The Royal Philatelic Collection*, London, 1952, p. 54.

5 *Ibid.*, p. 69.

6 RA GV/DVD/1897: 15 February.

7 *Stamp Collector's Fortnightly*, 1912, p. 57.

8 RA PS/GV/PS/1558/1/STAMP: 29 September 1913.

9 *Ibid./2*: 2 October 1913.

10 *Ibid./3*: 17 October 1913.

11 Wilson, *Royal Philatelic Collection*, London, 1952, p. 55.

12 RA PS/GV/PS/12139/1/ STAMP: 1 December 1913.

13 Account Book, Royal Philatelic Collection.

14 Wilson, *Royal Philatelic Collection*, p. 55.

15 RA PS/GV/PS/11558/3/STAMP: 17 October 1913.

16 RA PS/GV/PS/11558/04/STAMP: 20 October 1913.

17 *Ibid./15*: 28 December 1913.

18 *Ibid./7*: 31 October 1913.

19 Wilson, *Royal Philatelic Collection*, p. 56.

20 RA PS/GV/PS/11558/11/STAMP: 20 November 1913.

21 *Ibid./07*: 31 October 1913.

22 RA PS/GV/PS/121391a/01/STAMP: 28 December 1913.

23 *Ibid.*

24 RA PS/GV/PS/12139a/02/STAMP: 8 January 1914.

25 Bennett, Russell, and Watson, James, *Philatelic Terms Illustrated*, London, 1972, p. 101.

26 Wilson, *Royal Philatelic Collection*, Great Britain, p. 50.

27 *Ibid.*, GB13 illustration.

28 RA PS/GV/PS/12139a/01/STAMP: 7 January 1914.

29 *Ibid.*

30 RA PS/GV/PS 25063/5/STAMP: 5 March 1914.

31 *Ibid./06*: 6 March 1914.

32 RA PS/GV/PS 25063/8/STAMP: 7 April 1914.

33 RA PS/GV/PS 25063/20/STAMP: 23 June 1914.

34 *Ibid./20*: 23 June.

35 Wilson, *Royal Philatelic Collection*, pp. 42, 43.

36 Duke of York to Tilleard, letter book, Royal Philatelic Collection: 21 March 1897.

37 RA PS/GV/PS/6682/1/STAMP: 2 July 1912.
38 *Ibid./*4.
39 RA GV/GVD/1906: 15 July.
40 *Ibid.,* 13 March.
41 Ponsonby, Sir Frederick, *Recollections of Three Reigns,* London 1951, p. 281.
42 Wilson, *Royal Philatelic Collection,* p. 40.
43 Personal comment to author.
44 Sir David Wilson Bt to author.
45 *London Philatelist,* vol. XXIII, 1914, p. 38.
46 *Ibid.,* vol. X, 1901, p. 171.
47 *Ibid.,* vol. LV, 1946, p. 80.
48 *Ibid.,* vol. XVIII, 1909, p. 168.
49 *Ibid.,* p. 169.

CHAPTER 7

1 *London Philatelist,* vol. XXIV, 1915, p. 103.
2 *Ibid.,* p. 189.
3 *Philatelic Journal of Great Britain,* vol. XX, 2 August 1910, p. 146.
4 *Ibid.,* vol. LXVIII, 1959, p. 19.
5 RA PS/GV/Q832/268: 25 August 1916.
6 *Ibid/*268: 20 October 1916.
7 RA PS/GV/Q 832/269a: 3 November 1916.
8 Wilson, Sir John, Bt, *The Royal Philatelic Collection,* London, 1952, British Africa, p. 10.
9 *Ibid.,* p. 20.
10 *London Philatelist,* vol. XXIII, 1914, p. 121.
11 *Ibid.,* vol. X, 1901, p. 235.
12 Anglesey, The Marquess of, *A History of the British Cavalry 1819–1919,* London, 1986, p. 174.
13 *The Shorter Oxford English Dictionary,* 1982, p. 1256.
14 Wilson, *Royal Philatelic Collection,* British Africa, p. 13.
15 *Ibid.*
16 Wilson, *Royal Philatelic Collection,* introduction to British Africa, p. 1.
17 RA GV/AA50/19: 4 April 1900.
18 *Ibid./*33: 4 June 1900.
19 Williams, L. M. & M., *Encyclopaedia,* Geneva, 1993, p. 104.
20 Emilio Diena, quoted in *London Philatelist,* supplement December 1999, p. 21.
21 *Ibid.,* p. 15.
22 RA PS/GV/PS/25063/29/STAMP: 17 November 1915.

23 RA *Ibid./*32: 30 November 1915.
24 RA PS/GV/o 844/1:14 December 1915.
25 RA PS/GV/o 844/3: 29 December 1916.
26 *London Philatelist,* vol. XXV, 1916, p. 79.
27 RA PS/GV/PS 17627 *et seq:*/1/STAMP: 19 April 1916.
28 *Ibid./*2: 19 April 1916.
29 *Ibid./*3: 20 April 1916.
30 *Ibid./*4: 20 April 1916.
31 *Ibid./*12: 12 May 1916.
32 *Ibid./*13: 13 May 1916.
33 *Ibid./*14: 15 May 1916.
34 *Ibid.*
35 Nicolson, Harold, *Diaries and Letters about King George V,* London, 1948, pp. 181, 182.
36 *Ibid.,* p. 78.
37 RA PS/GV/PS 17627/17/STAMP: 7 May 1916.
38 Wilson, *Royal Philatelic Collection,* Great Britain, p. 74.
39 RA PS/GV/PS 17627/20/STAMP: 7 May 1916.
40 *Ibid./*21: 24 May 1916.
41 *Ibid./*29: 29 May 1916.
42 *Ibid./*32: 24 May 1916.
43 *Ibid./*35: 21 June 1916.
44 *Ibid./*36: 30 June 1916.
45 *Ibid./*37: 30 July 1916.
46 Wilson, *Royal Philatelic Collection,* Great Britain, p. 74.
47 Wilson, p. 36.
48 Quoted in *Stanley Gibbons' Monthly Journal,* vol. 14, 1904, p. 166.
49 Williams, L. M. & M, *Encyclopaedia,* Geneva, 1993, p. 290.
50 RA PS/GV/PS 18061/1/STAMP: June 1916.
51 Williams, *Encyclopaedia,* Geneva, 1993, p. 197.
52 *Ibid.*
53 Wilson, *Royal Philatelic Collection,* British Asia, p. 16.
54 Storr, p. 196.
55 RA PS/GV/Q 2521/ 92: 13 August 1916.
56 Lawrence, M. R., *The Home Letters of T. E. Lawrence and his Brothers,* Oxford, 1954, p. 85.
57 RA PS/GV/Q 2521/93, 18 September 1916.
58 Graffey-Smith, Laurence, *Bright Levant,* London, 1970, p. 22.
59 RA PS/GV/P 739/23, 5 July 1917.

CHAPTER 8

1   Gore, John, *King George V, A Personal Memoir*, London,1941, p. 306.
2   Wilson, Sir John, *The Royal Philatelic Collection*, London, 1952, p. 59.
3   RA GV/GVD/1906: 6 February.
4   *Ibid.*, 11 May 1906.
5   *Chambers's Encyclopaedia*, vol. 6, p. 81.
6   Hobson-Jobson, *The Anglo-Indian Dictionary*, Bombay, 1886, p. 299.
7   Williams, L. M. & M., *Stamps of Fame*, London, 1949, p. 193.
8   Williams, L. M. & M., *Encyclopedia*, Geneva, 1993, p. 150.
9   Wilson, *Royal Philatelic Collection*, p. 23.
10 *Ibid.*
11 *Moorabbin News*, (Australia), 19 January 1966.
12 Williams, L. M. & M., *Encylopedia*, Geneva, 1993, p. 223.
13 *Moorabbin News*, 19 January 1966.
14 RA GV/GVD/1919: 28 May.
15 *London Gazette*, 27 August 1919.
16 Wilson, *Royal Philatelic Collection*, British America, p. 34.
17 Rose, Kenneth, *King George V*, London, 1983, p. 386.
18 Drysdale, Dr Alan R. and Criddle, Major Harold, *The Tête-Bêche Varieties of Transvaal*, Bournemouth 1993, p. 3.
19 *Ibid.*, p. 8.
20 Wilson, *Royal Philatelic Collection*, p. 67.
21 RA PS/GV/P1627/04, (12 September 1920).
22 *Ibid.*
23 *Ibid.*/06, (17 October 1920).
24 RA PS/GV/PS 31402/1/STAMP: 16 June 1920.
25 RA PS/GV/PS 31402/2/STAMP: 14 June 1920.
26 Wilson, *Royal Philatelic Collection*, p. 25.
27 *Ibid.*, p. 25.
28 *London Philatelist*, vol. XXXII, 1923, p. 267.
29 RA GV/GVD/1923: 17 May.
30 *London Philatelist*, vol. XXXII, 1932, p. 103.
31 *Ibid.*
32 *Ibid.*
33 Wilson, *Royal Philatelic Collection*, p. 23.
34 *Philatelist*, vol. II, April 1868, p. 49.
35 Williams, L. M., and M., *Bibliographies*, Geneva, 1997, p. 116.
36 *Ibid.*, p. 150
37 Wilson, *Royal Philatelic Collection*, British Africa, p. 11.
38 Williams, L. M. & M., *Encyclopedia*, p. 153.
39 RA PS/GV1/PS 00245/39/STAMP: 21 July 1941.
40 Williams, L. M. & M., *Biographies*, Geneva, 1997, p. 24.
41 Wilson, *Royal Philatelic Collection*, p. 26.
42 *Catalogue of the International Philatelic Exhibition*, Melbourne, Australia, October 1928, p. 15.
43 *Stamp and Collectors Review*, October 1938.
44 *London Philatelist*, vol. XXXV, 1926, p. 291.
45 RA GV/GVD/1930: 19 May.
46 Wilson, *Royal Philatelic Collection*, Plate 1.
47 *Ibid.*, p. 27.
48 Beale, P. O., *The Postal Service Sierra Leone, Its History, Stamps and Stationary until 1961*, London, 1988, p. 175.
49 Rogers-Tillstone, Captain Benjamin (ed.), *The Royal Philatelic Society 1869–1969*, Glasgow, 1969, p. 68.
50 RA GV/GVD/1935: 12 May.
51 Wilson, *Royal Philatelic Collection*, p. 59.

CHAPTER 9

1   *London Philatelist*, vol. XV, 1906, p. 125.
2   Jefferies, Hugh, *The Queen's Stamps*, London, 2000, p. 5.
3   RA GV/GVD/1905: 18 April.
4   RA PS/GVI/PS 00245/002/STAMP: 28 January 1936.
5   *Ibid.*,/003: 6 February 1936.
6   RA PS/GVI/PS 00241/001/STAMP: 6 February 1936.
7   RA PS/GVI/PS 00246/001/STAMP: 18 February 1936.
8   Kirk, A. J., *King Edward VIII, A study of the stamps in the reign of King Edward VIII*, London, 1974, p. 1.
9   RA PS/GVI/PS 00874/1/STAMP: 10 July 1936.
10 *Ibid*/2: 12 July 1936.
11 RA PS/GVI/PS 01793/02/STAMPS: 24 March 1937.
12 RA PP/GVI/4327: 28 April 1938.
13 *Ibid*: 28 October 1936.
14 *Ibid*: 7 December 1936.

15 *Ibid*: 18 May 1938.
16 *Ibid*.
17 *Ibid*.
18 *Ibid*: 5 June 1938.
19 *Ibid*: 7 June 1938.
20 *Ibid*.
21 RA PP/GVI/4358: 27 June 1938.
22 *Ibid*.
23 *Ibid*: 17 December 1938.
24 *Ibid*: 6 September 1939.
25 RA PP/GVI/5287: 27 November 1939.
26 *Ibid*.
27 *Ibid*: 8 December 1939.
28 Sir David Wilson Bt, to author.
29 RA PS/GVI/PS 00246/03/STAMP: 2 September 1943.
30 *Ibid*./04: 3 September 1943.
31 *Ibid*./05: 9 September 1943.
32 *Ibid*./06: 13 September 1943.
33 Sir David Wilson Bt, to author.
34 RA PS/GVI/PS 00241/118/STAMP: 4 June 1945.
35 *Ibid*./122: 26 June 1945.
36 RA PS/GVI/PS 02313/24/STAMP: 18 February 1946.
37 *Ibid*./25: 19 February 1946.
38 RA PP/GVI/7130: 16 January 1947.
39 RA PP/GVI/5287: 19 December 1947.
40 *Ibid*: 15 January 1948.
41 *Ibid*: 19 December 1947.
42 Wilson, Sir John, Bt, *The Royal Philatelic Collection*, London, 1952, p. 63.
43 *London Philatelist*, vol. LIX, 1950, pp. 158–163.
44 Quoted in Rose, Kenneth, *King George V*, London, 1983, p. 128.

CHAPTER 10

1 Personal comment to author.
2 Potter, David, *British Elizabethan Stamps*, London, 1971, p. 18.
3 Williams, L. M. & M., *Commemorative Postage Stamps of Great Britain, 1890–1966*, London, 1967, p. 39.
4 Farleigh, John, *Graven Images*, London, 1940, p. 186.
5 Williams, L. M. & M., *Stamps of Fame*, London, 1949, p. 144.
6 *London Philatelist*, vol. LXXXIV, 1975, p. 48.
7 *Ibid*., vol. LXXIX, 1970, pp. 180, 181.
8 Benn, Tony, *Out of the Wilderness, Diaries 1963–67*, London, 1987, pp. 165, 166.
9 *Ibid*., p. 192.
10 Williams, *Commemorative Postage Stamps*, p. 76.
11 Benn, *Out of the Wilderness*, p. 219.
12 *Ibid*., p. 230.
13 *Ibid*., p. 235.
14 *Ibid*., p. 238.
15 Sir David Wilson Bt. to author.
16 Benn, *Out of the Wilderness*, p. 361.
17 *Ibid*., p. 407.
18 *Ibid*.
19 *Ibid*., p. 430.
20 Potter, *Elizabethan Stamps*, p. 64.
21 Personal comment to author.
22 Lady Marriott to author.
23 Charles Goodwyn to author.
24 Personal comment to author.
25 *Ibid*.
26 Personal comment to author.
27 Spink, *Stamps and Covers from the Royal Philatelic Collection*, Thursday 17 May 2001, p. 6.
28 Michael Sefi to author.
29 Jefferies, Hugh, *The Queen's Stamps*, London, 2002, p. 3.